IDEA GROUP PUBLISHING

Hershey, PA, USA • London, UK

Series in Information Technology Management

The surge in information technology during the latter part of the 20th century has forced organizations to meet its challenges with an increased use and management of information resources. This series takes an indepth look at trends, current practices, and problem resolution in information technology management and offers you a first-class source for expanding the reader's knowledge in this ever-growing field.

Books in this series:

- **Cases on Information Technology Management in Modern Organizations (Mehdi Khosrowpour and Jay Liebowitz)**
- **Information Systems Outsourcing Decision Making: A Managerial Approach (L.A. de Looff)**
- **Information Technology and Organizations: Challenges of New Technologies (Mehdi Khosrowpour)**
- **Management Impacts of Information Technology (Edward Szewczak)**
- **Managing Information Technology Investments with Outsourcing (Mehdi Khosrowpour)**
- **Business Process Change: Reengineering Concepts, Methods and Technologies (Varun Grover and William Kettinger)**
- **Reengineering MIS: Aligning Information Technology and Business Operations (Kevin Coleman, Jim Ettwein, Clelland Johnson, Dick Pigman and Deborah Pulak)**
- **Organizational Information Systems and Technology Innovation and Diffusion (upcoming) (Tor Larsen and Eugene McGuire)**
- **The Virtual Workplace (upcoming) (Magid Igbaria and Margaret Tan)**

For more information, or to submit a proposal for a book
in this series, please contact:

Idea Group Publishing
1331 E. Chocolate Avenue
Hershey, PA 17033-1117
Tel: 1/800-345-4332 or 717/533-8845
Fax: 717/533-8661
E-mail: jtravers@idea-group.com
Website: http://www.idea-group.com

Author guidelines also available at http://www.idea-group.com

Other IDEA GROUP Publishing Books

Excellent additions to your library!

Information Systems Outsourcing Decision Making: A Managerial Approach

Table of Contents

The research project described in this book was supported by the Dutch Ministry of Internal Affairs.

Preface

Organizations are increasingly considering outsourcing part or all of their information systems activities to external suppliers. Some client organizations have very high expectations of outsourcing, fed by positive media attention and eloquent suppliers. Other clients doubt whether the improvements attributed to outsourcing will arise and fear that they will become overly dependent on external suppliers. The main conclusion of the research presented in this book is that outsourcing only leads to the improvements decision makers expect if specific conditions are fulfilled, and that it may otherwise even appear to be detrimental to the organization. Improvements from outsourcing are never achieved automatically but must be supervised, and enforced if necessary, by the client organization.

The question of outsourcing is an inherent part of organizing the IS function of any organization. It is an important decision, that can have far reaching short and long term consequences, both positive and negative. The management of any organization should, when (re)organizing the IS function, decide what part of the IS function is to be performed internally and what part could be better outsourced to external suppliers.

IS outsourcing decisions should be taken with care, as today the IS function plays an important role in most organisations. The IS function is the aggregate of activities and resources needed to establish and sustain the information systems an organization needs. The IS function often takes up an increasingly large part of an organization's expenditures. Nowadays almost every organization depends to some extent on computerized information systems and the IS function is often of strategic importance to the organization. Furthermore the strategy of an organization can be supported or limited by the possibilities of information technology. Innovative information systems can even support and pave the way for new products or services. The question of who is to provide these information systems is therefore very important.

The research described in this book is intended to support the management of organizations that are considering or have chosen to outsource. A model for IS outsourcing decision making is provided in this book. Managers can use this model during analysis to decide whether outsourcing will be sensible and beneficial for their organization. The model is also intended to be used during the supplier selection process and to design and manage the outsourcing relationship. The model is based upon established organizational theories and case study research. The model is described in chapter 5, which can be read and used independently from the other chapters of this book.

Recommendations for IS suppliers are given which can used when developing marketing strategies and strategies for the acquisition and tendering process.

The result of this research is intended to be used in practice, I therefore look forward to receiving comments and suggestions, and I am willing to answer questions from practitioners implementing the guidelines provided in this book.

Leon de Looff
LLoof@mc.mey.nl
Delft, November 1996

ACKNOWLEDGMENTS

Many people have contributed to the research project described in this book. I was very fortunate to have Bas Brussaard as an inspiring supervisor. He stimulated me to be critical towards claims about IS outsourcing. His extensive practical experience was invaluable and his sincere interest in our research was a great motivation.

Paul Mantelaers guided my Masters project and stimulated me to start this endeavor. His continuous personal interest in my research and his extensive comments have improved this book considerably.

Egon Berghout and I had many discussions on research methodology, and he gave me a healthy skepticism about the validity of any scientific result. Ronald Losekoot read The Economist, Der Spiegel and the Harvard Business Review for me and pointed me to articles on IS outsourcing. My colleagues Hans de Graaff, Abraham Guyt, Stephan and Mariëlle den Hengst, Roeland van der Spek and Victor van Reijswoud became my personal friends. We solved many of the world's ethical and political problems over lunch. A number of fellow researchers from other Dutch universities gathered at the Research platform on Information Systems and Economics (RISE), gave me the opportunity to present my findings, and their comments improved the research design.

This research was supported by a grant from the Dutch Ministry of Internal Affairs. Han van den Broek was a cooperative mediator with a genuine interest in the subject.

Peter van der Vlis worked on the pilot study for this research. His thoroughness and working speed were far above that of the average Master's student. Our cooperation gave me a running start. The Dutch Council for Information Technology (Raad voor de Informatie Technologie) supported the pilot project and provided case study organizations.

A number of Dutch organizations agreed to cooperate in the longitudinal case studies. I want to thank the persons who created the necessary commitment within the case study organizations: Arnold Ten Cate and Jan Geerts (Directorate General of Public Works and

Water Management), Jos van Ham (Ministry of Social Affairs and Employment), Sietse Brouwer (Dutch Railway Company) Reinier Maarschalkerweerd and Nico Duynisveld (DSM), Hans Stol and Wim Camp (Central Bureau of Statistics) and Agnes Ovington and Joop Bruurs (municipality of Eindhoven). I also thank the interviewees for their time and suggestions.

Frans Berkelaar, Dick Stevens and Anton Winkels, students from the Department of Information Systems, contributed to this research project and provided me with empirical data and refreshing ideas.

Miranda Aldham-Breary not only corrected my grammar, but also improved the style and clarity of the book. I enjoyed our conversations about classical music and applaud her sympathy for brass players.

I thank my parents for providing me with the opportunities and stimulation to get to where I am now. They also supplied me with empirical examples of IS outsourcing in transport and in local government. My brother Remco helped me by organizing a management conference that 'coincidentally' covered my research area. I thank my wife Ellen for her support and enthusiasm and for reminding me of the human side of decision making.

Leon de Looff
Delft, November 1996

CHAPTER 1

Introduction

Information systems (IS) outsourcing implies commissioning an external IS supplier to perform certain IS activities for an organization, such as information planning, system development, or maintenance and operation of information systems. This may include transferring IS staff and resources to the supplier. An organization may choose to outsource its IS function because of a temporary shortage of IS personnel or computer capacity. Another organization may assume that a large, specialized, IS supplier will provide a better service at a lower cost, compared to an internal department. A further reason can be that an organization wants to pursue a technological change in a short time and hires external IS staff to save the time needed to retrain the organization's IS personnel.

Before client organizations decide to outsource, they often have high expectations of outsourcing. IS suppliers predict large cost reductions and improvements in quality and responsiveness if organizations hand over their IS function to them. Public outsourcing reports are often overly optimistic (Lacity and Hirschheim, 1993). Some organizations that have chosen to outsource have found themselves locked into unfavorable contracts or, with reorganization, have internalized previously outsourced IS activities (Douglass, 1993). Organizations are sometimes faced with unexpected fees for work above the agreed baseline. Some contracts are too open-ended to be enforced. In other cases, the supplier has not delivered the agreed products or services or has even gone bankrupt. Therefore, many organizations are currently in doubt as to whether they can expect benefits from outsourcing (Lacity and Hirschheim, 1993).

1.1 Renewed attention for IS outsourcing

IS outsourcing is not a new phenomenon. Outsourcing options have existed since the dawn of data processing. As early as 1963, Perot's Electronic Data Systems (EDS) handled data processing services for Frito-Lay and Blue Cross (Lacity and Hirschheim, 1992). Activities such as software programming, operation of large computers, time-sharing and purchase of packaged software have to some extent been outsourced since the 1960s (Markus, 1984).

IS outsourcing has received renewed interest in the past few years. In the United Kingdom £800 million was spent on IT outsourcing in 1993, and this is projected to rise to £1.72 billion by 1998 (Fitzgerald and Willcocks, 1993). In 1992, a Yankee Group report estimated that every Fortune 500 company would evaluate IS outsourcing and 20% would sign outsourcing deals by 1994 (Lacity and Hirschheim, 1992). In 1994, up to 72% of the Fortune 1000 companies were planning to use external companies to augment their IT capabilities (Computing Canada, August 1994).

The first contract where the term 'outsourcing' was used, was announced in April 1988, when Wisconsin's Department of Administration outsourced facilities management to Omni Resources (Loh, 1992a). The first widely published large-scale outsourcing operation was announced in July 1989, when Eastman Kodak outsourced its data center operations to IBM and its microcomputer systems operations to Businessland (*Wall Street Journal,* July 26, 1989). This outsourcing operation was a critical event that influenced the diffusion pattern of outsourcing as it ".. represented a higher level of visibility .. than prior user-vendor relationships due to the prominence of the two companies and the magnitude of the contract ($500 million)" and ".. seems to have provided a major impetus for managers in other organizations to seriously evaluate outsourcing" (Loh, 1992a).

In the trade literature, the term IS outsourcing first appeared in 1990 (e.g. Gantz, 1990; Rochester and Douglass, 1990). The first results of scientific research on IS outsourcing were published in 1992 (Loh and Venkatraman, 1992abc; Willcocks, 1992; Lacity and Hirschheim, 1992).

Though the concept of IS outsourcing is not new, there has been renewed attention in practice as well as in the professional and scientific literature. Several changes may have caused this renewed attention. The next sections describe these changes originating from the demand side, i.e., organizations that are considering or have chosen to outsource part of their IS function, and from the supply side, i.e., the suppliers that are offering IS products and services.

1.1.1 Changes originating from the demand side

Focus on core business. Organizations in the past few years have shown a tendency to focus on their core business. Functions that are not considered to be part of the core business are outsourced to external suppliers. Organizations are tending to focus on a smaller part of the production chain and at the same time to increase their scale by mergers and take-overs. Managers are no longer buying only the products and services they can not provide internally: they now make internally only what they can not buy from external suppliers. The IS function is often not considered to be part of the core business and is therefore outsourced.

Need for flexibility. Organizations face an increased need for flexibility, as a consequence of a faster changing competitive environment and rapid developments in information technology. Consequently, the information systems also need to change, often just as rapidly. This calls for an IS function that can respond adequately to these changing demands. Some managers assume that this flexibility can be achieved by outsourcing, as the capabilities and capacity of an internal IS function are limited by the capabilities and capacity of the current IS staff and technology.

Need for reduction of costs and staffing levels. Tough economic and competitive climates have led to a need for cost reduction (Lacity, Willcocks and Feeny, 1995) and a reduction of staffing levels. Many organizations, even thriving, profitable ones, strive for continuous reduction of costs and staffing levels. They assume that outsourcing reduces costs, because it introduces the market mechanism and increases economies of scale. Selling IS assets can also produce a cash infusion. Outsourcing of IS personnel decreases the staffing levels of an organization and a reduction of staffing levels is assumed to reduce costs and to increase flexibility.

Decentralization of IS function. Many companies that in the past were organized around functions and had centralized support functions, have reorganized into autonomous self-contained business units, each of which is responsible for specific product/market combinations. Support functions, such as the IS function, are decentralized to the business units (Mantelaers, 1995). Organizations have found that dividing the IS function among business units decreases the level of specialization within the IS function and thereby decreases the level of efficiency and effectiveness. Outsourcing the IS activities of the business units to large suppliers can regain some of the economies of scale of the former central IS department, while maintaining the autonomy of the business units.

Negative perception of internal IS function. As users become more aware of the possibilities and limitations of information technology, they tend to become more critical of the IS function. Ever increasing IS budgets and doubts about the resulting benefits have led to questions about the legitimacy of investments in information technology (Berghout, 1995). Internal customers sometimes have a negative perception of the quality and responsiveness of the internal IS function. Some internal IS departments are perceived to be outdated, inflexible, expensive, unmanageable and not customer-oriented. This negative perception, whether it is right or not, often acts to initiate discussions about outsourcing. Organizations in this situation consider outsourcing as a way of solving problems with their internal IS function and of breaking the power of the central internal IS department. Vollmer (1993) considers outsourcing, in conjunction with downsizing of hardware and increased end user computing, to be a symptom of what he calls the legitimacy crisis and the game for power over the information systems.

Marketing and sales of IT products and services. Some internal IS departments have unique knowledge and skills, provide useful IT products and services or have excess capacity that can be sold to other organizations. These internal IS departments often lack the commercial skills and facilities for marketing and selling these products and services. Outsourcing gives them access to the external market and yields the opportunity to deploy their potential.

Career opportunities for IS staff. Organizations can not always provide their IS staff with sufficient career opportunities to remain an attractive employer. External IS suppliers can often provide IS staff with more opportunities to specialize in certain areas, to work at the edge of technological developments and to promote to higher general management positions.

Market ideology. New management theories put a higher emphasis on using external markets to obtain products and services. Organizations participate in networks of buyers and suppliers and the obligation to take services from internal staff departments is lessened. Government organizations have been privatized in the public sector of many western states as a direct consequence of this market oriented ideology.

Technological changes. Developments in information technology, such as downsizing, client/server technology and object oriented development methodologies, arise at a pace that some organizations have trouble following. Users and managers often do not want to wait until the internal IS department has hired or retrained staff to implement new technologies, and turn to external suppliers that are already familiar with the new technology. In other organizations, the internal staff is too much burdened with maintaining the old systems to be able to implement new technology. In these situations, the maintenance and operation of the old systems is sometimes outsourced, to give the internal staff time to learn and implement new technology.

The changes in the demand for IS services, given above, act as triggers for reconsidering the role of the IS function, and in particular for considering outsourcing. This does not imply that each point is a valid reason for outsourcing and that the expected improvements will be achieved automatically. Each point is based on many implicit and unproved assumptions. There is no conclusive theoretical or empirical support for the assumption that outsourcing will always lead to more focused organizations, higher flexibility, lower costs and staffing levels, economies of scale and to the solution of all problems with internal IS departments.

1.1.2 Changes originating from the supply side

New types of outsourcing. Many innovative types of outsourcing have emerged in the past few years. Today, IS staff and resources are often transferred to the IS supplier to which the activities are outsourced. IS suppliers often take responsibility for entire projects and sub-contracting by main suppliers is common practice. Client organizations and IS suppliers engage in strategic relationships that exceed individual projects and systems. Contracts sharing risks and rewards, based on some output measures of the client organization, are becoming more common. Joint ventures are formed between organizations and IS suppliers, in which the parties take a share in each other or establish a jointly owned IS organization.

Availability of products and services. Ready made software packages have become available for an increasing number of applications and industries, and can often be customized to the client's needs. Fourth generation languages and tools make it easy for end users to do part of the development. The relative need for tailor-made systems has decreased (Rands, 1993).

Higher market pressure. As the IS market matures, competition among IS suppliers is increasing, tariffs have decreased and margins for IS suppliers have become less exorbitant. There has been a shake out among IS suppliers, and mergers and take-overs among IS suppliers have become common practice. On one hand, an increase in competition is a positive trend for customers: IS suppliers that deliver insufficient quality or charge too much, will disappear from the market. On the other hand, take-overs and bankruptcies can be very harmful to current customers. Mergers have led to the outsourcing market being concentrated in the hands of a relatively small number of IS suppliers and these are interrelated in many ways. In the USA, a 56.7% share of the outsourcing market is held by seven companies (Arnett and Jones, 1994). In the Netherlands, a 75% share of the market for outsourcing of facilities management is held by nine suppliers (IDC, 1990). This may limit a client organizations choice of IS suppliers for specific activities to a very few or to only one IS supplier.

Focus on customer groups. Today, customers demand that their supplier is familiar with their business processes. It is no longer acceptable for an IS supplier to ask the client organization to explain the organizations business processes and markets. To meet this demand, small suppliers are focusing increasingly on specific client groups. There are IS suppliers that focus on technical design automation, environmental management, local government, and so on. Large IS suppliers have changed their internal structure from being organized around functions and technical disciplines to product/market oriented units, each of which focuses on a specific group of clients. Some suppliers even suggest that they can contribute to the business of their clients, by assisting in developing the business strategy and identifying opportunities for innovative applications of information technology. The focus on customer groups is a positive trend for client organizations, because less time is needed for the IS supplier to get acquainted with the organizations business processes and the result is better suited to the organizations needs.

1.2 Relevance of IS outsourcing

IS outsourcing is relevant at the macro-economic level: a considerable part of the IS activities of organizations is being outsourced and the IS suppliers form a large industry. It is difficult to determine the exact size of the IS outsourcing market, because market research reports use different definitions and research methods.

IS outsourcing is relevant to individual client organizations and IS suppliers. Outsourcing can have a high positive or negative impact on the performance and the added value of an organizations IS function. IS suppliers depend upon client organizations for their revenues.

1.2.1 Size and growth

Many large scale outsourcing operations have been reported on in the popular literature. Large, well-known, organizations have outsourced a considerable part of their IS function (Loh, 1992a).

It is difficult to determine the total amount of outsourced versus internal IS activities, or the absolute or relative growth of outsourcing. Several reports have been published on the actual and predicted size and growth of the IS outsourcing market. The market for IS outsourcing in the Netherlands is estimated to be 1,000 to 2,000 million Dutch guilders. More accurate estimations can not be given, because definitions of IS outsourcing differ between market surveys (Buijs and Van der Kaa, 1996). Definitions of IS and outsourcing are often lacking or unclear. The costs are often not determined in an economically correct way. The accuracy of the market information depends on the accuracy of the financial administration on IS spending by the organizations that respond. Surveys are sent to functionaries who spend a few minutes on answering the questions on behalf of an entire organization spending up to millions of guilders on IS, often dispersed over many autonomous business units. Sample sizes and research design are often not described in market reports (Borgers, 1995). Response rates are often very low, as are the absolute number of responses. The IT Outsourcing Survey by PA Consulting, for example, based conclusions on 80 responses out of over 10,000 questionnaires (Telecommagazine, December 1995).

Clear and uniform terminology and agreement on research methods is necessary to get more reliable market data. Talks on this matter between several marketing research organizations and FENIT, a Dutch association of organizations in the IT industry, have not yet, however, led to agreement.

1.2.2 Relevance to client organizations

Today information systems are essential to many organizations. Adequate information systems can be used to improve the effectiveness and efficiency of business processes, to make changes in these processes possible, or even to produce new products and services that would be unattainable without information technology. The success of an organization depends to a large extent on the effectiveness and efficiency of its IS function.

The effectiveness and efficiency of an organizations IS function is affected by the way the IS function is organized. This has been demonstrated in studies of organizational issues, such as the position of the CIO (chief information officer), decentralization of IS activities, and internal transfer pricing of IS services (Mantelaers, 1995).

The IS function is fundamentally different from other functions that can be outsourced, because it is not a process at the beginning or the end of an organizations production chain but an integrated part of it. Information systems are integrated parts of almost all processes within an organization, and influence directly how these processes are performed. This is especially the case for information systems that support primary processes, and even more so if these primary processes are essentially information processing. The IS function can not be isolated and separated as easily as other processes and the requirements for information systems can not be specified in general terms that are independent of the organizational context. IS outsourcing can therefore not be compared to outsourcing of catering, security, logistics, legal services or advertising, or the procurement of raw materials and components, and needs a separate specific outsourcing theory. This does not imply that nothing can be learnt from outsourcing of these other functions. General organizational theories and procurement literature are useful, but must be adapted and enhanced to the specific nature of IS outsourcing (see Chapter 3).

Outsourcing, as one of the possible organizational changes, can have a high positive or negative impact on the effectiveness and efficiency of the IS function. Cost savings of up to 40% have been reported. Suppliers sometimes achieved improvements in quality and

Other organizations have experienced that improvements promised by suppliers did not materialize. Some suppliers have charged excessive fees for work above the agreed baseline or have made unreasonable demands during contract renewal. Other suppliers simply have not delivered according to requirements or have not been cooperative when major changes in volume, technology or functionality were needed (Lacity and Hirschheim, 1995). Client organizations have sometimes had insufficient knowledge or IS staff to keep up to date with developments in IT and to manage and control their supplier. At the end of outsourcing contracts, or even before, some client organizations had changed to another IS supplier or even re-internalized IS activities (Douglass, 1993).

These examples of major improvements as well as major problems after outsourcing show that managers should be very careful and take outsourcing decisions after careful consideration of all the possible consequences. Knowledge of all the expected effects of specific types of outsourcing in specific situations is therefore essential.

1.2.3 Relevance to IS suppliers

Providing IS products and services is the core business of IS suppliers. It is very important for IS suppliers to know the motives and expectations that client organizations have for outsourcing. IS suppliers can adjust their products and services and their marketing strategy to these motives and expectations, and thereby improve their market share and customer satisfaction.

Traditional IS products and services, such as payroll processing and operation of mainframes, have reached the maturity stage of the product life cycle, where total demand has stabilized and suppliers compete on price to retain their market share (Borgers, 1995). IS suppliers are offering new types of outsourcing in search of new opportunities with higher added value. Knowledge of the needs and expectations of customers can be used to support this search for innovative products and services.

1.3 IS outsourcing decision making

Given the relevance and impact of outsourcing on the performance of the IS function, an outline of how decisions on IS outsourcing are taken is given in the following sections. Whether these decision processes are satisfactory, and whether current knowledge and methods support the decision process adequately, will also be discussed.

1.3.1 Current practice

Before starting the research reported on here, a pilot study was conducted on current practice in IS outsourcing decision making (Van der Vlis, 1993; Van der Vlis, Berghout and De Looff, 1993), in cooperation with RIT. The RIT (Raad voor de Informatie Technologie, Council for IT) is a Dutch organization aimed at pre-competitive cooperation between IT suppliers and user organizations. The pilot study was conducted in association with a work group on Facilities Management. The interviews were held mainly at member organizations of the RIT.

The purpose of the pilot study was to determine whether the subject justified further research and to identify areas that needed additional investigation. The pilot study consisted of 30 interviews, of personnel from client and supplier organizations involved in outsourcing decisions. The study focused on the way organizations take outsourcing decisions. The questions asked during the interviews considered the steps in the decision process, the functionaries involved in the decision process and the arguments they used. Conclusions on the actual effects of outsourcing could not be drawn, because the interviews focused on the expectations of stakeholders shortly after the outsourcing decision was taken.

Comparing the decision processes that the organizations went through revealed many differences. The actual outsourcing decision was sometimes taken at a very early stage and sometimes not until the analysis of proposals was finished. The motives for outsourcing ranged from expected reductions in costs and improvements in quality, to solving IS management problems and facilitating technological changes. Decision makers differed in the emphasis they put on the different effects of outsourcing. Some decision makers, for example, only considered cost reduction, while others emphasized improvements in quality of service, or a reduction in staffing levels.

The terminology that was used in the cases was far from clear. Decision makers and IS suppliers used different terms for different concepts, without clear definitions. This often led to disagreements between client organizations and IS suppliers about the interpretation of agreements and contracts.

Formal methods and a theoretical foundation for IS outsourcing decisions were found to be lacking. Decisions were taken largely based on ideology, trends, wishful thinking and personal expectations instead of systematic analysis of actual consequences in comparable situations. Interviewees were dissatisfied with this basis for decision making, but had no alternatives to hand. The decision process was often an isolated project, not based upon or incorporated in the information strategy process, even though interviewees acknowledged that a strong interdependency between outsourcing and information strategy existed.

Different arguments were mentioned for different types of outsourcing and for different types of information systems, IS components and IS activities. Arguments were also found to be dependent on the characteristics of the specific situation, such as the organization and responsible persons, the information systems in use, the competitive environment and the availability of appropriate IS suppliers.

Interviewees indicated that they had difficulty in choosing the right outsourcing arrangement and in managing the outsourcing relationship. The contracts offered by IS suppliers were not always in the best interest of the client organization. Monitoring and controlling the IS supplier appeared to be very different from managing an internal IS department.

IS suppliers have had difficulty in determining the client organizations motives for outsourcing, which makes it hard to develop marketing strategies and strategies for handling client interactions.

The pilot study highlighted a need for a basis for IS outsourcing decision making. There is a particular need for clear terminology and a theoretical foundation, and empirical research is needed into the actual consequences of IS outsourcing.

1.3.2 Available support

The apparent need for a basis for outsourcing decision making is not complemented by sufficient available decision support. Publications on outsourcing are abundant, but most do not step beyond describing individual outsourcing cases (e.g. Douglass, 1993), enumerating advantages and disadvantages of outsourcing (e.g. Wagner, 1992), and giving check lists for contracting (e.g. Radding, 1991). Publications seldom state under what conditions and for which information systems or IS activities these advantages apply and under what circumstances the pros outweigh the cons, or vice versa. Empirical or theoretical support is scarce. The terminology that is used is far from clear, which makes the research results less useful and comparable. The research that has been undertaken by other researchers is summarized below and is analyzed further in later chapters of this book.

Conceptual studies. Richmond, Seidmann and Whinston (1992) use mathematical models of incomplete contracting to investigate outsourcing of systems development. They have determined the effects of information asymmetry and different profit sharing rules when deciding whether to outsource or to use an internal development team.

Ang (1994) introduces three conceptualizations of organizational boundaries to improve conceptual clarity with regard to outsourcing: geographical, legal ownership and behavioral control boundaries. Rands (1992, 1993) has developed a framework for software make or buy decisions, based on the required IT service level, the application delivery portfolio and external software supply conditions.

Empirical studies. Buck-Lew (1992) investigated the outsourcing of applications development in three organizations; she gives a set of criteria for managers to use when deciding what projects are likely candidates for outsourcing. Ang and Beath (1993) investigated hierarchical elements in software contracts and analyzed the content of six actual software contracts.

Lacity and Hirschheim (1992, 1993, 1994) have conducted an in-depth multiple case analysis of thirteen large service or manufacturing companies in the USA. The cases were investigated from a transaction cost economics, and a power and politics perspective. The authors exposed several outsourcing myths and presented a number of stringent contract negotiation strategies.

Willcocks and Fitzgerald (Willcocks 1992; Willcocks and Fitzgerald 1993, 1994) conducted a series of open-ended telephone interviews, a postal questionnaire, and a series of semi-structured interviews which resulted in 30 detailed cases. They investigated the effect of six factors: in-house expertise with IT, coupled to the stability of the technology; business uncertainty; systems interconnectedness and complexity; IS as a business differentiator or a commodity; the activity's relationship to business strategy; and in-house capability relative to the external market. The survey of over 1,000 senior managers and directors found that many outsourcing contracts were incomplete. Partnership relationships may not be appropriate in all circumstances and should be based on shared risk and benefits, instead of a give-and-take relationship.

Willcocks, Lacity and Fitzgerald have combined their research results on IT outsourcing in Europe and the USA (Willcocks, Lacity and Fitzgerald, 1995; Lacity, Willcocks and Feeny, 1995), to draw conclusions on tight and loose contracting, measures and service levels, IT outsourcing contracts, and the importance of retaining in-house capability, and they advise selective outsourcing to maximize flexibility and control.

Several case studies have been conducted in the USA (Buck-Lew, 1992, Huber, 1993) and in European countries (Auwers and Deschoolmeester, 1993; Saarinen and Saaksjarvi, 1993; Heinzl, 1993; Griese 1993).

A nationwide survey in the USA by Arnett and Jones (1994) that received forty useful responses revealed several structural and managerial characteristics of organizations that outsource one or more IS activities.

Aubert, Rivard and Patry (1993, 1994) conducted ten case studies and a survey among 630 firms in Canada. They analyzed the effects of asset specificity, uncertainty, frequency and measurability on governance modes, and found a strong correlation between measurability and the use of outsourcing.

Loh and Venkatraman (1992a) concluded from an analysis of 58 IT outsourcing announcements that the stock market reacts favorably to announcements about IT outsourcing decisions. Using the same sample, Loh and Venkatraman (1992b) observed that the degree of outsourcing is related positively to both business and IT cost structures and related negatively to IT performance.

Decision models. Minoli (1995) has proposed a decision process in three steps, based on a model of the current IS function, strategic objectives for the IS function and an analysis of internal and external alternatives.

The Euromethod model (Euromethod consortium, 1994; Verhoef and Van Swede, 1995) is the result of a project funded by the European Commission and performed by a multi-national project team. The aim of Euromethod is to improve customer-supplier relationships when outsourcing IS development and modification. Euromethod is decision and delivery oriented and takes a situation driven approach towards managing the transactions between the main actors of the client organization and the IS supplier during a project.

The Gartner Group (Terdiman, 1993) has published check lists and factors that can be used to reach an outsourcing decision. Consultancy firms often have their own method of supporting clients in outsourcing decisions, but have not published their methods.

Van der Vlis (1993) has developed a model that can be used to determine the risk of outsourcing using seven guidelines to describe the ongoing IS situation. The advantages and disadvantages of outsourcing are then analyzed. The combination of the risk, advantages and disadvantages leads to a recommendation for or against outsourcing.

The Dutch Ministry of Home Affairs (CCOI, 1990) has issued guidelines for the privatization of government IS activities.

Hoogeveen (1994) has proposed a ten step checklist when reviewing an outsourcing decision, from the specification of the problems and goals of the IS function to the negotiation of the contract and the evaluation of outsourcing. Beulen (1994) gives a decision model, based on four approaches towards outsourcing: the political, fundamental, cultural and transaction cost approaches. External and internal factors are scored and a total score is calculated from the scores and weight factors.

1.3.3 Evaluation of needs and available support

Surveys of outsourcing decisions made by organizations have not led to conclusive results regarding the factors that influence outsourcing. Most of the case studies conclude with warnings, check lists and recommendations. Researchers have not used their results to develop a comprehensive decision model for IS outsourcing.

The pilot study led to a number of criteria that a decision model should meet to give adequate support to client organizations in all phases of IS outsourcing decision making. A model must be based on established theories and on systematic empirical research. A model should cover all phases of IS outsourcing, from the initial decision to possibly outsource, to the management and termination of outsourcing. Differences between different types of outsourcing should be acknowledged and incorporated in the model. A model should incorporate recognition of the fact that the attractiveness and approach of outsourcing depends on the specific situation of the client organization. Guidelines should be provided for analyzing situational factors. Managers of client organizations must be able to use the model, which should therefore be elaborate and action-oriented, and include instructions for use. Indications of the relative strengths and weaknesses of the decision models available currently are presented in Table 1.1.

Euromethod, and the models of Van der Vlis and Beulen are the only decision models that acknowledge explicitly that the consequences of outsourcing depend on the specific situation. Euromethod is however, only aimed at managing the client-supplier relationship during IS development projects and does not address the actual outsourcing decision and other IS activities. The model of Van der Vlis is aimed only at the initial sourcing decision and does not acknowledge differences in importance of goals and differences between IS activities. Beulen makes implicit assumptions on the (positive) effects of outsourcing and fits all factors into one computational model.

Outsourcing both extends and limits the options for IS strategy and the IS strategy must be taken into account in outsourcing decisions. The IS strategy in turn depends upon and influences the organizations business strategy. None of the studies acknowledges explicitly this interdependency between outsourcing, IS strategy and

Models	Criteria					
	theoretical foundation	empirical research	covering all phases	outsourcing types	situational factors	elaborate and useable
Beulen (1994)	+	o	-	-	+	+
CCOI (1990)	-	-	-	+	o	o
Euromethod (1994)	+	-	-	+	+	+
Hoogeveen (1994)	+	+	+	-	o	o
Lacity and Hirschheim (1995)	+	+	+	o	o	+
Minoli (1995)	-	-	o	o	o	+
Terdiman (1993)	-	-	-	-	o	o
Van der Vlis (1992)	-	+	-	-	+	+

+ = model is strong on criterion
o = model is average on criterion
- = model is weak on criterion

Table 1.1 Evaluation of existing decision models

planning, and organizational strategy.

1.4 Narrowing the scope

The field of IS outsourcing decision making is a large and diverse research area with many aspects that can and need to be investigated. The intended contribution of this book to the field is demarcated in this section, and a description of the objectives, the research questions and the limitations of the research is given.

1.4.1 Research objectives

The pilot study showed that many organizations are in doubt about what effects they can expect from IS outsourcing, and that decision makers need clear terminology and a model to use when making outsourcing decisions. The literature and research results that are currently available do not completely meet this need. The objective of the research presented in this book is to fulfill this need. The objectives are:

- to support management of client organizations when making the decision whether or not to outsource (parts of) the organizations IS function,
- to support management of client organizations when designing and managing an IS outsourcing relationship,
- to support IS suppliers with their marketing strategy.

The underlying objective is to maximize the performance or added value of the IS function. This objective will be elaborated in chapter 2. Improving the IS function has been the subject of many studies in IS and many different measures have been proposed. This research is confined to organizational measures, and to outsourcing decisions in particular.

1.4.2 Research questions

Supporting outsourcing decisions requires information on several aspects of outsourcing. These aspects lead to the research questions for this research:

1. How can the variables that are relevant to IS outsourcing be described systematically?
2. What are the actual consequences of IS outsourcing in the short and long term?
3. What situational factors are relevant to IS outsourcing decision making and how should these factors be taken into account?

4. What are the options for designing and managing an outsourcing arrangement, and what options should be chosen in a specific situation?
5. How should the outsourcing decision process be organized?
6. How can IS suppliers use the answers to these questions when developing their marketing strategies?

The result of this research is a model for IS outsourcing decision making that can be used to indicate what part of the IS function in a specific situation can best be outsourced, and what part the organization should perform internally. The model can also be used to guide decision makers when organizing the outsourcing relationship.

The model contains guidelines for organizing the decision making process and the actual decision. The model can be used by organizations that are considering IS outsourcing, and by organizations that have outsourced and want to evaluate or reorganize their outsourcing relationship.

IS suppliers are supported by a number of guidelines that they can use as a basis for their marketing strategy. These guidelines are based upon conclusions drawn from the research on the motives and expectations of customers that have chosen to outsource.

1.4.3 Limitations of the research

IS outsourcing decisions are a part of IS management, which consists of identifying and selecting useful and economically justifiable information systems, and organizing the IS function, i.e., the resources and activities needed to establish and sustain these information systems (Brussaard, 1992). This research is aimed only at organizational measures to improve the IS function, and is not aimed primarily at for example technical, legal or financial measures, or the improvement of system development methodologies and tools. These organizational measures are further restricted to decisions on the division of tasks and responsibilities between client organizations and IS suppliers, and to designing and managing the outsourcing relationship. The research is not per se aimed at organizing the internal IS function and not at the internal organization of IS activities performed by a supplier.

It is furthermore assumed that the organizations current and future needs for information and information systems are known. This is necessary because the decision model is based partly on the characteristics of these information systems. In practice, the interrelationship between outsourcing and information planning has to be taken into account, because the degree and type of outsourcing both limits and extends the possibilities for maintaining existing systems and developing new systems. The extent to which outsourcing influences the ability of the organization to determine the future need for information systems is included, as it is assumed that there is a relationship between outsourcing and planning ability.

The empirical results are based on a limited number of cases, and focus mainly on qualitative variables. These choices are justified in chapter 4. Large-scale quantitative data on the size and growth of the outsourcing market have not been gathered. Conclusions on costs of internal and external provision and on other benchmarks for efficiency and industry standards have not been drawn; the decision model does however provide a conceptual framework to structure these types of analysis.

Information systems do not necessarily contain computer hardware and software. This research does not focus on manual information systems but on systems that contain hardware and software as well as people, data and procedures.

Outsourcing of the use of information systems is not considered in this research. The use of information systems is interpreted as the gathering, entering, processing, storing and presenting of information by the users of the information systems. Outsourcing of, for example, the entire pay roll processing, from data entry to payment, or gathering and processing of market data by a market research bureau, is not included. These types of outsourcing are very relevant and suppliers do offer information processing services. The choice between gathering or buying information is however not included in this research. The research only addresses the outsourcing of planning, development, implementation, maintenance and the operation of information systems that are used by the client organization.

1.5 Research approach

Several research strategies were followed to achieve the research objectives. The research phases are summarized in Figure 1.1, together with the numbers of the corresponding chapters.

Following on from the pilot study, a descriptive framework was developed, to describe different types of outsourcing in a structured way (chapter 2). The descriptive framework was used for the case study research, and can be used by decision makers to describe alternatives in IS outsourcing decisions. Several organizational theories were analyzed and elements that appeared relevant to IS outsourcing decision making were used to establish relationships between situational factors, types of outsourcing and the effects of outsourcing (chapter 3). The findings from the organizational theories were formulated as propositions in terms of the framework (section 3.6).

In-depth case study research was conducted in a further six organizations, to analyze and refine the propositions (chapter 4). In this phase, the actual consequences of 23 outsourcing decisions were investigated, retrospectively, from up to ten years ago, and longitudinally, over a period of two years after the initial decision.

A model for IS outsourcing decision making was developed, based on the findings from the case studies (chapter 5). This decision model is aimed at supporting the management of organizations when making IS outsourcing decisions. The model covers all phases of IS outsourcing decision making, from the initial sourcing decision to managing and terminating the outsourcing relationship. All parts of the IS function are covered, and differences between information systems, IS activities and IS components are incorporated. Guidelines are given for the actual decisions and for the process of decision making.

The case study results are also used to provide strategies for IS suppliers (chapter 6). Strategies are suggested for determining attractive product market combinations, entering new market segments, identifying and approaching client organizations, and responding to calls for tender.

The overall conclusions, evaluations and directions for further research are presented in chapter 7.

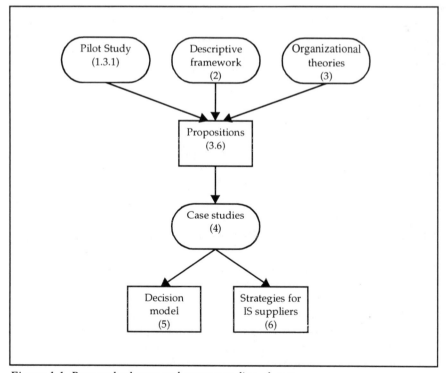

Figure 1.1 Research phases and corresponding chapters

CHAPTER 2

IS Outsourcing Framework

The terminology used in IS outsourcing is far from clear; researchers and practitioners use many different terms and concepts in ambiguous ways. This leads to difficulties in comparing research results and to disagreements between client organizations and IS suppliers.

A descriptive framework that can be used to describe different types of outsourcing systematically is described in this chapter. The framework is used in chapter 3 to classify guidelines for IS outsourcing derived from established organizational theories, and to describe the case studies presented in chapter 4. The framework is also used as a basis for the decision model presented in chapter 5.

2.1 Introduction

The term outsourcing is used for many different types of external relationships, for example for:

- hiring an external consultant to select a data base management system;
- having a new order system developed, maintained and operated by an IS supplier;
- transferring an entire internal IS department, including hardware, software and IS personnel, to an IS supplier.

Many terms to describe these and other types of outsourcing have been introduced in the literature, and in practice. Lacity and Hirschheim (1993), for example, distinguish body shopping (contracting personnel to meet short term demand), project management (outsourcing a specific portion of IS work) and total outsourcing (putting the vendor in complete charge of a significant piece of IS work). They differentiate between outsourcing data processing, telecommunications, planning, strategic systems or the entire IS department.

Other terms that are used in practice include: systems integration, facilities management, data center privatization, service bureau and third party maintenance. There is no consensus about the meaning of these terms and many classifications are neither complete nor mutually exclusive (Ang, 1994). This makes analysis of theory and practice difficult and complicates decision making. Ang (1994) states that "the concept of outsourcing remains nebulous ... [which] leads to disagreements about the underlying motivations in outsourcing decisions. Second, it leads to contradictory projections about the consequences of outsourcing".

The descriptive framework for IS outsourcing is intended to meet the need for consistent terminology. The framework is intended to be used to describe existing outsourcing situations and to describe outsourcing options that are under consideration.

2.2 Information systems function

Most authors on outsourcing indicate that outsourcing may involve the entire IS function or only part of it. Lacity and Hirschheim (1995) call this total versus selective outsourcing and Buck-Lew (1992) calls it pure versus hybrid outsourcing. Selective outsourcing is an important notion, because it is very unlikely that any organization will outsource the entire IS function or outsource nothing at all, and because today many organizations already have several outsourcing contracts in place (Zoetmulder, 1995).

2.2.1 Definition of IS function

The following definition of the IS function of an organization is used (derived from Brussaard 1992):

Definition 1: *The IS function of an organization is the aggregate of activities and the associated human and other resources needed to establish and sustain the information systems needed by the organization.*

The IS function is not restricted to a central IS department or data center. It is a concept that is independent of departments and functionaries. Parts of the IS function can be performed by IS specialists in IS departments, but parts can also be performed by non-specialists in user departments. The decision as to which parts of the IS function are to be performed by IS specialists and which by users or line managers is in fact one of the most important design decisions in organizing the IS function (Mantelaers 1995).

2.2.2 Classification of IS function

If an organization outsources only part of the IS function, there has to be terminology to indicate which part is outsourced and which part is kept in house. Several authors on IS outsourcing provide classifications of the IS function, to indicate selective outsourcing (see Table 2.1).

The classifications given in Table 2.1 are not disjunctive, nor are they complete or widely accepted in IS management literature. There is an intermingling of classifications of activities, such as development, operation, management, planning and programming, with classifications of components, such as software, data and hardware, and classifications of systems, such as strategic versus non-strategic

Authors	Parts of the IS function
Buck-Lew (1992)	data communications data center functions management and technical 　　support of computer systems development of applications
Richmond et al. (1992)	facilities management software development systems integration network management
Arnett and Jones (1994)	facility management hardware maintenance contract programming software support systems integration
Aubert et al. (1993)	software development operations
Eggleton and Otter (1991)	telecommunications computer operations systems development other services
Ketler and Walstrom (1993)	operations or facilities management contract programming education/training network management telecommunications systems integration systems conversions
Klepper (1991)	system development system and data center operation IS management
Lacity and Hirschheim (1992)	data processing telecommunications planning strategic systems IS department

Table 2.1 Classifications of the IS function

systems.

In the classification of Arnett and Jones (1994), for example, hardware maintenance is a separate type of outsourcing, while software maintenance is not mentioned. Facility management usually includes hardware and software maintenance. Arnett and Jones' classification does not include software development; this may be part of systems integration or contract programming in their terminology.

A disjunctive and complete classification of the IS function should cover all IS activities, IS components and information systems. Information systems can, as can all dynamic open systems, be described in analytical, functional and temporal terms (Brussaard, 1995). In functional terms, an information system is described by the business process it supports. In analytical terms, an information system is described by the components it consists of. In temporal terms, an information system is described by the activities needed during the life cycle of the system to establish and sustain the system.

The IS function can be classified according to the three dimensions by which information systems are described: the information systems the IS function provides, the components that make up the information systems, and the activities necessary to establish and sustain the information systems. These three dimensions are elaborated in the following sections.

2.2.3 Classification of information systems

The first dimension classifies the IS function by the functional information systems the IS function establishes and sustains.

Definition 2: *An information system is defined, functionally, as a system to support or perform a specific business function, by providing the information required to perform this function.*

A functional classification of information systems is derived from classifying the business functions that are supported by the systems. Porter (1980) divides business functions into primary functions and secondary functions. Primary activities are those involved in the physical creation of the product, its marketing and delivery to buyers, and its support and servicing after sale. Secondary activities provide the inputs and infrastructure that allow the primary activities to take place. Primary functions include such activities as product design, production, sales and distribution, while secondary functions include finance and human resources management. The information systems that support these functions can be classified accordingly. Systems supporting primary functions can be divided into systems that actually execute primary information processes, and systems that support physical or information primary processes (see Table 2.2). Information

Category	Description	Examples
primary systems	systems that execute informational primary processes	land registry IS, claims processing IS, electronic banking IS
primary support systems	systems that support primary processes	production scheduling IS, project planning IS, materials requirements IS
secondary systems	systems that support secondary processes	personnel IS, financial IS, archives IS

Table 2.2 Functional classification of information systems

primary processes can be aimed at delivering abstract products or services that materialize in information, such as financial transactions, insurance policies or registry of rights, or at delivering information as a product, such as market information, consultancy, news, and medical advice.

Other functional classifications of information systems exist, for example classifications along the goal of an information system (efficiency, effectiveness, strategic, transforming) or target group (operational staff, management, clients). These classifications may also be relevant to outsourcing, but the classification used in this book is more fundamental, as it considers the inherent nature of the systems and indicates the strong relationship between information systems and the processes they support or execute.

Information systems can also be classified into strategic and non-strategic systems. This distinction is relevant to this research because it is often suggested that strategic information systems should not be outsourced (Fitzgerald, 1994; Hewett, 1994; Ketler and Walstrom, 1994). Willcocks (1995) defines strategic information systems as systems that are essential for the continuity of an organization. Fitzgerald (1994) distinguishes 'key strategic areas' that make a major contribution to the company and its goals and objectives. Deitz (1996) describes strategic systems as information systems that influence the business strategy and are to some extent risky, innovative, and oriented externally. Other authors hold that strategic systems are systems that are directed at suppliers or buyers, such as airline reservation systems with terminals at the reservation agencies (see IJpelaar, 1993). In this research, strategic systems are defined as follows:

Definition 3: *Strategic information systems are systems that distinguish an organization from its competitors.*

2.2.4 Classification of IS components

The second, analytical, dimension that can be used to describe the IS function is the dimension of the components that information systems consists of.

Definition 4: *IS components are the analytical parts of information systems. IS components can be classified into hardware, software, people, procedures and data.*

Each system consists of one or more instances of different types of components. Information systems do not necessarily contain all five categories of components. Manual information systems do not contain computer hardware and software. Automated information systems, such as robots in a computer integrated manufacturing (CIM) environment, contain no people and manual procedures.

Each of the five types of components can be classified further. Hardware can, for example, be classified into input, storage, processing, communication and output hardware. An extensive overview of classes and subclasses of components can be found in Looijen (1996).

There is not always a one-to-one relationship between components and information systems. A piece of hardware can, for example, be used by several information systems, and an information system can use several classes of data that are also used or created by other information systems. The distinction between the analytical dimension of components and the functional dimension of information systems is necessary because each of the analytical components can be used by more than one functional information system, and vice versa (Brussaard, 1992).

The distinction between components and systems is relevant with regard to outsourcing, because outsourcing a certain component may have consequences for several information systems, and outsourcing a certain information system may have consequences for other information systems with which the system shares components. The relationships between information systems and IS components can be depicted in a "systems versus components" table (see Table 2.3).

IS components can be classified into infrastructural and non-infrastructural components. This distinction is relevant to this research because establishing and sustaining an IS infrastructure is often organized in a different way than activities for non-infrastructural components (Renkema, 1995). Infrastructure is defined by Renkema (1995) as "the shared system of people, non human resources and organizational procedures in the field of information technology, that an organization has at its disposal for the longer term." In this book, IS infrastructure is defined as follows:

Definition 5: *The IS infrastructure of an organizational unit is* *the aggregate of IS components that are part of a relatively large number of the unit's information systems.*

A "systems versus components" table such as Table 2.3 can be used to identify infrastructural components. If a certain row has a relatively large number of marked cells, then that component is considered to be part of the IS infrastructure.

Hardware and system software, i.e., operating systems, database management systems, and so on, will often be part of the IS infrastructure, as they are often used by multiple information systems. The same holds for IS users, who usually work with more than one information system. Application software is often not part of the IS infrastructure, because each application will usually be part of only one information system.

2.2.5 Classification of IS activities

The third dimension of the IS function is a classification of the activities that make up the IS function.

Types of components	Examples of components	Examples of information systems		
		license registry system	license inspection planning system	license inspection reporting system
hardware	AS/400 mini computer 1	x	x	
	AS/400 mini computer 2			x
	personal computers	x	x	x
software	database tool X	x	x	x
	reporting tool Y			x
	license application	x		
	planning application	x		
	reporting application		x	
people	users at head office	x	x	
	users at bus. units	x	x	
	IS staff	x	x	x
procedures	proc.s for commissioning	x		
	proc.s for inspection	x	x	
	proc.s for reporting		x	
data	licences	c	u	u
	inspections	c	u	

x = component is part of information system
c = data category is created by information system
u = data category is used by information system

Table 2.3 Example of "systems versus components" table

Definition 6: *IS activities are the activities needed, over time, to establish and sustain information systems. IS activities can be classified into planning, development, implementation, maintenance and operation.*

The classification is based on the systems development life cycle and is similar to the state model of Looijen (1996).

In particular situations, the terminology may be different and it may be necessary to refine certain activities. The IS activities are described in Table 2.4, and some examples of refinements into sub activities are given. A more detailed classification of all IS activities is given by Looijen (1995), who provides an extensive classification of activities into tasks, task areas and task fields. The Information Technology Infrastructure Library (CCTA, 1994) includes a description of maintenance and operation activities. Further classifications of development activities can be found in system development methodologies.

IS activity	Description	Examples of sub activities
planning	determining the information strategy as a basis for developing, maintaining or terminating information systems	• IS strategy • project planning
development	designing and building an information system	• definition or problem analysis • basic or functional design • detailed or technical design • construction or programming • testing
implementation	installing a purchased, developed or adapted information system and making it ready for use	• user acceptance • installation • data conversion • user training
maintenance	keeping the IS appropriate for the intended use, by changing the functional or technical characteristics of the system.	• preventive maintenance • corrective maintenance • perfective maintenance • adaptive maintenance • additive maintenance
operation	operating information systems to allow for the uninterrupted use, without changing functional or technical characteristics of the system	• help desk • capacity management • problem management

Table 2.4 Description of IS activities

The classification of IS activities should not be interpreted as a classification of functionaries or departments. Several IS activities can be performed by one department or functionary, and a single IS activity can be performed by several specialized or non-specialized departments or functionaries. Planning, for example, often involves IS management as well as user management and top management of an organization. End users sometimes perform simple operation and maintenance activities, such as solving minor problems and making backups of personal data files. Current system development tools make it possible for end users to develop systems for personal use.

IS activities can be performed on specific information systems or specific IS components. This distinction is relevant with regard to outsourcing, because outsourcing of a certain IS activity may have consequences for several information systems. Or, outsourcing of a certain information system may have consequences for other information systems on which the same activities are performed. The relationships between information systems and IS activities can be depicted in a table (see Table 2.5).

The IS function can thus be classified using the three dimensions described above: information systems, IS components and IS activities. A specific part of the IS function is denoted by the IS activities that are performed with specific components of the pertinent information systems. This can be depicted in a three-dimensional figure such as Figure 2.1. The development of the software of the financial information system, for example, is depicted by the cube in Figure 2.1.

2.3 IS outsourcing

Managers of any organization have to make decisions about which of the organization's IS activities are to be performed within the

IS Activities	Information systems		
	IS 1	**IS 2**	**IS 3**
planning central	central IS department	central IS department	IS department
development	business unit's IS department	supplier A	supplier A
implementation	business unit's IS department	business unit's IS department	business unit's IS department
maintenance	business unit's IS department	supplier A	supplier A
operation	supplier B	supplier B	supplier B

Table 2.5 Example of "activities versus systems" table

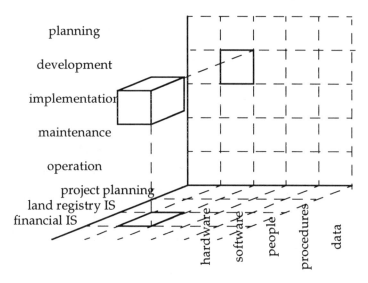

Figure 2.1 Dimensions of the IS function

organization and which activities should be outsourced to other organizations. In this section, the concept of IS outsourcing is elaborated. A number of concepts from organizational science that are relevant to defining IS outsourcing are summarized, current definitions of IS outsourcing are analyzed and the definition that is used in this book is given. The distinction between outsourcing and internal provision is not as sharp as it may seem, and a number of intermediate types of sourcing are distinguished.

2.3.1 Horizontal and vertical integration

Mintzberg (1979) describes the process of organizing to be that of dividing activities among organizational units and establishing coordination between these units. On the level of entire organizations, organizing consists of dividing activities among autonomous organizations and coordinating these activities between the organizations. In organizational science, division of tasks among organizations is described by the part of the production chain an organization encloses (De Leeuw, 1989, Gurbaxani and Whang 1991, Porter 1980). An organization's span of activities can increase or decrease in two dimensions, resulting in four possible changes: diversification, specialization, differentiation and integration (see Figure 2.2).

Diversification is the process of increasing the number of products and services the organization produces. An example of diversification would be the vendor of office supplies that decides to add personal computers to their assortment. The opposite of diversification is specialization: providing a smaller number of products or services.

Differentiation, sometimes called disintegration, is the process of

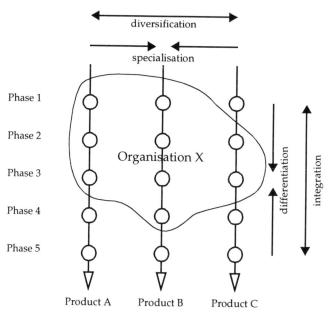

Figure 2.2 Span of production chains

decreasing the number of subsequent phases of the production chain. The opposite of differentiation is integration: performing a larger number of phases of the production chain. Backward vertical (des)integration refers to (des)integrating preceding phases in the production chain. An example of backward vertical disintegration would be the car manufacturer that decides to buy assembled engines instead of buying components and assembling the engines. Forward vertical (des)integration refers to (des)integrating of following phases in the production chain. An example of forward vertical integration would be the consultancy firm that offers to implement suggested changes for customers.

In this book, outsourcing is interpreted as vertical disintegration: decreasing the number of phases of the production chain encompassed by the organization, by commissioning activities to other organizations. Outsourcing of support functions, such as the IS function, is backward vertical disintegration.

Backward vertical (des)integration is sometimes called the market versus hierarchy decision (Williamson, 1985), because management of an organization that needs a certain product or service can decide to buy that product from the market or to produce it within the hierarchy. Other authors call it the make or buy decision (Rands, 1992).

2.3.2 Definition of IS outsourcing

Many definitions of IS outsourcing can be found in the literature.

A number of these definitions is listed in Table 2.6. Common elements in these definitions are:

- the notion of two or more parties, where one party (company, user organization, firm) outsources to one or more other parties (outside party, external vendor, third party vendor)
- the notion that the other party is an external organization that is not part of the user organization
- the notion that the other party agrees to perform some activities (fulfill, subcontracting, provide, commissioning) for the user organization.

The definitions differ mainly in two respects. First, the definitions given in Table 2.6 are ambiguous as to whether activities are outsourced

Authors	Definition
Buck-Lew (1992, p.3)	"a company .. requests the services of an outside party to fulfil a function or functions that involve computer systems"
Eggleton and Otter (1991, p. 1)	"contracting out all or part of the information systems activity"
Ketler and Walstrom (1993, p. 449)	"the process of transferring part or all of the information systems functions to an external vendor"
Klepper (1991, p. 5)	"the contracting of information systems hardware, software and systems functions or services to external vendors"
Lacity and Hirschheim (1994, p. 363)	"the use of a third party vendor to provide information products and services that were previously provided internally"
Loh (1993, p. 29)	IT sourcing is "the positioning of the locus of decision rights for technological resources, human resources, or technical procedures associated with the entire or specific components of the corporate information infrastructure with respect to the user organization and the vendors"
Richmond, Seidmann and Whinston (1992, p. 459)	"the subcontracting of some or all the information systems functions by one firm to another"
Willcocks and Fitzgerald (1993, p. 224)	"the commissioning of third party management of IT assets, people and/or activities to required results. This can and often does involve a degree of transfer of assets and staff to the third-party organization"

Table 2.6 Definitions of outsourcing

or the human and other resources to perform the activities are outsourced. Loh (1993) defines IT sourcing in terms of the decision rights over the resources. Willcocks and Fitzgerald (1993) refer to activities as well as resources ("IT assets, people and/or activities") and add explicitly "This can and often does involve a degree of transfer of assets and staff." The other authors quoted in Table 2.6 define outsourcing as the transfer of activities.

Second, outsourcing can refer to the static state of external provision, as opposed to the state of internal provision, and to the dynamic transition, or change process, from internal to external provision, as opposed to insourcing (see Figure 2.3).

Lacity and Hirschheim's (1993) definition refers to the transition ("products and services that were previously provided internally"), as do Ketler and Walstrom (1993), who speak of "transferring". The other definitions given in Table 2.6 can be understood in both ways. In this research, IS outsourcing is defined as:

Definition 7: *IS outsourcing is the commissioning of part or all of the IS activities an organization needs, and/or transferring the associated human and other IS resources, to one or more external IS suppliers.*

Definition 7 refers to the dynamic transition from internal provision to external provision. In this book, the term outsourcing will be used for the *transition* as well as the resulting state of external provision. A number of elements of this definition are elaborated in the following sections.

The term *IS outsourcing* is preferred to the term *IT outsourcing*, because IT is sometimes interpreted to be hardware, systems software

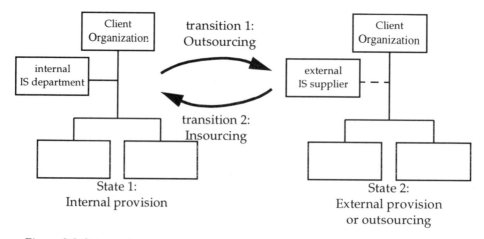

Figure 2.3 Outsourcing as state and as transition

and ready-made software packages. Tailor-made software, people, data and procedures are however also included in this research. The term sourcing will be used for deciding between insourcing or outsourcing.

Outsourcing is different from selling a department or divesting a product or service, because outsourcing concerns activities that remain needed by and are performed for the client organization. Strong relationships remain between the supplier that establishes and sustains the information systems, and the client that uses the information systems.

2.3.3 Activities or resources

Outsourcing can comprise IS activities or IS resources, or both. IS resources include: IS personnel; the hardware and software required to perform IS activities; procedures, such as development methodologies, user support procedures, change procedures; and data, such as information plans, system designs, system documentation. Three types of outsourcing are therefore possible.

Outsourcing activities but not resources occurs if IS activities that were previously performed internally are outsourced. The IS staff and other resources that performed these activities become available and can then be used for other activities, such as developing new information systems or switching to a new technology. The supplier has to have or to obtain staff and other resources to perform the activities that the client organization has outsourced.

Outsourcing activities and resources means that an organization outsources activities as well as the staff and other resources required to perform these activities. The same staff perform the same activities, but from within the supplier organization. The supplier that takes over the activities and resources may, over time, decide to use other resources to perform these activities for the customer, or to deploy the customer's former resources in activities for other customers.

Outsourcing resources but not activities implies that a supplier takes over the IS staff and other resources from a client organization, but not the activities the staff perform. If the client organization wants to continue the activities, they have to obtain other resources. The IS supplier has to find other activities for other customers to deploy the staff and resources they have taken over. This third type of outsourcing is uncommon, because suppliers will usually be prepared to take over staff and resources only if a certain amount of work is guaranteed by the client, at least for as long as it takes to obtain new clients to deploy the staff and resources.

2.3.4 Market or hierarchy relationship

The outsourcing decision is sometimes presented as the choice between provision by the market or within the organization's hierarchy (Williamson, 1985). The dichotomy of markets and hierarchies is however, not as sharp as it may seem. Organizational arrangements vary between the extremes of pure market and pure hierarchy relationships.

According to traditional microeconomics, a pure market relationship is a relationship in which a buyer buys a product or service from one of a large number of suppliers, and transactions take place instantaneously (Douma and Schreuder 1992). Prices are based on the value buyers put on the product or service delivered and on the size of total supply and demand. Buyers and suppliers are independent of each other.

A pure hierarchy relationship is a relationship in which the client organization has full hierarchical power over the supplier, by means of a labor contract that gives the client organization the right to order the supplier to do anything that is within legal and moral boundaries.

In practice, there are market relationships that do not meet the criteria for pure markets and have some characteristics of hierarchical relationships, and vice versa. Williamson (1985), for example, mentions neoclassical contracting, where flexibility and goodwill are more important than the letter of the contract, and relational contracting, based on the relationship as it has developed through time. Ang and Beath (1993) found hierarchical elements in IS development contracts, such as progress meetings and informal dispute resolution mechanisms. Fitzgerald and Willcocks (1994) distinguish six types of contracts, some of which have hierarchical elements, such as cost based pricing and incentive schemes. Conversely, Mantelaers (1995) found that market elements are applied in some hierarchical IS settings, such as internal transfer pricing and internal contracts.

2.3.5 Internal or external IS supplier

The distinction made in definition 7 between internal and external IS suppliers is not straightforward. A number of types of IS suppliers are listed below, ordered from more or less internal to more or less external:

- a business unit's IS department,
- a central IS department at the parent company,
- a dedicated company that is owned jointly by the client organization and an IS supplier.
- an IS supplier the organization has a relationship with, spanning multiple transactions, such as guaranteed spending, fixed tariffs or

a preferred position,
- an IS supplier who depends heavily on the client for most of their business,
- an independent IS supplier with no connection to the client.

This list is neither complete nor disjunctive, and combinations occur. The IS supplier may be the client's former internal IS department. A number of examples of client-supplier relationships in the Netherlands in which it is not immediately clear whether to speak of an internal or an external IS supplier, are listed in Table 2.7.

Simon (1989) distinguishes between internal and external suppliers, which he denotes task organizations and market organizations. If an organizational unit performs a function for one other organizational unit, and is thereby strategically dependent upon the unit, the term

Client organization	IS supplier	Situation in 1996
Fokker Aircraft Company	Debis Systemhaus	In 1992, Fokker decided not to outsource the IS function, after reviewing several proposals of IS suppliers. In 1995, Fokker outsourced its IS department of 140 employees to Debis Systemhaus, the IS subsidiary of Daimler/ Benz, which is the parent company of Fokker. After the bankruptcy of Fokker in 1996, the remaining IS staff were taken over by IBM.
Philips	BSO/Origin	In 1990, Philips outsourced its IS development department of 1,000 employees to BSO, a Dutch software house. Philips took a 40% share in BSO/Origin and around 40% of BSO/Origin's revenues still come from Philips. BSO/Origin have cooperated with Philips' data centre, C&P, in many projects. Recently, BSO/Origin and C&P have merged and operate as Origin.
Dutch central government	RCC (State Computer Centre)	RCC serves the Dutch Ministries and other (central) government organizations. In 1992, the RCC was privatized and is now a private company, though fully owned by the state. Most of its revenue still come from the central government and the public sector in general. In the near future, shares in RCC may be floated on the open market.
NS (Dutch Railways)	CvI (Centre for Information processing)	CvI has been a fully owned but separate subsidiary within NS for over twenty-five years, but has always depended on NS for over 90% of its revenue. In 1995, CvI was outsourced to EDS, a large IS supplier that has taken over many internal IS departments.

Table 2.7 Examples of client-supplier relationships

task organization is used. A task organization is evaluated and paid by another organizational unit, that determines the goals and the continuity of the task organization and takes a binding decision in the case of conflicts

If an organizational unit is independent of other units, then it is called a *market organization*. A market organization has clients that are essentially indifferent to the continuity of the organization. Payment is based on a reward per transaction for products or services delivered. Strategic choices are made by the management of the market organization, and clients are free whether or not to buy the products or services. Conflicts are eventually settled in court.

The examples given in Table 2.7 and the distinctions made by Simon (1989) highlight a number of characteristics of internal and external IS suppliers. Do the client organization and the IS supplier have joint hierarchical authorities? Do they belong to the same legal entity? Does the client organization own the IS supplier? Does the supplier depend upon one client organization for most of its business? Are conflicts resolved by a common superior or in court? Are the IS supplier and the client organization free to chose their business partners, or is the client organization obliged to take services from one supplier and is the supplier not allowed to offer services to other client organizations?

Each of these criteria is relevant and will be used as decision variables in section 2.4.2. The criterion of joint hierarchical authorities is used to define the concept of external suppliers. This follows Wierda (1991), when he defines interorganizational information systems as "information systems that are jointly developed, operated and/or used by two or more organizations that have no joint executive."

Definition 8: *An IS supplier is an organization that performs IS activities for one or more client organizations*

Definition 9: *An external IS supplier is an IS supplier with which a client organization has no joint hierarchical authorities*

The notion of internal and external IS suppliers is a relative distinction. An IS supplier is internal or external with regard to a specific client organization. An IS supplier can be internal for one client organization and external for another, for example if an internal IS department also serves external client organizations.

IS suppliers can themselves outsource certain IS activities and thereby be a client organization in another outsourcing relationship. An IS supplier can, for example, outsource IS activities for their own information needs, such as the pay roll system, or subcontract to other IS suppliers part of the activities it performs for its own clients.

2.4 IS outsourcing decision making

Many different variables play a role in IS outsourcing decision making. In this section, these variables are classified, by modelling IS outsourcing decision making from a systems theory perspective. Each of the classes of variables will be discussed below.

2.4.1 A systems theory perspective

Decision making is intended to change a situation. A systems theory perspective is useful when modelling the variables relevant to a particular decision. One application of systems theory is the *information paradigm* (Brussaard, 1992): "Every open and dynamic system can be modelled as a combination of an information system (IS) and a real system (RS), where the information system controls the behavior of the real system". The IS contains information about the RS and controls the behavior of the IS. The RS has incoming and outgoing physical and/or information flows. The IS has incoming and outgoing information flows. The RS can be a physical transformation process, but can also be an informational process, for example if an organization's primary process is information processing, as is the case for banks and insurance firms and the majority of public sector organizations.

In Figure 2.4, the information paradigm is used to model the problems of IS outsourcing decision making. The decision makers and the decision making process are part of the IS and the IS function makes up the RS. The IS function uses IS resources (arrow (1) in Figure 2.4) to establish and sustain information systems (arrow (2) in Figure 2.4). IS outsourcing decision making requires information on the characteristics of the IS function, such as information about the current information systems that are in use and the size and the quality of the IS staff (arrow (3) in Figure 2.4). Information is also required on characteristics of the client organization, such as the degree of decentralization, and the environment, such as the availability of IS suppliers, developments in technology, and the stability of the client organization's competitive environment (arrow (4) in Figure 2.4). IS outsourcing decision making results in decisions about the IS function, such as the degree of externality and the type of outsourcing (arrow (5) in Figure 2.4). The decision makers report their considerations and results to higher management (arrow (6) in Figure 2.4).

The variables influenced directly by IS outsourcing decisions are called decision variables. The internal and external characteristics that are taken into account by the decision makers are denoted situational factors. The variables used to indicate the actual or required performance of the IS function are called goal variables.

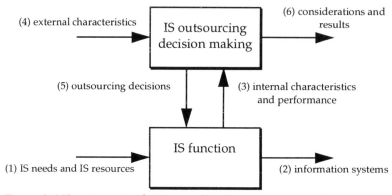

Figure 2.4 IS outsourcing decision making in systems perspective

2.4.2 Changing roles of variables

The classification of variables described in the previous section is not fixed. Specific variables can take different roles depending on the specific situation. In specific situations, decision makers have to decide which variables they must or want to take as situational factors, which decision variables they can and want to change, and on which goal variables they want to optimize.

In the following sections, a number of possible decision variables, situational factors and goal variables are presented. In practice, certain variables often have other roles, that may even change during decision processes. The number of internal IS specialists may, for example, be one of the decision variables in a specific outsourcing decision; it may also however be a situational factor, if for example higher authorities have decided not to hire additional IS staff. The number of internal IS staff may also be a goal variable, if the decision makers have as an objective the reduction of IS staffing levels, irrespective of other consequences.

It should be noted that the distinction between situational factors and decision variables is independent of the question of whether certain variables can be changed. At a sufficiently high level, most of the situational factors can be influenced. The range of possible values of the decision variables will in practice, often be limited. These limitations can, for example, result from the time horizon of the decisions, because some variables may only be adjustable over the long term, or from restrictions of the authority of certain decision makers, because the decision makers may not have the authority to overrule decisions taken earlier or by higher management.

2.4.3 Decision variables

Decision variables are used to describe existing outsourcing situations and the alternative outsourcing options that are considered in a decision process. The decision variables used in this research are based on the aspects that distinguish market relationships from hierarchy relationships and internal IS suppliers from external IS suppliers, as described in section 2.3, and on distinctions that other authors on IS outsourcing have made.

In this section, the variables will be presented separately and without stating the advantages and disadvantages of certain values of the variables. Propositions about the relationships between decision variables and the considerations for closing the appropriate values are derived in chapter 3. The decision variables are classified into five categories (see Table 2.8). Each of the variables is discussed below.

Relationship

Legal relationship

This variable indicates the legal relationship between the client organization and the IS supplier. The parties can be part of the same legal entity, for example if the IS supplier is an internal department of the client organization. They can be separate legal entities, but be part of the same parent company, with which they have a holding-business

---

relationship
- legal relationship
- economic relationship
- transactional relationship
- choice of business partners

division among suppliers and contracts
- number of suppliers
- division among suppliers
- number of contracts
- division among contracts

management structure
- requirements specification
- pricing mechanism
- lead time mechanism
- quality control mechanism
- conflict resolution mechanism
- coordination mechanisms

operational structure
- location
- ownership
- employment
- exclusiveness

internal organization of outsourcing coordination
- decentralization
- line or staff
- outsourcing of outsourcing coordination

Table 2.8 Decision variables

unit relationship or a shareholder relationship. A client organization can also own its IS supplier, totally or partially, or have a joint venture with other client organizations or with an IS supplier.

Economic relationship

Regardless of the formal legal relationship, a client organization and an IS supplier may in practice have a strong economic relationship.

In this book, an IS supplier is said to have a strong economic relationship with a client organization if the client organization represents a considerable part of the IS supplier's business volume, or if the client organization outsources a considerable part of its IS activities to the IS supplier.

An indication of the economic relationship between an IS supplier and a client organization is the percentage of the IS supplier's business volume the client organization represents, and the percentage of the client organization's IS costs that are spent on the IS supplier. The higher these percentages are, the stronger the economic relationship.

Transactional relationship

In the traditional model of a market, transactions take place instantaneously, and buyers and sellers have no relationship before or after the transaction. In practice, client organizations and IS suppliers may have relationships that span multiple transactions and that take place over time.

An informal *working relationship* may evolve after an IS supplier has conducted several activities for the client organization. If the client organization is satisfied, the IS supplier will be invited to write a proposal if new activities are to be outsourced.

A working relationship between a client organization and an IS supplier can be formalized in a *cooperation agreement*. This can, for example, include an agreement on standard contractual conditions, on tariffs and volume discounts or on requests for proposals. Some client organizations have cooperation agreements with a small number of preferred suppliers that are always invited to tender.

If an outsourcing operation involves the transfer of IS staff, then a cooperation agreement can include guaranteed spending, which means that the client organization agrees to spend a certain amount of money over a certain number of years with the IS supplier that takes over the staff, for example an amount comparable to the costs of the IS staff transferred.

Choice of business partners

In a pure market situation, buyers and suppliers are free to chose their business partners. In a pure hierarchy, all transactions take place between units within the organization.

In an organization that has an internal IS department, business units may be obliged to take services from the internal IS department, or have the freedom to chose whether to do business with the internal department or with external IS suppliers.

An internal IS department can be obliged to offer services only to the internal business units, or be allowed to offer products and services to other client organizations.

Division among suppliers and contracts

Number of IS suppliers and division among suppliers

A client organization can outsource to one IS supplier or decide to outsource different parts of the IS function to different IS suppliers.

Client organizations can chose different IS suppliers for different information systems, for example by outsourcing office systems to one IS supplier and secondary systems to another. IS components can also be outsourced to different IS suppliers. Some IS suppliers specialize in certain IS activities; therefore, client organizations can for example outsource development and operation to different IS suppliers.

Number of contracts and division among contracts

The part of the IS function a client organization outsources to one IS supplier can be arranged in one all-encompassing long term contract, or be split into a number of separate contracts.

Similar to dividing work among different IS suppliers, outsourced activities can be divided into separate contracts for separate information systems, IS components and IS activities. A client organization can, for example, decide to outsource development, maintenance and operation of an information system to one IS supplier, but make four separate contracts: a development contract, a software maintenance contract, a hardware maintenance contract and an operation contract.

Management structure

Requirements specification

Decision makers at client organizations can specify the requirements for activities outsourced in broad terms or in great detail. They can also specify requirements in functional terms, for example by describing the information a new information system must deliver, or in technical terms, by describing the components and the working of a system.

Pricing mechanism

A pricing mechanism is needed if an external supplier is involved or if an internal IS supplier charges other business units for its products and services. Fitzgerald and Willcocks (1994) distinguish six types of contracts, each with a different pricing mechanism (see Table 2.9).

Contract	Payment based on
Time and materials	the actual use of personnel and materials
Fixed fee	a lump sum for a defined work load or service
Fixed fee plus variable element	predicted changes in, for example, work loads or business circumstances
Cost plus management fee	the real costs incurred by the vendor plus a percentage
Fee plus incentive scheme	some benefits that accrue to the client company or performance over and above an agreed baseline
Share of risk and reward	how well the client company or a joint venture performs

Table 2.9 Outsourcing contracts (Fitzgerald and Willcocks, 1994)

In this research, the pricing mechanism of a "fixed fee plus variable element" contract is called "workload pricing." "Incentive schemes" can be used in combination with most of the other pricing mechanisms. "Cost plus management fee" is a special case of "time and materials" pricing. The following pricing mechanisms are distinguished:

- *no pricing*, if the IS supplier is an internal department and there is no internal transfer pricing
- *time and materials*, an input based pricing mechanism, based on the actual use of personnel and materials
- *fixed fee*, a lump sum for a defined work load or service
- *work load*, an output based pricing mechanism, based on a fixed fee per unit of work
- *benefits to client*, pricing mechanisms based on the performance of the client, such as increases in revenues or reduction of business costs.

Combinations of pricing mechanisms can occur, such as a fixed fee for a certain service plus a tariff per unit of work, or a time and materials pricing mechanism with a fixed maximum fee.

Lead time mechanism
A client organization can chose to determine a fixed lead time or not to put a limit to the time the supplier may take to perform the IS activities outsourced. If the client organization chooses a fixed lead time, provisions must be made in case the supplier does not meet the agreed deadline.

Quality control mechanism

Quality control mechanisms can be divided into mechanisms for assessing the end product and mechanisms for monitoring the process and intermediate results. Client organizations can also chose who is to assess the quality: having the supplier write quality reports, having the client organization test the quality or having a third party conduct a quality audit.

Conflict resolution mechanism

Conflicts may arise between a client organization and an IS supplier over the activities that were outsourced to the IS supplier. The two extremes in conflict resolution are a binding decision by a joint hierarchical superior in a hierarchy situation, and legal action and a court decision in a market situation. More or less formal dispute resolution mechanisms exist between these extremes.

Ang and Beath (1993) found hierarchical elements in market relationships for IS development, amongst which were procedures for conflict resolution before parties take legal action. This may involve escalation procedures in which the higher management of both parties or a third party try to resolve the dispute.

Coordination mechanisms

The client organization can use different mechanisms to coordinate the IS supplier. Ang (1994) distinguishes two general strategies of performance evaluation: (1) behavioral or process control, i.e., control over the manner in which work is performed: and (2) outcome control, i.e., control over the results of the work. Outsourcing may include the client organization relinquishing behavioral or process control and only controlling the outcome of the activities.

Willcocks and Fitzgerald (1993) make a similar distinction between commissioning of a third party to manage a client organization's information technology assets, people and/or activities, which they call outsourcing, and contracts that call for the market to provide resources to be deployed under the buyer's management and control, which is called insourcing by Feeny et al. (1993).

Mintzberg (1989) distinguishes six coordination mechanisms (see Table 2.10). Standardization of work process is what Ang (1994) calls behavioral or process control. Standardization of output is similar to outcome control.

All five coordination mechanisms may occur in outsourcing relationships, though client organizations have to rely mainly on standardization of skills and standardization of output (Van den Broek, 1990). In this research, the control a client organization has over an outsourcing relationship is denoted by stating which of Mintzberg's coordination mechanisms are used.

Coordination mechanism	Examples in IS outsourcing
mutual adjustment	user participation, clarification of requirement specification
direct supervision	progress meetings, change requests
standardization of work process	prescription of development methodology, quality system, tools to be used
standardization of output	specification of the product or service required
standardization of skills	selection of IS supplier, selection of supplier's staff
standardization of norms	transferring norms, values and beliefs to the supplier

Table 2.10 Examples of Mintzberg's (1989) coordination mechanisms in IS outsourcing

Operational structure

Location

Ang (1994) describes outsourcing using three conceptualizations of organizational boundaries: geographical, legal ownership and control (see Table 2.11). Outsourcing of control is covered by the coordination mechanisms described above.

The first conceptualization, geographical outsourcing, refers to the location of the activity. IS activities that are outsourced can be performed on the premises of the IS supplier, but there can also be reasons to locate the activities at the client organization's premises.

The location can be different for different IS components. Certain pieces of hardware can be held at the IS supplier's premises, while users and other pieces of hardware reside with the client organization. With modern operation tools, IS staff can operate large computers at

Conceptualization	Description
geographical outsourcing	business activity is performed or located away from the premises of the business entity
outsourcing of ownership employment	an organization relinquishes legal ownership of and those physical assets required to conduct and execute business activities, and/or uses non-employee agents to execute the business activities
outsourcing of process control	an organization relinquishes process control and relies on outcome control over external service-providers

Table 2.11 Conceptualizations of organizational boundaries (Ang 1994)

other locations, by remote operation. External IS developers can work in the IS supplier's office or at the client organization.

Not all combinations of locations and components will occur. Software and data are bound to the location of the processing and storage hardware. Software and data can however be developed and gathered at another location than where it is going to be operated and used. Users are bound to the location of the data entry and presentation hardware. Procedures can not be said to have a location.

Ownership

Ang's (1994) second conceptualization of outsourcing, outsourcing of ownership, refers to the ownership of the physical assets and to the employment relationship between client organization and IS staff.

Ang defines legal ownership boundaries using property rights associated with the ownership of assets. Ownership refers to a bundle of property rights that an economic agent or a group of agents is legally entitled to exercise over a tangible or intangible asset. The three main components in this bundle of rights are: (1) the right of utilization or determination of use, (2) the right to possess the products of the asset for the costs of its use, and (3) the right to alienate or dispose of the asset.

This variable should not be confused with the variable "legal relationship" which was defined earlier. "Legal relationship" refers to whether the client organization owns the IS supplier. "Ownership" refers to whether the IS components are owned by the client organization or by the IS supplier.

Ownership of the IS components can reside with the client organization, even when the activities performed on those components are outsourced. With outsourcing of software development, for example, the client organization often becomes the owner of the resulting software. Operation of computers can be outsourced without selling the computers to the IS supplier.

Employment

IS staff can have an employment relationship with the client organization or with the IS supplier. In the latter case, the supplier's staff works for the client in a contractor relationship instead of an employment relationship (Ang, 1994).

Exclusiveness

A client organization can decide to have exclusive use of IS components or to allow other organizations to use the components.

Dedicated use of components that are developed and maintained by an external IS supplier means that the IS supplier is not allowed to let other client organizations use the components.

Shared use of components in an outsourcing situation means that the IS supplier is allowed to offer the components to other client organizations. Examples of shared use are ready-made software packages, time-sharing on large computers, and IS staff working for several client organizations at the same time.

Shared use of components of an internal IS department means that the internal IS department offers the products and services it develops for internal clients to other organizations. Internal IS departments sometimes develop software that can be useful for other organizations, without harming the interests of the parent organization. Some client organizations offer the excess capacity of their large computers or their wide area network to other organizations.

Internal organization of outsourcing coordination

Decentralization
Outsourcing coordination can be centralized in one unit that coordinates all outsourcing relationships that the client organization has, or be decentralized so that each business unit manages its own outsourcing relationships.

Line versus staff
Outsourcing coordination can be allocated to line managers and users, or to staff units. This dimension is sometimes called vertical (de)centralization (Mintzberg, 1979).

Outsourcing of outsourcing coordination
The capacity and skills required for outsourcing coordination may not be available within the client organization. Some of the outsourcing coordination activities can however also be outsourced. This would mean that an external organization or expert assists the client organization and designs and manages the outsourcing relationship on behalf of the client organization.

2.4.4 Situational factors
One of the assumptions of this research is that no single solution or outsourcing option is best for every situation. The optimal IS outsourcing decision will depend on the specific situation. One of the objectives of the research was to determine which characteristics of a specific situation are relevant and how these situational factors should be taken into account when making outsourcing decisions.

In this book, situational factors are divided into three categories. The first category contains characteristics of the IS *function* and the *information systems* that are to be established and sustained. The second category are characteristics of the client organization and its environment. The third category consists of characteristics of the IS market and suppliers. A few examples of situational factors are given in Table 2.12.

Categories	Examples
IS function and information systems	scale, complexity, uniqueness, variability
client organization and environment	IS maturity, information intense business processes, IS usage by competitors
IS market and suppliers	number of IS suppliers for certain activity, supplier concentration, availability of market information

Table 2.12 Categories and examples of situational factors

2.4.5 Goal variables

The IS activities, whether performed internally or by an external supplier, can be evaluated in terms of goal variables. The primary criteria on which an activity is evaluated is whether the activity is performed within cost and time constraints and whether the result meets the specified requirements. Costs, lead time and quality must always be considered in conjunction. It is useless, for example, to talk of reducing costs without stating that lead time and quality must remain the same. Other goal variables that are distinguished in this research are flexibility, controllability and continuity.

Costs

The costs of an IS activity are interpreted in this book as the costs incurred by the client organization for having that activity performed. All direct and indirect costs of the IS function have to be determined and allocated to the pertinent part of the IS function, according to standard micro economic allocation criteria.

The costs of IS activities that are performed internally consist of the costs of performing the actual activities, management and other overhead costs, and costs incurred by non-IS specialists.

The costs of outsourced IS activities include the money paid to the IS supplier, the internal costs of searching for and selecting an IS supplier, negotiating a contract, and monitoring the performance of the IS supplier. The payments to the IS supplier include, above the costs of actually performing the activity, management and other costs and the costs of searching for and getting clients, negotiating a contract and reporting to the client organization.

costs
lead time
quality
flexibility
controllability
continuity

Table 2.13 Goal variables

Lead time

In this book, lead time is defined as the time between the moment requirements for an activity have been specified and the moment the result of the activity is accepted.

If the activity is performed internally, the lead time not only includes the time to actually perform the activity, for example to develop certain software, but also includes the time it takes to hire or retrain IS staff, if necessary, and the time until the internal IS department has capacity available to start the activity.

If the activity is outsourced, the lead time also includes the time it takes to search for appropriate IS suppliers, to develop a request for proposals, to evaluate proposals, to select an IS supplier, to negotiate a contract and to get the IS supplier acquainted with the organization and the business process of the client organization.

Quality

In this book, quality is defined as the degree to which activities are performed according to specified requirements. The desired result of an activity is defined in terms of functional and technical requirements.

Flexibility

Changes in business processes, information needs or available technologies may ask for changes in information systems. Flexibility of the IS function is defined as the degree to which IS activities that are needed can be started at any time. The flexibility of IS activities is defined as the degree to which requirements can be changed or terminated at any time.

Controllability

Controllability is the client organization's ability to ensure that the activities are performed satisfactorily. Controllability applies to the first three goal variables and is defined as the degree to which costs, lead time and quality can be predicted, measured and if necessary be enforced.

Continuity

Continuity is defined as the probability that a certain product or service will be delivered satisfactorily for as long as the client organization has a need for it.

Continuity includes more than the probability that the IS supplier will not go bankrupt. Continuity also depends on a number of other factors, such as whether the IS supplier will keep serving the particular group of clients, whether new versions of software packages and tools will be released and whether the technology used will remain up to date. Mergers and take-overs between IS suppliers may cause disruptions in service. Continuity also depends on the continuity of internal or external IS staff, especially if certain critical knowledge resides with a small number of people, or turnover is high.

2.5 Conclusions

The descriptional framework developed in this chapter is intended to fulfil the need for clear terminology in IS outsourcing. The framework can be used by management in organizations, to evaluate existing IS outsourcing situations, or to describe different outsourcing options in a decision process. The framework consists of a classification of the IS function, decision variables, situational factors and goal variables.

The *IS function* is classified by the information systems, the IS activities and the IS components it contains (see Figure 2.1). A specific part of the IS function that is under consideration of a decision process can be described along these three dimensions: what activities are performed with what components of what information systems?

Outsourcing decisions are described using decision variables (see Table 2.8). These variables can be used to describe an existing situation or to express a certain change, for example, changing the location and the employment of the IS staff. Alternative outsourcing options can be characterized by choosing a value of the decision variables for each of the alternatives.

Situational factors are the characteristics of the specific situation that are relevant to outsourcing decisions (see Table 2.12). In an existing outsourcing situation, the situational factors can be analyzed to determine whether the current situation is optimal. The factors can also be used to chose among alternative outsourcing options. The relationships between situational factors and outsourcing decisions will be derived from organizational theories, in chapter 3, and the case studies, in chapter 4.

An IS outsourcing situation is evaluated in terms of *goal variables* (see Table 2.13). Evaluating an existing situation should be done by assessing the situation with regard to each of the goal variables. Alternative outsourcing options in a decision process can be compared by assessing the value of the variables for each of the alternatives.

The use of the framework will be described more extensively in chapter 5, where the prescriptive model for IS outsourcing decision making is presented.

CHAPTER 3

Theoretical
Perspectives

The question of outsourcing is the subject of various organizational theories. A number of established organizational theories are analyzed in this chapter and elements that appear applicable are adapted to the issue of IS outsourcing. The guidelines resulting from the organizational theories are investigated in practice (chapter 4), to provide a theoretical and empirical basis for the prescriptive model for IS outsourcing decision making presented in chapter 5.

3.1 Introduction

The theories that appear to be useful for analyzing IS outsourcing are mostly economic theories considering markets and organizations, as outsourcing is an organizational decision with many economic consequences. Economic approaches to organizations focus specifically on the economic problem of optimal allocation of scarce resources. The descriptions given in this chapter are based mainly on Douma and Schreuder's (1992) book, *Economic Approaches to Organizations*, which provides an excellent and coherent overview of the economic theories involved.

The theoretical perspectives are used pragmatically and as a source of guidelines for IS outsourcing. The research presented is in the area of IS management, and is not an economic or organizational study; therefore it should not be judged as such. Economics and organizational science serve as reference disciplines, while the core discipline of this research is IS management. Not all elements of the theories are used and no pretence is made that the descriptions in this chapter are complete and comprehensive reviews of the economic theories discussed below.

To apply an economic theory to the field of IS outsourcing is not a matter of simply filling in the variables of the various theories. Economic notions, such as standardization, products, services, economies of scale, and specificity, need to be adapted to IS to be applicable to IS outsourcing.

Literature on procurement (e.g., Van Weele, 1992; Kraljic, 1983) is not treated separately in this chapter, but a number of findings from this body of literature is included implicitly. There is little scientific literature on procurement (Van Weele, 1992), and the literature that is available is based mainly on the organizational theories that are analyzed in this chapter. Procurement literature is focused mainly on procurement of raw materials and components and less on procurement of client-specific services and capital goods. The procurement of IS products and services is fundamentally different, as information systems are integrated parts of business processes instead of separated processes at the front or the end of an organization's production chain.

A number of theoretical perspectives is presented below. Each section starts with an outline of the theory. Elements of the theory are then adapted to IS outsourcing, by interpreting the goal variables, the decision variables, the situational factors, and the relationships between these variables, to IS outsourcing. Some theories distinguish intermediate variables that influence the goal variables and are influenced by the decision variables and situational factors. Some of the theories given have also been applied to IS outsourcing by other researchers, and their conceptual and empirical conclusions are included in this chapter.

The theories are described from a contingency perspective. The pilot study for this research revealed that the arguments used in outsourcing decisions and the actual decisions taken depend on the specific situation. In this research, a contingency perspective is taken, which rests on the belief that "no universal set of strategic choices exists that is optimal for all businesses, irrespective of their resource positions and environmental context" (Ginzberg and Venkatraman, 1985). Thus, effective strategies are those which achieve a fit or congruence between environmental conditions and organizational factors; therefore, there are situations under which outsourcing may or may not be appropriate (Cheon, Grover and Teng, 1995). In this chapter, contingency factors, or situational factors, will be derived from established organizational theories.

3.2 Division of labor and coordination

Organizational activities are usually divided among employees and organizational units. This division of labor has certain advantages, but also introduces the need for coordination. Coordination is basically information processing, and consists of providing organizational units with the information necessary to perform their tasks.

Activities can be coordinated using market coordination, by

organizational coordination, or by intermediate or combined types of coordination. Market coordination relies mainly on the price mechanism, while organizational coordination uses authority and other procedural coordination mechanisms.

The actual mix of coordination mechanisms to be used in a given situation, will depend mainly on the information requirements inherent in the situation. Ideal markets are characterized by the operation of prices as "sufficient statistics." That is to say, the price contains all the information needed for the coordination of transactions. In very many situations however, the price mechanism is complemented or substituted by organizational coordination mechanisms. Apparently, there are many situations in which a price cannot absorb all the necessary information to enable the execution of transactions, because of fundamental information problems which cannot be resolved by the price system. Thus, organizations arise as solutions to information problems.

The choice between market coordination or organizational coordination is the basic question in IS outsourcing, and therefore, the findings of coordination literature are very relevant to IS outsourcing decision making.

3.2.1 Division of labor

Adam Smith is usually credited with being the founding father of modern economics (Douma and Schreuder, 1992). He accords great importance to the division of labor and holds that it has improved productivity to a great extent. Division of labor refers to the splitting of composite tasks into their component parts and having these parts performed separately. Division of labor is a fact of life. Nobody is completely self-supporting and everybody buys certain goods or services. Most people work in organizations, where they usually perform only a small part of the entire organizational task.

Division of labor occurs within organizational units between individual employees at the micro level, but also between more or less autonomous organizational units at the meso level, and between the public and the private sector and all intermediate forms at the macro level (Brussaard, 1994).

There are economies of labor specialization to be gained through increased division of labor. Specialized production is more efficient, because workers become good at their specialized tasks. They can devote all their attention to improving their performance, they can learn form experience and can devise methods and instruments which will further improve their execution of the task. They will lose less time when switching from one type of work to another during operations.

Specialization improves performance, but also restricts choice options for deploying employees and resources. To individuals, the limits of specialization are reached when the satisfaction gained from higher performance and the corresponding reward is outweighed by the dissatisfaction arising from a too narrow area of skills application.

Increasing the scale at which activities are performed may yield economies of scale, because the larger scale increases production efficiency and labor specialization. Production efficiency is increased on the larger scale by better utilization of the capacity of staff and resources, by re-use of knowledge and skills across activities and by increased motivation of employees due to optimal use of their qualities and better career perspectives (Mintzberg, 1979).

3.2.2 Market coordination

Standard microeconomic theory focuses on how economic decisions are coordinated by the market mechanism. Economic decisions have to be made by consumers and by producers. Consumers can choose between a large number of goods and must decide how much they are going to consume. Producers must decide how much they are going to produce and how they are going to produce.

Outline of market coordination. The total demand for a certain good depends on the price for that good. If the price of a certain good goes down, and everything else remains the same, then total demand will generally go up. The relationship between price and quantity demanded is called the *demand curve*. The total quantity supplied also depends on the price. If prices go up, and everything remains the same, then total supply will generally go up. The relationship between price and quantity supplied is called the *supply curve*. Market equilibrium occurs where the demand curve and the supply curve intersect.

The theory of demand assumes that each consumer derives a certain satisfaction from having a specific good, which is called the consumer's utility of that good. The theory of production describes a firm as an entity that maximizes an objective function, normally profit, or the value of the firm on the stock market. A production function describes the relationship between any combination of inputs and the maximum output that a firm can produce with those inputs. In competitive markets prices are determined by the process of market interaction. Individual firms cannot set their own prices and maximize their profit by setting the quantity of their supply to the value that maximizes the difference between their costs and their revenues, as described by their production function.

In a competitive market a firm can earn no economic profit in the long run. Economic profit is profit in excess of normal profit, where normal profit is defined as the profit that a firm needs to stay in business, that is the opportunity cost of the equity capital provided by the owners of the firm. If profit is lower than the opportunity cost of equity capital, the owners may decide to take their capital out of the firm and employ it elsewhere. If there are economic profits, new firms will enter the market, supply will increase, price would go down and the economic profits will vanish.

In an ideal market, buyers and sellers only need to know the price of a certain good and need not have any kind of personal contact because the price system forms the coordinating device which takes care of allocation. The price contains all the information a buyer needs to base the transaction on.

Assumptions of market coordination. The model of perfect competition is based on a number of assumptions. There are three assumptions that, when relaxed, lead to other models within the context of standard microeconomics:

1. There are a *large number of buyers and sellers,* each of which is too small to affect the market price.
2. There is *free entry and exit* of firms, and no barriers to keep new firms from entering or to keep existing firms from exiting the market.
3. The industry is characterized by *homogeneous, standardized* products and consumers do not differentiate between products from different sellers.

These assumptions are relaxed in other models of standard microeconomics such as the models of monopoly and oligopoly. Four additional assumptions underlay all the models of standard microeconomics (Douma and Schreuder, 1992):

4. Firms are viewed as *holistic units* and everyone within a firm takes all decisions solely with the firm's objective in mind.
5. Firms are assumed to have a *single objective,* either to maximize profits or to increase the value of the firm on the stock market.
6. There is *perfect information;* every buyer and seller knows everything that is relevant to making decisions on consumption and production, and the price is the only remaining variable.
7. The behavior of producers and consumers is described as *maximizing behavior;* parties know all alternatives and they are able to compare all decision alternatives and to choose the one that maximizes the objective function.

In practice, most markets do not comply to one or more of these assumptions.

Information required for market transactions. One of the assumptions of the model of perfect competition deserves special attention: the assumption that buyers and sellers have perfect information and that the price is the only remaining variable. Since coordination is essentially information processing, it is relevant to analyze what additional information buyers and sellers may need, and why market coordination may not be able to provide that information.

In the model of perfect competition, knowledge of the price is sufficient because in this model each buyer and seller only has to decide how much to buy or to produce of a homogeneous good. In practice, prices are often not enough and parties need additional information. If products are not homogeneous, buyers base the price they want to pay on the *quality* of the product or service. For some products, quality is standardized, while for others, buyers want to inspect the quality before buying the product.

The quality of a product or service may not be known to anyone at the time the transaction is closed. In this case there is uncertainty as to the future quality of the product. Parties might agree to base prices on the actual quality to be inspected at the time of delivery in a *contingent claims contract.* Such a contract is possible only if there is a way, which is acceptable to both parties, to determine the quality of the product. Markets are however, not able to handle very much uncertainty, because of the cognitive limitation of human mind which is unable to juggle a large number of uncertain factors simultaneously.

If information is available but it is unevenly distributed, there is an *information asymmetry.* Sellers may not always want to reveal this information, because disclosure sometimes decreases the value of the information. Information asymmetries arise from uneven distribution and unobservability of information relevant to the distribution of benefits of a transaction, and from a lack of incentive for the party to disclose information. If uncertainty is high or if significant information asymmetries exist between buyer and seller, then organizational coordination may be necessary to meet the information requirements of the buyer and the seller to avoid the abuse of information asymmetries.

3.2.3 Organizational coordination

Mintzberg (1979) has synthesized the organizational literature on the structure of organizations. He poses coordination as the central problem of organization design. He does not recognize however, that coordination is essentially information processing, and therefore he does not offer a basis for designing and managing information systems and IS management. His findings are however, relevant for describing coordination mechanisms and analyzing what coordination mechanisms are best suited for specific situations.

Coordination mechanisms. Mintzberg (1989) distinguishes six types of organizational coordination mechanisms:

1. *mutual adjustment,* which achieves coordination by the simple process of informal communication between operating employees,

2. *direct supervision*, in which coordination is achieved by having one person issue orders or instructions to several others whose work is interrelated,
3. *standardization of work processes*, which achieves coordination by specifying the work processes of people carrying out interrelated tasks,
4. *standardization of outputs*, which achieves coordination be specifying the required results of an activity,
5. *standardization of skills*, in which work is coordinated by specifying the education and training the workers must have received,
6. *standardization of norms*, where the norms determining the work are controlled, usually for the entire organization, so that everyone functions according to the same standards.

All six coordination mechanisms are alternatives to the pricing mechanism for communicating information. The type of information requirements present in any situation will determine the actual mix of coordination mechanisms in that situation. Mintzberg (1989) distinguishes six types of organizations, which he calls *configurations*, that have different dominant coordination mechanisms, determined by the type of work involved and other contingency factors.

• *Entrepreneurial organizations* use direct supervision as the dominant coordination mechanism, as a single person can oversee the entire organization and have knowledge of all operations.
• *Machine organizations* rely on standardization of work processes; this is only possible if technological developments are slow and production is rationalized.
• *Professional organizations* are organizations that have a high amount of professional work, such as research and development, or systems design. Professional work cannot be standardized; all an organization can do is standardize the skills required for executing this work, for instance by demanding a certain type of training.
• *Diversified organizations* are often controlled by standardizing the output of the divisions, in terms of product specifications and financial results, leaving them considerable autonomy as to how to achieve these goals.
• In *innovative organizations*, a high degree of innovative work requires the collaboration of many different specialists, who coordinate by mutual adjustment.
• *Missionary organizations* standardize the norms and values of their work force.

Uncertainty and information processing. Galbraith (1973, 1977) gives a theoretical basis that incorporates the interconnection between organizing and information processing. His theory states that each organizational unit has to cope with uncertainty about the tasks to be performed. Uncertainty is defined as the difference between the information the organizational unit has to hand and the information that is needed to perform the task. The degree of uncertainty is determined by the diversity of production resources, the diversity of products or services to be delivered, the efficiency demanded and the length of the period of time available for completion of the task. Organizational forms must be chosen so that these information needs can be fulfilled. If the information needs can not be fulfilled by rules, objectives and hierarchical coordination, four additional strategies can be followed:

•To reduce the need for information. This involves a decrease in productivity. The need for information can be reduced by:

❐ creating *slack resources* for the execution of the tasks, by for example, increasing stock levels, allowing lower utilization of production resources, or loosening time schedules,
❐ creating *self-contained units* with less mutual dependencies and therefore, a reduced need for information; units have their own support functions and specialties instead of using centralized services.

• To improve the information processing. This increases the costs of coordination. Information processing can be improved by:

❐ building *vertical information systems* to provide for structured information that is known in advance,
❐ creating *lateral relationships*, which are forms of organization and communications that go across hierarchical structures, to provide for unstructured information that is not known in advance.

3.2.4 Intermediate coordination

Organizational coordination and market coordination are not mutually exclusive. Markets may also exist within organizations, and many markets are organized to some extent.

Organizational markets. Within large diversified organizations, transactions between divisions may take place, which are often effected against an internal transfer price. Transactions can include the delivery of goods, but also the delivery of capital, since corporate management allocates its funds between the divisions, and allocates labor force, when divisions compete for the best human resources.

Organized markets. Markets can be organized to some extent. Most markets are controlled by government regulations and sometimes supervised by a board or commission. Informal communication, which is mutual adjustment, often takes place between suppliers, for example to divide markets between them or to set prices. Culture, which is standardization of norms, influences business practices. A client and a supplier seldom use only contract clauses and legal action to coordinate their efforts.

3.2.5 Application of division of labor and coordination to IS outsourcing

Outsourcing is a form of division of labor found at the meso level, between client organizations and IS suppliers. Adapting the variables and relationships to IS outsourcing leads to the following proposition, which is elaborated in the following sections:

Outsourcing is beneficial if suppliers have more economies of scale than the client, if there is sufficient market pressure, and if the client organization retains control.

Intermediate variables and situational factors

Economies of scale

Economies of scale depend on the scale and similarity of activities, the inherent possibilities for economies of scale, and the presence or absence of barriers to re-use.

IS suppliers have more economies of scale than client organizations only if they perform the pertinent activities and if the IS supplier performs the specific activities on a considerably larger scale. This may seem very trivial, but in practice suppliers are often assumed to have economies of scale, regardless of whether their scale of working is actually larger. Scale is not a matter of comparing the size of the client organization's IS function with the size of the IS supplier. The total size of the IS supplier is not very relevant if the pertinent activity is only a small part of the supplier's portfolio. If a client organization for example, outsources the development of a specific environmental control system, then a large supplier with little or no experience in developing environmental systems will have no economies of scale over the client organization.

Activities of multiple clients must be similar enough to enable the supplier to use the same staff and resources for multiple clients. If clients have unique or idiosyncratic needs, then suppliers must designate staff and resources and can not achieve economies of scale.

IS activities differ in their *inherent possibilities for economies of scale.* Some activities require considerable scale to be performed efficiently, while the efficiency for other activities hardly improves with increasing scale. The inherent possibilities for economies of scale are large for activities that require large initial, step-wise investments, such as mainframe operation and disaster recovery services, or large investments in training and learning time, such as developing systems with innovative development tools, programming languages or system software. The inherent advantages of scale are small for activities that are extremely dispersed, such as user support and personal computer maintenance, or when little capital investment is needed, such as with consultancy.

The possibilities for the IS supplier to achieve economies of scale also depend on possible barriers to re-use, that is, whether the supplier is allowed and enabled to share knowledge, skills and resources among multiple clients and is able to integrate the activities for multiple clients in one unit. If a client organization demands the exclusive use of certain staff, resources or components, then the IS supplier will not be able to achieve the advantages of a larger scale.

Market pressure

Market pressure on IS suppliers depends on the number of IS suppliers, the barriers to entry and exit, whether products are homogeneous, and the availability of market information

Specific market segments comply to a greater or lesser extent to the conditions of the ideal market. If a market segment is fairly close to an ideal market, then the market pressure on IS suppliers is high and suppliers must deliver good products or services at a reasonable price to avoid being outperformed by competitors and going bankrupt.

The *number* of IS suppliers refers to the number of suppliers that provide a particular IS product or service. If a client organization wants to outsource the maintenance of software for processing insurance claims, then it is not the total number of IS suppliers that is relevant, but the number of suppliers that have the knowledge, skills and experience to maintain software for processing insurance claims. If this number is very small, then the market pressure on these few suppliers is not very high and outsourcing is not advisable.

The *barriers* to enter or exit are high for activities that require large investments, such as mainframe operation or disaster recovery facilities, and for activities that require lengthy learning times and have a large learning curve.

The assumption of a *homogeneous* product and indifferent buyers does not hold for most IS products and services. Features and quality are relevant and buyers are not indifferent to differences between IS products and services offered by different suppliers. The only IS products that are fairly homogeneous are certain types of hardware, such as IBM-compatible personal computers, but even with personal computers, prices vary by a factor of two and brands differ in features, quality, reliability and service.

The availability of market information is essential for market pressure. Client organizations must know what products and services are available from what suppliers, they must know the features and quality of IS products and services and the specialties and qualities of the IS suppliers, and they must know what are reasonable prices and lead times for IS activities. This is very difficult in most segments of the IS market. Products and services are not standardized and there is no universal agreed terminology to describe products and services unambiguously. Products of different suppliers are seldom interchangeable. Even prices and tariffs are not widely known and are difficult to obtain.

Control

Client organizations can retain control only if output measurability is high and if uncertainty and information asymmetry are low.

Client organizations that have outsourced IS activities are restricted to coordinating external IS suppliers mainly by standardization of output and skills. Output can be controlled by specifying the requirements in the contract, and skills can be controlled by selecting an IS supplier with the necessary knowledge and experience to perform the activities, and sometimes by selecting the personnel that the supplier deploys.

The *outcome measurability* of many IS activities is however often not enough to be controlled solely by skills and output. Many IS activities are not standardized enough and requirements are not quantifiable enough to rely only on output (De Wijs, 1995). Since these activities can not be managed by output or skills, they should not be outsourced. Innovative IS activities and activities requiring highly professional skills can not be controlled by output, and outsourcing these activities will endanger the client organization's control.

The factors that determine uncertainty, according to Galbraith (1973), can be adapted to determine the uncertainty found in IS activities. Uncertainty depends on the diversity of IS production resources, such as the different IS skills and tools necessary to develop and operate information systems. The diversity of IS products and services is another factor that determines uncertainty. The efficiency demanded is operationalized as the costs that may be incurred to perform the IS activities. The length of the period of time for completion is operationalized as the lead time for IS activities, such as the lead time demanded for developing a system or the lead time before a maintenance request is handled by the IS supplier.

Information asymmetries arise if IS suppliers have information that the client organization does not have. The IS area is still relatively new and developing fast, so users and managers do not always know all the possibilities and limitations of information technology as a good IS supplier should do. Information asymmetries increase when IS products and services are less standardized.

Decision variables

Coordination mechanisms

If IS activities are outsourced, the client organization can coordinate the IS supplier using mainly standardization of skills and output. The other coordination mechanisms are also applicable to some extent.

1. *Mutual adjustment* can be used, for example, by holding regular meetings with the IS supplier's staff, by having the supplier's staff interview the users to determine the user requirements, or by having the users call the supplier's help desk when problems arise.
2. *Direct supervision* of the supplier by the client occurs if project management is performed by a client organization's employee, or if the client organization hires the IS supplier's staff to work under its own management.
3. *Standardization of work processes* of the IS supplier includes prescribing the development methodology, data modelling technique, format of documentation, and the project management tool the supplier must use.
4. *Standardization of outputs* implies defining the requirements for the product or service the IS supplier must deliver. This is usually part of the contract, but determining the requirements can also be part of the activities themselves, for example when developing a new information system.
5. *Standardization of skills* involves selecting the IS supplier with the necessary skills, and possibly selecting the personnel to be deployed by the IS supplier.
6. *Standardization of norms* involves imposing some of the client organization's norms and culture on the IS supplier and having the IS supplier's staff act according to these norms.

Strategies for reducing uncertainty

If the amount of uncertainty for outsourced IS activities is high, then Galbraith's (1973) strategies for uncertainty reduction can be applied to the outsourcing relationship:

• creating *slack resources*, by lowering the demands on the supplier, by not monitoring the supplier's performance very closely, or by having the supplier deploy more personnel or resources,

- creating *self contained units* that reduce the need for the supplier to coordinate with the client organization, such as including users in a project team for system development, or outsourcing activities that are interconnected to one supplier,
- building *vertical information systems*, such as a repository of system design data shared by the client and the supplier, automated monitoring by the client of performance and resource utilization, and providing automated reports of the suppliers progress for the client,
- creating *lateral relationships* between the client organization and the IS supplier, such as a joint steering committee, a supplier's help desk at the client organization's office, and employees of the client organization working temporarily with the IS supplier.

3.3 Transaction cost theory

Transaction cost theory is a perspective that has been applied to IS outsourcing by several academics, such as Beath (1987), Klepper (1993), Lacity and Hirschheim (1993). These authors state that it provides a theoretical framework for describing and explaining the IS outsourcing phenomenon (Willcocks, Lacity and Feeny, 1995).

3.3.1 Outline of the transaction cost theory

The idea of a transaction cost was introduced by Coase (1937) and developed principally by Williamson (1975, 1979, 1985). Williamson developed transaction cost theory when he became troubled by a discrepancy between economic theory and organizational reality (Lacity and Hirschheim, 1993). Economic theory predicts that goods and services are most efficiently produced in specialized companies that are able to achieve economies of scale. Why then, Williamson questioned, has the twentieth century witnessed the growth of large bureaucracies that produce many functions internally? (Perrow, 1986).

Coase (1937) maintained that usually there is a cost for using the price system. There is a cost for finding out what the relevant prices are and to drawing up a contract, and there may be conditions under which it is hardly possible, or extremely costly, to reach an adequate contractual agreement. In those cases, organization may provide an alternative. Within organizations, the price system is replaced by authority as a coordination mechanism.

Transaction cost theory assumes that, in practice, markets are not perfect, and that these imperfections lead to costs. The theory acknowledges explicitly the imperfections of the market mechanism, and maintains that the organization of economic activity depends on balancing production costs against the cost of transacting (Cheon, Grover and Teng, 1995). Transactions are here, the exchanges of goods or services between economic actors, who are technologically separate units, found inside or outside the organization (Williamson, 1985).

Decision variables

Governance structure
For a given transaction, managers can chose between two governance mechanisms to govern the transaction:

- hierarchical governance: produce the transaction internally,
- market governance: purchase the transaction from a vendor.

In later publications, Williamson distinguishes a third governance mechanism, clans or ritual communities, relatively small, closed groups of actors with a shared culture, where transactions are based on trust and oral agreements. Williamson distinguishes three types of market governance:

- market governance using a contract equal to sale,
- market governance using a trilateral contract, in which third-party arbitrators resolve disputes,
- market governance using a bilateral contract, where the mutual obligations of both parties are spelt out.

Contracts
Williamson (1979) describes three types of contracts that can be used to organize transactional relationships:

- *classical contracts*, where buyer and seller exchange a discrete, homogeneous product or service,
- *neoclassical contracts*, in which not all future contingencies are spelled out, but a mechanism for solving disputes is established in the contract, such as third party arbitration to resolve arguments and evaluate performance,
- *relational contracts*, where a buyer and seller develop a relationship and the contract may be adapted as the relationship between buyer and seller changes over time.

Goal variables

Transaction cost theory holds that the firm considering the market versus hierarchy option will behave in a cost-economizing way. Williamson (1975) claims that costs come primarily from two sources, production and coordination. These costs must be considered when determining whether the appropriate governance structure for a transaction is a market or a hierarchy. *Coordination costs*, i.e., transaction costs, are the costs associated with planning, adapting and monitoring task completion (Williamson, 1979), which requires defining, negotiating and enforcing contracts and monitoring and coordinating activities across organizational borders. Production costs are the costs associated directly with the handling of the task (Williamson 1979). The most efficient choice is a trade-off between production costs and coordination costs.

Intermediate variables

Production costs are influenced by the intermediate variable economies of scale. Transaction costs are caused by five factors: two human factors, namely opportunism and bounded rationality, two environmental factors, namely uncertainty/complexity and the number of suppliers, and the atmosphere of a transaction (see Figure 3.1). Opportunism is treated here as an intermediate variable, because opportunism influences transaction costs and is influenced by the other factors in the transaction cost framework. The factor atmosphere is not used in this research.

Economies of scale

Williamson assumes that markets provide lower production costs than hierarchies, due primarily to the economies of scale that a service provider enjoys. This assumption is only valid under certain conditions, as was shown in section 3.2.1.

Opportunism

Opportunism extends the notion that people act in their own self-interest to "self-interest seeking with guile" (Williamson, 1975). People may not always be trustworthy, honest, or purport unfair representations. Buyers and sellers have different interests. The buyer wants good products or services at low cost, while the seller wants high revenues and low costs.

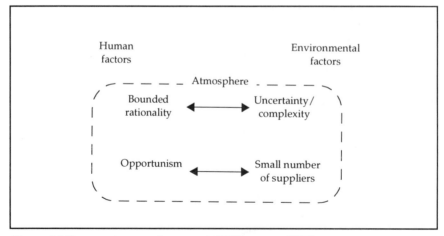

Figure 3.1 Transaction cost framework (Williamson, 1975)

Effects on governance structure

Williamson assumes that markets cause companies to incur higher coordination costs than if the transaction was handled internally, because there is a greater likelihood of opportunistic behavior on the part of the supplier than would be expected from internal sources, thus giving rise to the need to monitor the supplier more closely.

Hierarchies should have lower transaction costs because employees have less opportunity for opportunistic behavior and because mechanisms to monitor employees are already in place. Within the organization, it is not necessary to predict all future contingencies, and situations can be treated as they arise. This relaxes the problems of bounded rationality. Opportunism will be less because organizational units have a shared profit motive. Internal motivation and control mechanisms are more sophisticated and conflict resolution will be much cheaper.

Production costs and market costs therefore have opposite effects on the efficiency of governance structures (see Table 3.1). The trade-off between production costs and transaction costs depends on the characteristics of the transactions and the parties involved.

Situational factors

A number of situational factors determine under what circumstances a hierarchy is more efficient than a market. Most of these situational factors are related to the information needs of the parties. The market model is chosen if all the relevant information is readily available to all parties. If uncertainty is too high to be dealt with by the price mechanism, the hierarchy model is chosen, which provides the information via planning and budgeting procedures and management information systems.

Asset specificity

Asset specificity refers to the degree of customization of the transaction and is defined as the degree to which the transaction will produce an asset that is dedicated to a special purpose with poor alternative uses. A transaction is highly asset specific if it cannot readily be used by other companies because of site specificity, physical asset specificity, or human asset specificity.

• *Site specificity* refers to transactions that are available at a certain

Governance structure	Production costs	Coordination costs
Markets	Low	High
Hierarchies	High	Low

Table 3.1 Cost structures of markets and hierarchies (Malone, Yates and Benjamin, 1987)

location and can only be transported at a great cost.
- *Physical asset specificity* refers to how specialized the equipment must be to complete the transaction. Some transactions are homogeneous and do not require any special equipment or special production line configurations. Other transactions must be tailored to meet a company's particular needs.
- *Human asset specificity* refers to how specialized the required knowledge must be to complete the transaction. Special training, learning on the job and knowledge of a company's processes are examples of specific human assets required to complete a transaction.

Asset specificity should not be confused with the total investment needed by the supplier to provide the transactions. Telephone services, for example, require huge investments, but these investments are usually not specific to certain buyers.

Williamson classifies transactions into three categories, according to their asset specificity:

- non-specific transactions, which require standard equipment and non-specialized knowledge because the transactions do not have to be tailored to the buyer,
- idiosyncratic transactions, which require specialized equipment or knowledge,
- mixed transactions, which have attributes of both.

Frequency
Frequency refers to how often a transaction occurs, either occasionally or recurringly. The frequency dimension refers to buyer activity in the market, i.e., how many times a company seeks to initiate the transaction (Williamson, 1975).

Setting up a specialized governance structure, such as a vertically integrated firm, involves certain initial and fixed costs. If certain transactions occur only once or infrequently, then these initial costs often can not be justified. The costs of a specialized governance structure are more easily recovered for high frequency transactions. Williamson matches the most efficient governance strategies with the transaction types determined by the situational factors frequency and asset specificity (see Table 3.2).

Frequency	Asset specificity		
	non-specific	**mixed**	**idiosyncratic**
occasional transaction	market governance with contract	market governance with trilateral contract	
recurrent transaction	equivalent to a sale	market governance with hierarchical bilateral contract	governance

Table 3.2 Efficient governance strategies (Williamson, 1979)

Number of suppliers

Opportunism is only a threat when there are few suppliers available to provide a specific service. Markets with a large number of suppliers minimize opportunism because rivalry among larger numbers of bidders will render opportunistic inclinations ineffectual (Williamson, 1975). With few alternatives, the company is in a poor position to bargain with the supplier.

Williamson (1975) distinguishes *ex ante* and *ex post* small numbers. Initially, the buyer may select a supplier based on who provides the required service for the lowest cost. If few adequate suppliers exist, Williamson speaks of *ex ante* small number bargaining.

If many suppliers provide the required service, and the buyer has selected a supplier, that supplier usually acquires valuable knowledge about the customer's organization. At the end of the contractual period, the supplier has an advantage over the other vendors in the marketplace and other suppliers will be at a competitive disadvantage, which leads to ex post small number bargaining. The degree of *ex post* small numbers depends on the advantage a supplier acquires during the first transaction and on the costs of switching to another supplier. Williamson argues that companies can buy transactions from markets with few suppliers if they negotiate appropriate contracts (see Table 3.3).

Uncertainty and complexity

Uncertainty refers to the possibility of gathering all the information required to make an informed decision. Buyers may face uncertainty in the environment which will impact on the contract and its fulfillment. Uncertainty may be high as a result of unpredictable market, technological, or economic trends, contractual complexity and quality of outputs.

Complexity is a characteristic of a specific decision situation and refers to the number of alternatives in a decision situation, and the number of variables and the relationships between these variables.

Uncertainty and complexity may lead to opportunism because client organizations can not oversee all alternatives and prescribe the

Frequency	Asset specificity		
	non-specific	**mixed**	**idiosyncratic**
occasional transaction	classical contracting	neo-classical contracting	
recurrent transaction		relational contracting	

Table 3.3 Appropriate contracts for transaction types (Williamson, 1979)

necessary actions before the transaction starts, and must therefore postpone decisions about appropriate actions until the moment problems arise. At this time, suppliers will be in a better negotiating position and may abuse their resulting bargaining power.

Bounded rationality

Bounded rationality refers to the cognitive limitations of the human mind which makes it difficult to evaluate fully the consequences of all possible decisions (Simon, 1960). The degree to which bounded rationality is present depends partly on the knowledge and skills the buyer has to specify requirements, to select appropriate suppliers, to draw a tight contract and to manage and control suppliers.

3.3.2 Application of the transaction costs theory to IS outsourcing

The transaction cost approach offers a method of evaluating the relative advantages of the different internal and external organization forms for handling transactions. This theory also provides an excellent framework for analyzing the outsourcing option, since the essential choice here is between using an outsourcing service provider, a market mechanism, and providing in-house services, an organizational hierarchy. The theory also appears to be useful for reducing transaction costs in an outsourcing situation and thereby improving the benefit one can realize through outsourcing (Cheon, Grover and Teng, 1995).

Decision variables

The concept of governance structures applies directly to IS outsourcing. IS transactions are the IS activities an organization needs and wants to be performed. Client organizations are buyers and internal or external suppliers are sellers of IS transactions. Outsourcing corresponds to market governance, while insourcing or internal provision is equivalent to hierarchical governance.

Goal variables

The assumption of cost-optimizing can be maintained for IS outsourcing, because cost reduction is one of the main objectives client organizations want to achieve with IS outsourcing. The notion of costs is interpreted very broadly in the transaction cost theory. Costs include all negative consequences of governance mechanisms and are not restricted to financial consequences. The distinction between production and coordination costs is also maintained.

Intermediate variables

IS outsourcing leads to lower production costs and higher transaction costs. IS outsourcing should be chosen if the savings on production costs caused by economies of scale outweigh the increase in transaction costs caused by the threat of opportunism.

Economies of scale

The conditions under which IS suppliers can achieve economies of scale are discussed in section 3.2.1.

Opportunism

Opportunism can also be found in IS outsourcing relationships. IS suppliers may for example, misrepresent their abilities or abuse their knowledge advantage to sell hardware or software the client has no need for or could obtain cheaper elsewhere. They may abuse their bargaining position at the time the client organization wants to change requirements for system development or wants to decrease the volume of usage of network capacity. The degree to which a particular relationship is in danger of opportunism is determined by situational factors.

Situational factors

Situational factors that determine transaction types and thereby the likelihood of opportunism can be translated into characteristics of IS transactions.

The probability of opportunism, and thereby transaction costs, depends on asset specificity, frequency, the number of suppliers, on uncertainty and complexity, and the degree of bounded rationality.

Asset specificity

Asset specificity is relevant in IS outsourcing because many IS transactions are customized to the pertinent client organization. The following types of specificity arise:

- *Site specificity* can be present with IS outsourcing if, for example, the hardware needs extensive provisions such as air conditioning and physical security measures. It also applies when regular face-to-face contact between the staff of the client and supplier is required, such as required for user support, training or consultancy.
- *Physical asset specificity* refers to how specialized the equipment must be to complete the transaction. Equipment is here interpreted as the IS resources, excluding human resources, needed to perform the IS activities, such as the hardware for system development, the programming languages and tools, the data base repositories, and the systems operation tools. Although these tools are often not developed specifically for one client organization, certain transactions may demand a unique combination or the application of tools

that suppliers have no experience with.

- *Human asset specificity* refers to how specialized the workers' knowledge must be to complete the transaction. The knowledge and skills needed to perform IS activities for a client organization can be highly specific, because many IS activities require knowledge of the client's business processes. System development, for example, requires an analysis of the business processes that are to be supported or performed by the information system.

Frequency

The frequency dimension refers to how often a client organization seeks to initiate a certain IS transaction. The transaction costs of internal provision are high if transactions are infrequent, because then the initial and fixed costs of setting up an internal IS unit to provide the transaction must be allocated to a small number of transactions.

Frequency of outsourcing IS operation and maintenance can be interpreted in two ways. Aubert, Rivard and Patry (1993) do not take the variable into account for their research into the outsourcing of IS operations, because operation is a continuous activity. Frequency of operation is incorporated in this book, because frequency refers to the number of times an organization initiates a transaction. Organizations can outsource different operation activities and contracts can be renewed, changed or terminated.

Frequency of planning, development and implementation refers to the number, the size and the fluctuation in projects. Information planning is, for example, often conducted only once a year, while system development and implementation may occur more often.

Small number of suppliers

The total number of IS suppliers is high, but the number of adequate suppliers for specific IS transactions may be low if there is only a small number of IS suppliers that specialize in the pertinent technologies, activities and client's business processes.

Ex post small numbers situations will occur often, as IS transactions require extensive learning times and learning curves and switching costs are considerable. The client organization has limited choices, particularly during contract renewal or when large changes in existing contracts are required.

Uncertainty and complexity

Many IS transactions are conducted under uncertainty, especially if the transactions involve products or services that have yet to be developed. Uncertainty with regard to the requirements or volume of IS transactions may be caused by unpredictable IS markets and technological developments, but also by unpredictable developments in the client organization's business processes and environment.

The complexity of IS transactions will be high if the information systems support complex business processes, or if the technical complexity is high. Information systems that require many different types of hardware and software to interconnect and have a large, dispersed and heterogeneous user community are very complex to develop and maintain.

Bounded rationality

Bounded rationality in the IS outsourcing context refers to the ability of client organizations to evaluate fully the consequences of all possible decisions on selecting and managing IS suppliers. The degree to which bounded rationality is present in IS transactions depends partly on the knowledge and skills of the client organization to specify requirements for IS activities, to select appropriate suppliers, to draw a tight contract and to manage and control IS suppliers.

Empirical support

Aubert, Rivard and Patry studied the effect of asset specificity, uncertainty and measurement problems on outsourcing of IS operations in a very detailed survey of 250 large Canadian firms (Aubert, Rivard and Patry, 1993), and IS development in ten in-depth case studies (Aubert, Rivard and Patry, 1994). Both studies largely confirmed the expected relationships between the three factors and the degree of outsourcing.

In Aubert, Rivard and Patry's (1993) survey of IS operations, a strong relationship was found between the parties' ability to measure and predict activities, and the use of outsourcing. Asset specificity did not show the expected effect on governance mode. The authors conclude that IS operations may involve very limited business knowledge and skills.

Aubert, Rivard and Patry's (1994) case study of IS development demonstrated that the components of transaction cost theory displayed significant explanatory power. Software development activities requiring significant business and organizational knowledge were kept in-house, indicating the importance of asset specificity in software development. Measurement problems were also an important decision factor in the governance mode of software development activities. Frequency was also useful in explaining outsourcing decisions. The organizations studied showed a tendency to keep their work force at a stable level and to rely on external assistance when their needs increased on a temporary basis.

Loh and Venkatraman (1992b) studied asset specificity and uncertainty as determinants of IS outsourcing but found no significant relationships.

Lacity and Hirschheim (1993) interpreted thirteen IS outsourcing case studies from a transaction cost perspective and conclude that this perspective explains many of phenomena observed in the outsourcing decision processes.

3.4 Agency cost theory

The agency cost theory, developed by Ross (1973) and Jensen and Meckling (1976), examines the reasons for principal-agent relationships and the problems inherent in them. Jensen and Meckling (1976) define an agency relationship as "a contract under which one or more persons (principal(s)) engage another person (the agent) to perform some service on their behalf which involves delegating some decision making authority to the agent."

3.4.1 Outline of the agency cost theory

Agency relationships can be found within firms, such as a manager and a subordinate, or the shareholder and the manager of a firm, and between firms, such as licensing and franchising or other client-supplier relationships.

Two streams of literature can be distinguished within agency theory: the positive theory of agency and the theory of principal and agent. In the positive theory of agency, the firm is viewed as a nexus of contracts. The theory deals with the effects of contracts on the behavior of participants and the origin of certain organizational forms. In the theory of principal and agent the central question is how the principal should design the agent's reward structure. Both streams have their antecedents in the literature on the separation of ownership and control. The *theory of principal and agent* forms the core of modern agency theory (Douma and Schreuder, 1992), which will be used in this book.

Agency theory rejects the classical image of a firm as a holistic profit-maximizing unit and replaces this with a model of a firm as an agency relationship based on a set of contracts between a principal and a number of agents, that strive for their own goals.

Goal variables

Agency theory is aimed at minimizing the agency costs, which are the costs incurred as a result of discrepancies between the objectives of the principal and those of the agents. The agency costs are the sum of the monitoring costs, the bonding costs, and the residual losses of a principal. Monitoring costs are incurred by the principal to assess the performance of the agent. Bonding costs are incurred by agents to assure the principal of their commitment. Residual loss is the remaining loss resulting from an agent performing a task.

Intermediate variables

Agency costs are caused by the fact that agents often act in a manner that is inconsistent with maximizing the welfare of the principal, specifically by:

- *goal incongruence*, the goals of the principal and the agent are often inconsistent with one another; in the theory of principal and agent, it is assumed that the agent wants to receive more money and does not want to deliver more effort, while the principal wants to maximize profit,
- *information asymmetries*, agents will usually have more information on their efforts than the principal, and the principal will not be able to obtain this information in full and without cost.

Another problem is that the principal and the agent may have different attitudes towards risk (Eisenhardt, 1989). Agency theory assumes that the agent is more averse to risk than the principal, because the principal can often diversify, that is, have contracts with several agents and by this reduce most of the risk.

Decision variables
The focus of the agency theory is centered on determining the most efficient contract to govern the relationship between a principal and an agent.

Agency theory proposes to make the agent's reward totally or partially dependent on the results of the agent's performance, such as profits made or amount produced, to ensure that the agent acts in the principal's best interest. The results of an agent's action will however, always be influenced by the efforts of the agent on one hand and circumstances over which the agent has no influence on the other hand, such as market conditions or prices of raw materials. If agents are averse to risk, they will not accept that the reward depends on factors that they can not influence, and will only accept a reward structure based on their own efforts. The following two extreme types of contracts are possible:

- A *wage contract* implies a fixed salary for the agents, independent of the pay-off of the their efforts. The principal takes all the risk and the agents have no incentive whatsoever to do a good job.
- A *rent contract* means that the agents receive the pay-off and the principal receives a fixed amount. The agents have the maximum incentive to do their very best, but also bear the entire risk. If the agents are averse to risk, they will accept more risk only if this is offset by a higher expected income.

The optimal contract usually involves risk-sharing between agent and principal. Reward mechanisms that share the risk between agent and principal include contracts with a fixed base salary and a bonus for above average performance.

Situational factors

Agency costs are determined by five factors (Eisenhardt, 1989):

- Outcome uncertainty can be high due to, for example, government policies, economic climate, technological change, and competitor action. If outcome uncertainty is high, then an agent would demand higher risk compensation.
- The degree of aversion to risk of the agent determines the amount of risk compensation the principal must pay to have the agent accept a risk-sharing contract.
- Programmability is the degree to which appropriate behavior of the agent can be specified by the principal in advance, which reduces the necessity and effort required to bond, and to monitor the agent's actions.
- Outcome measurability is the extent to which the principal can measure the efforts of the agents and the outcomes of their actions. Measurability is improved if the principal can monitor the agents using information systems. Measurability decreases if tasks require a long time to complete, involve joint team effort, or produce soft outcomes.
- The length of the agency relationship determines whether the principal can learn about the agent and thus be able to assess behavior more readily.

Agency theory and profit center management

Merchant (1989) focuses on a particular principal-agent relationship: the relationship between corporate management and business unit management, particularly profit centre management. Merchant defines a business unit as an organizational unit that purchases from and sells to an external market. The contract between corporate management and profit centre managers is aimed at letting the profit centre manager act in the interest of the organization as a whole. Corporate management however, often has insufficient knowledge of the business and of the day to day operations to control the business unit directly. Profit centre managers therefore must be controlled indirectly, by motivating them to act in the interest of the organization.

Merchant observed practices by profit centre managers that were not in the interest of the organization, such as negotiating for the largest possible budget, and hiding or delaying extra profit. He explains these practices as the result of inadequate contracts between corporate management and profit centre managers, that have focus especially on short term results, the inclusion of irrelevant evaluation variables and compensating for uncontrollable factors. This induces profit managers to postpone or cancel investments that yield only in the long term and to take operational decisions that will be negative in the long run, such as lowering quality and enforcing high overtime.

Profit center managers should not be evaluated on factors that are outside their control, either because of the prescriptions of corporate management or because of uncontrollable external influences. Corporate general and administrative expenses should be charged to business units only if the business unit managers have an influence on these expenses, either individually or collectively.

3.4.2 Application of the agency cost theory to IS outsourcing

Outsourcing is not included explicitly in agency theory. Principal-agent relationships are present within and between organizations, and agency theory therefore applies to outsourcing as well as insourcing. The amount of agency costs will however, in general, be different. Goal incongruence will be higher between organizations that each have their own profit motive than within a single organization. Information asymmetries will be less within organizations, because monitoring internal employees is generally easier than monitoring external suppliers. Therefore, outsourcing is advisable only if agency costs are low.

Agency costs are higher with outsourcing, because goal incongruence and information asymmetries are higher. Outsourcing should only be chosen if agency costs are low.

Goal variables

Agency costs are present in IS outsourcing because client organizations must monitor and enforce the IS supplier's performance. Monitoring costs are the client organization's costs to monitor the IS supplier's performance, for example by testing software that has been developed, inspecting documentation that has been delivered or changed, and testing disaster recovery facilities. Bonding costs are those incurred by the IS supplier to keep the client organization informed about progress and performance, and includes the costs of for example, progress reports, project meetings, informing users, quality reports, external audits, and reporting on the availability and response time of networks.

Intermediate variables

Goal incongruence
Agency relationships between client organizations and IS suppliers will induce agency costs, as goal incongruence is also present

between client organizations and external IS suppliers.

Information asymmetries
Information asymmetries are increased by the terminology used in the information systems field, which is known to be difficult to understand for users and clients.

Situational factors
Agency costs depend on the outcome uncertainty, the aversion to risk of the supplier, the programmability of the IS activity, the outcome measurability and the length of the outsourcing relationship.

Outsourcing is not recommended if monitoring the IS supplier is difficult, if outcome uncertainty is high, if the aversion to risk of the supplier is high, if the aversion to risk of the client organization is low, if the goal conflict between client organization and IS supplier is high, if task programmability is low, if outcome measurability is low, or if the length of the agency relationship is expected to be short.

Outcome uncertainty of IS activities is high if the client organization can not specify all requirements in advance. The factors determining uncertainty are described in section 3.2.5.

The aversion to risk of the supplier is the willingness of IS suppliers to take part of the risk, for example by accepting fixed price fixed date contracts or by making large initial investments in resources needed by the client organization.

Programmability is the degree to which the IS activities can be performed using prescribed procedures and working instructions.

Outcome measurability is the extent to which the client organization can measure the efforts of the IS supplier and determine whether the supplier complies to requirements. Measurability is improved if the principal can monitor the agent using information systems. Measurability decreases if tasks require a long time to complete, which is the case for example with many software development projects. Measurability is also low if the activities involve joint team efforts, especially if the client organization and the supplier are working very closely together and the supplier needs input from the client organization; it is then difficult to determine whether the supplier has taken his share of the work and whether problems can be attributed to the supplier or to the client organization. The same holds if different suppliers must work together closely to perform certain IS activities for one client organization, which is the case for example if hardware, software, networks and user training are all provided by different IS suppliers. A further cause of low measurability can be that activities result in soft outcomes that can not be measured by objective and mathematical criteria. The quality of information planning, consultancy, user support and problem solving, for example, can not be measured using objective and deterministic criteria.

The *length* of the IS outsourcing relationship determines whether the client organization can learn about the IS supplier and will be able to assess the supplier's performance more easily. In a long-term relationship, the client organization becomes conversant with the reports and the working procedures of the supplier and learns how to evaluate the supplier's performance.

Decision variables

The main decision variable of the agency theory is the type of contract. A wage contract in the IS outsourcing context means that a fixed salary is paid to an internal IS staff or IS staff is hired from an external IS supplier for a fixed tariff and a fixed period of time. The client organization receives all the pay-off of the staff's efforts, but takes all the risks, including the risk that the staff must be paid even if no work is available to deploy the staff.

The other extreme type of contract is the rent contract, where the client organization receives a fixed amount and the supplier takes all the risks and receives all the pay-offs. This type of contract occurs for example if a supplier rents the excess capacity of a client organization's computer network for a fixed fee, and tries to lease the network capacity to other clients. Another example would be a client organization allowing a supplier to sell tailor-made software to other clients, in exchange for a one-time reduction of the development fee.

Many intermediate contract types will occur. Some risk can be transferred to the supplier by hiring IS staff from a supplier only when the client organization has a need for it. This transfers the risk of having to pay the staff if there is no work to the supplier. The supplier will therefore usually charge a higher tariff if staff are hired ad hoc than if staff are hired for a longer period.

With a contract with a fixed fee for a fixed amount of work the supplier takes the risk that the actual costs per unit of work may be lower or higher than the fixed tariff. The same holds for a contract based on a fixed tariff per unit of work, but then the supplier also takes the risk that the total amount of work is higher or lower than expected, which may leave the supplier with an excess or shortage of resources.

Even more risk is transferred to the supplier if the supplier's fee depends not on the amount of work, but on the benefits of the product or service to the client organization. A supplier may for example agree to develop and operate a new inventory management system and be paid a percentage of the savings in inventory costs. Suppliers take a very high risk in this type of contract, because many factors that influence the outcomes are out of their control, such as the cooperation of the users, developments in the client organization's market, and the inventory demands of the client organization's business units.

3.5 Competitive Strategy

A number of organizational theories focus on strategies for organizations and organizational units to compete for power, market share and continuity.

Porter (1980, 1985) investigated threats that influence an organization's competition and strategies to improve an organization's competitive position. IS outsourcing decisions influence the efficiency and effectiveness of an organization's IS function, which in turn often can be a source of competitive advantage and at least be part of competitive strategy. The market of IS suppliers is also competitive, and client organizations may benefit or suffer from competition among suppliers.

Quinn, Paquette and Doorley (1990ab) and Prahalad and Hamel (1990) propose a particular strategy, focusing on core competencies, to improve the organization's competitive position and continuity. The two theories are analyzed and adapted to IS outsourcing in the following sections.

3.5.1 Competitive forces and competitive advantage

Porter (1980, 1985) has extended traditional models of competitive strategy, in which only rivalry among existing firms is treated. He distinguishes five competitive threats (see Figure 3.2) :

- *rivalry among existing firms* depends *inter alia* on number and size distribution of firms, level of product differentiation, and cost structures,
- *threat of new entrants* depends on barriers to entry,
- *bargaining power of suppliers* depends on the number and size distribution of suppliers and the level of product differentiation,
- *bargaining power of buyers* depends on the number and size distribution of buyers
- *threat of substitute products or services* depends on whether products or services exist or may arise that can be used to perform the same function for buyers.

The intensity of competition in a specific industry is determined by the degree to which each of these five threats is present in the industry.

Application of competitive forces to IS outsourcing

Client organizations and IS suppliers both face competition in their industry. From the viewpoint of client organizations, IS suppliers are a category of suppliers which may pose a threat. From the viewpoint of the IS suppliers, client organizations in a specific industry are a category of buyers (see Figure 3.3). The chain of supply is

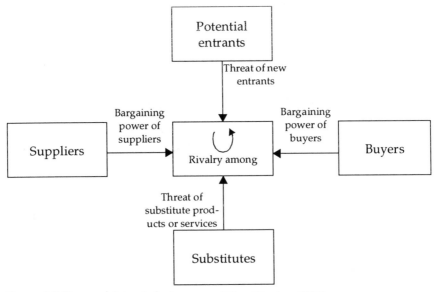

Figure 3.2 Forces driving industry competition (Porter, 1980)

simplified to two steps here, but as IS suppliers can themselves subcontract IS activities or be client organizations of other IS suppliers, the chain can and usual does contain several steps.

Bargaining power of IS suppliers

The competitive threat of IS suppliers to client organizations may be significant when the bargaining power of the IS supplier is high. Outsourcing is not advisable if this leads to a situation in which the supplier has a lot of power over the customer. The bargaining power of IS suppliers is determined by:

• the switching costs of IS suppliers, i.e., what it will cost the supplier

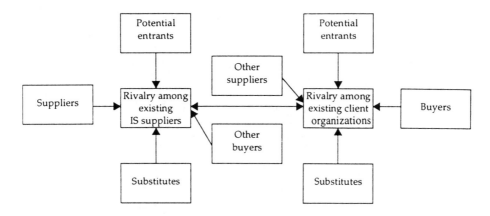

Figure 3.3 Competitive forces in IS supply and client organization industries

to switch to other clients,
- the switching costs of client organizations, what are the costs for the client of switching to another IS supplier,
- the supplier concentration; a few large IS suppliers have more power than many small IS suppliers,
- the importance of a client organization's volume to IS supplier; if the client represents only a small part of the supplier's business volume, then the client's bargaining power is very small,
- the impact of inputs on cost or differentiation; if the impact of the IS function is large and involves almost all processes in an organization, an IS supplier may derive significant power from this impact.

Bargaining power of buyers of the client organization
Some buyers demand or appreciate that their supplier outsources their IS activities to a stable IS supplier. Sometimes buyers demand their supplier to use a specific information system, for example the order entry system developed and operated by the buyer or by the buyer's IS supplier. The organization is then forced to outsource to that supplier.

Threat of new entrants in the client organization's industry
Client organizations can lower the threat of new entrants into the client's industry by raising barriers to entry. One of the possible barriers to entry is vertical integration of essential processes. If most firms in an industry have integrated their IS function, then few IS suppliers will exist with a knowledge of that industry. This means new entrants will also have to integrate their IS function, which increases the barriers for entry.

Threat of substitute products or services to the client organization
Existing product differentiation decreases the threat of substitutes. Outsourcing may influence the client organization's ability to use information systems for product differentiation. The IS function can contribute to product differentiation, for example by offering buyers information on the products they buy, or by allowing buyers to order products on-line, for just-in-time inventory management.

Rivalry among existing firms in the client organization's industry
It is often stated that information technology can be applied to create competitive advantage (Cash and Konsynski, 1985; McFarlan, 1984; Porter, 1985). The possible influence of outsourcing on the competitive use of information technology and information systems is discussed below in section 3.5.2.

Bargaining power of IS suppliers' suppliers
IS suppliers may buy IS resources and subcontract parts of the activities they perform for client organizations. An IS supplier produc-

ing tailor-made systems will usually buy hardware and system software from other suppliers. IS suppliers may have a higher bargaining power because they often buy on a larger scale than client organizations and receive volume discounts.

Bargaining power of client organizations

Client organization may have high bargaining power with regard to IS suppliers, which makes outsourcing more attractive to them. Buyer concentration, that is, the number and size of client organizations that buy specific IS products and services from a specific group of IS suppliers, increases the buyer's bargaining power. Client organizations outsourcing only a small part of the IS activities to a specific IS supplier, increase their bargaining power.

Threat of new entrants in IS supplier's industry

High barriers to entry and exit in a specific segment of the IS industry decreases competition in that segment and make outsourcing less attractive to client organizations. Barriers to entry and exit in the IS market are discussed in section 3.2.5.

Rivalry among existing IS suppliers

The intensity of rivalry among existing IS suppliers determines the intensity of competition. High competition in the IS industry increases the attractiveness of outsourcing to client organizations, because it increases the market pressure on IS suppliers and increases the options for client organizations to select the best supplier and to switch to another supplier if necessary. Heavy competition may however, also result in many bankruptcies, mergers and take-overs among IS suppliers, all of which may harm client organizations.

3.5.2 Core business and core competencies

IS outsourcing is often justified by the argument that IS is not the company's core business (Lacity and Hirschheim, 1993). The conventional interpretation of the core business concept as it is used in practice however, is inappropriate for making IS outsourcing decisions. The new paradigm of core competencies is better suited, because it acknowledges the strategic role that support services can play. These two paradigms are analyzed and applied to IS outsourcing in the following sections.

Core business

IS outsourcing is often presented as an innovative concept and as a way to become leaner and more focused (Douglass, 1993). Outsourcing is thought to decrease staffing levels and increase flexibility. Many firms and public sector organizations have a strategy to focus on their core business and outsource everything else (Porter, 1985), and do not see IS as part of their core business. Managers want to reduce the time they have to spend on managing IS, and free management attention and investment capital for core business activities. Their implicit assumption is that outsourcing will always and automatically lead to lower costs, less demands on their time, and higher flexibility.

The core business trend is a reaction to the expansion strategy companies followed in the 1980s. Companies expanded by internalizing activities upstream or downstream in the value chain, to control all phases of the production process of their end products. New products were derived from the existing portfolio and firms entered new markets that sometimes had little to do with their original focus (Quinn et al., 1990b).

As companies experienced that it is not possible to own all the service activities required, they started restructuring, decluttering and delayering (Prahalad and Hamel, 1990), and to go back to what they called their core business. Initially, core business was often taken to be the primary activities required to produce the end products that yielded the company the highest revenues or market share. When asked, managers often describe their core business in terms of their mission statement, such as "manufacturing light bulbs", "providing social security" or "producing chemicals." Staff functions and other secondary activities were reduced or outsourced. Business units that produced products or services outside the main focus of the company were sold or eliminated (Quinn et al., 1990a).

Can IS be part of the core business?
In line with this trend to focus on core business activities, the IS function was an obvious candidate for outsourcing (Lacity and Hirschheim, 1993). The conventional interpretation of core business as it is used in practice is, however, inappropriate for making IS outsourcing decisions. If the core business is taken to be the company's primary activities required to produce their original end products, all non-primary activities should be outsourced. Finance, human resources, marketing, logistics and even general management are not core business in this sense, as none of these functions contributes directly to the end products of the firm.

Providing IS products and services can be core business, in the sense that it is the primary product and source of revenues, only for IS suppliers. Following the "not our core business" argument, all other organizations should outsource their IS function. This is of course not a very distinctive criterion for IS outsourcing decision making.

Even if the IS function is not considered to be part of the core business, the function can not be separated as easily as security, catering and mail delivery. Most systems are integrated parts of the businesses they support and can not be taken away without interrupting processes that depend on the systems (Lacity, Willcocks and Feeny, 1995).

Most importantly, the core business argument neglects the strategic role IS can play in determining the added value and the competitive position of the company. Lacity and Hirschheim (1993) wonder: "During the 1980s, executives were advised of the strategic role that information and information systems could provide to organizations ... So what happened to the IS function in the past few years? Has IS suddenly become a commodity service that is best managed by a large supplier?" As Porter and Millar (1985) point out, "Information technology is permeating the value chain at every point, transforming the way value activities are performed and the nature of the linkages among them. It is also affecting competitive scope and reshaping the way products meet buyer needs. These basic effects explain why information technology has acquired strategic significance and is different from the many other technologies businesses use."

Core competence

Quinn, Doorley and Paquette (1990ab) offer a new paradigm that goes beyond the concept of core business. They argue that firms should not think of their strengths in terms of their end products and market shares, but in terms of activities or services. "The major value-added in most products today comes not from direct production or conversion processes. Knowledge bases, skill sets, and service activities are the things that generally can create continuing added value and competitive advantage." (Quinn et al., 1990b). These critical services are called a company's core competencies (Prahalad and Hamel, 1990).

According to the new paradigm, all activities that are not core competencies should be outsourced. "Focus on what gives your company its competitive edge. Outsource the rest. ... Whenever a company produces a service internally that others buy or produce more efficiently or effectively externally, it sacrifices competitive advantage" (Quinn et al., 1990a).

To analyze core competencies, the company should consider each overhead category as a service that the company could either "make" internally or "buy" externally. In many cases, companies find that specialized outside service sources can be much more cost effective than their internal groups because they "often provide greater economies of scale, flexibility, and levels of expertise for specialized overhead services than virtually any company can achieve internally" (Quinn et al., 1990b).

Strategic outsourcing of all activities that are not core competencies allows a company to focus all its attention on the areas in which it adds the most value; because they are leaner, these companies can respond faster to customers, their executives no longer need to waste time on peripheral activities and can concentrate more on their business' core strategic activities (Quinn et al., 1990a). If one supplier under-performs, the firm can quickly substitute competitors' components or services. If new technologies suddenly appear, it is easier to switch sources. If there is a cyclical or temporary drop in demand, the firm is not stuck with all the idle capacity and inventory swings of the entire production chain (Quinn et al., 1990b).

Core competencies should not be outsourced, because "the embedded skills that give rise to the next generation of competitive products cannot be "rented in" by outsourcing and OEM-supply relationships. In our view, too many companies have unwittingly surrendered core competencies when they cut internal investment in what they mistakenly thought were just "cost centres" in favor of outside suppliers" (Prahalad and Hamel, 1990).

There can be reasons to maintain activities in house that are not core competencies. "A company must maintain command of those activities crucial to its strategic position. … It is essential that the company plan and manage its outsourcing coalitions so that it does not become overly dependent on, and hence dominated by, its partner. In some cases this means consciously developing and maintaining alternate competitive sources or even strategically controlling critical stages in an overall process that might otherwise be totally outsourced if efficiency were the sole criterion" (Quinn et al., 1990b).

Can IS be a core competence?

Though IS is core business only for IS suppliers, a company's IS function and the way information technology is used can be a core competence. The IS function is a core competence if it lowers costs or improves value-added significantly, in a way that outperforms the company's competitors.

Information technology has the potential to improve a company's performance (Cash and Konsynski, 1985; Earl 1989;McFarlan, 1984). Information technology "is affecting the entire process by which companies create their products. Furthermore, it is reshaping the product itself: the entire package of physical goods, services, and information companies provide to create value for their buyers" (Porter and Millar, 1985). Information technology can be used to:

- change the nature of competition, by changing the structure of the industry or even changing the boundaries of industries
- create competitive advantage, by lowering cost, enhancing differentiation of changing competitive scope
- spawn new businesses, by making new businesses or products technologically feasible, or by using existing information-processing capacity to start a new business (Porter and Millar, 1985)

Apart from creating value and improving the competitive position directly, the use of information systems also influences all other value activities and the linkages among them. The IS function can be of strategic importance if it is essential to the company's chosen areas of strategic focus and core competencies.

This does not mean that information technology and the IS function is crucial to every company. In some companies and business processes information systems play only a minor role and do not give the company a unique advantage over its competitors. Before company managers consider outsourcing, they should analyze whether their IS function is a core competence, or essential to one or more other core competencies. Outsourcing should only be an option if IS is not a core competence or essential to other core competencies.

Outsourcing may effect the extent to which an organization is able to create competitive advantage with IT. If part of the IS function gives an organization competitive advantage, then outsourcing makes this advantage available for competitors. Simon (1989) poses that part of the competitive strength of an organization depends on the exclusiveness of its procurement. If an organization buys standardized products or services that are also available to competitors, these products or services will not yield competitive advantage. Buying tailor-made products or services can increase an organization's exclusiveness, and thereby its competitive strength, if the design of these products or services can be shielded effectively from competitors. This will not always be legally or practically possible. This strategy also decreases the supplier's possible economies of scale, as the re-use of knowledge and skills will be restricted, and enforces the supplier to charge all costs to the client organization.

Outsourcing IS activities and information systems that yield competitive advantage has the risk that knowledge of these activities and systems becomes available to competitors. One can also doubt whether an organization can still make competitive use of IT when they have outsourced their IS department. Suppliers often claim to be a strategic partner and able to assist in developing the IS strategy, but this requires inside business information, from both formal and informal circuits, about new products, markets and business strategies (Earl, 1989). One may question whether suppliers can obtain this information and whether it is wise for the customer to share this information with its IS supplier, who may also serve competitors.

Validity of the core competence paradigm

Even if certain external IS suppliers are able to provide a service at lower cost or with higher value this does not mean they will offer a lower price and higher quality. The core competence paradigm is too optimistic about the IS supplier sharing these advantages with its clients. Lacity, Willcocks and Feeny (1995) found that many client managers ignore the supplier's need to maximize its revenues and profits. Lessons learned from transaction cost economics (Williamson, 1975, 1985), agency theory (Jensen and Meckling, 1976) and theories on power (Pfeffer, 1981) show that suppliers can, and often do, use their power to get the most out of an outsourcing deal.

The core competence paradigm assumes that outside suppliers can be more efficient or effective, because they provide greater economies of scale, flexibility and specialization. Organizations that focus only on their core competencies become leaner, more focused and more flexible. Companies that outsource can easily switch sources if a supplier under-performs or technology changes. Executives no longer need to spend much of their time on peripheral activities. Each of this assumptions can be doubted. In section 3.2.1, it was stated that suppliers have economies of scale and specialization only under certain conditions, that is, if suppliers perform similar activities on a considerably larger scale, integrate these activities and are allowed to share knowledge and resources among clients. Switching is not as easy, and leads to considerable switching costs.

The core competence paradigm states: "focus on core competencies, outsource the rest". Only the first part of this paradigm is accepted here. If a specific part of the IS function is a core competence, then it should not be outsourced. If a part of the IS function is not a core competence, then outsourcing may be an option, but further analysis is necessary to determine whether outsourcing is useful and sensible.

3.6 Political model

Pfeffer (1980) investigates power in organizations, but his conclusions are also useful for analyzing and predicting power distributions between parties in an IS outsourcing relationship.

The political theory of organizational behavior attends to two main constructs, power and politics. Power is defined as the potential of an actor to influence the behavior of another actor on a particular issue (Tushman, 1977). Politics is defined as "the structure and process of the use of authority and power to effect definitions of goals, directions, and other major parameters of the organization" (Tushman, 1977). Power enables stakeholders to influence a decision, but political strategies enacted during the decision-making process may alter power-balances (Pfeffer, 1981).

3.6.1 Outline of the political model

Power

Power is a relative notion; an actor's power is only meaningful when compared to another actor's power on a particular issue. Power is derived from (Pfeffer, 1981):

- *authority;* an institutional code within which the use of power is organized and legitimized, determined by the structural position of actors in the organization,
- *resources acquisition;* the amount of resources an actor brings into the organization, determined mainly by budget allocation,
- *dependency and low substitutability;* offering something of value that few other sources can provide, determined by the attractiveness of the offer to the receiver and the availability outside the relationship,
- *absorbing uncertainty;* the actor who has access to information derives power from absorbing uncertainty.

Political tactics

Power is employed through the following legitimate political tactics (Pfeffer, 1981):

- *selective use of decision criteria;* if there is a lack of clearly defined decision criteria, actors attempt to influence the decision by appealing for criteria that promote their decision preferences
- *selective use of information;* actors can influence decisions by emphasizing or withholding information, either deliberately or unconsciously, by selective perception and retention.
- *use of outside experts;* outside experts legitimize a stakeholder's position by offering "objective" verification and providing an aura of rationality to the decision process
- *building coalitions;* temporary alliances to rally support and legitimize a stakeholder's position
- *co-optation;* swaying the opposition to favor one's position by giving the opposition representation on a committee, and thus confronting them with social influence and conformity pressures.

3.6.2 Application of the political model to IS outsourcing

Power and politics are phenomena that play a role in IS outsourcing decision making in three ways: in the decision process itself, in analyzing expected distribution after outsourcing, and in designing and managing the outsourcing relationship. Each of these three ways is discussed in the following sections.

Power and politics in decision processes

Power and politics play an important role during IS outsourcing decision processes. The aim in this book is to give an objective look on the consequences of outsourcing, but in practice decision makers may have other objectives than the best interest of their department or organization, and they may use other tactics than arguments and research results.

Lacity and Hirschheim (1993) examined power and political tactics in IS outsourcing decision processes. They found that the political model explained many of the outsourcing decision processes they analyzed. Some IS managers used political tactics to "prove" the efficiency of their department to top management, such as requesting bids from expensive suppliers or requesting bids for parts of the IS function the department was best at. Senior managers were found to use outsourcing evaluations to increase efficiency. Outside outsourcing experts or benchmarking firms were used to "confirm" the decision makers' perceptions of the IS function's (in)efficiency.

Lacity and Hirschheim (1993) also analyzed the power of the IS department relative to the power of other departments, and found that the IS department was the least powerful department. Senior managers view the IS function as a value-consuming function and are reluctant to spend money on information systems. The IS function was structured as an overhead account, the costs of which had to be minimized, and the IS manager was two or even three levels below the chief executive officer. They conclude that senior managers perceive their IS departments to be cost burdens.

Expected power and politics when considering outsourcing

During outsourcing decision making, decision makers should analyze the expected distribution of power between the client organization and possible suppliers. If they expect that an IS supplier will have a greater power and have more options for political tactics, they might decide not to outsource. A number of sources of power and political tactics are relevant to outsourcing evaluations:

- Resources acquisition; Client organizations can decide whether to award certain IS activities to a specific supplier and whether to award additional or follow-up contracts to the supplier. They can withhold payment, withhold future projects, damage a suppliers reputation, or threaten legal action. The power a client organization derives from these resources decreases the moment the client signs a contract, especially if it is a long-term contract for a high amount of money.
- *Dependency and low substitutability;* Pfeffer (1981) gives as an example computer programmers, who can deliberately increase their power by making the organization more dependent on them, for example by not documenting systems. IS suppliers can make their customers dependent on them in many ways, and make themselves difficult to substitute, for example by not complying to technical and methodological standards.
- *Absorbing uncertainty;* IS suppliers can, by their technical expertise, have more information on possibilities and limitations of information technology and on achievable costs and lead times. This will be the case particularly if the client organization has little knowledge of IT.

- *Selective use of information;* IS suppliers can withhold or disclose information on their performance, on actual costs of activities, and so on, thus influencing the client organization's perception of the supplier's performance.

There is also a power balance between internal IS suppliers and their internal clients. Some business unit managers may perceive the internal IS department to be too powerful, and use outsourcing to external suppliers to improve their power over their company's IS activities.

Balancing power and politics in IS outsourcing relationships

If client organizations have decided to outsource, they should design the outsourcing relationship in a way that balances the distribution of power between the client organization and the IS supplier, or possibly even give the client organization more power. Several sources of power and political tactics can be used:

- *Resources acquisition;* client organizations can maximize their power of resource acquisition by withholding part of the resources from the supplier, for example by splitting a project into phases and only awarding the first phase to the supplier, or by postponing a percentage of payments for a development project until the system has been proven to be error-free.
- *Dependency and low substitutability;* client organizations can minimize their dependency on suppliers by choosing technical components that confirm to industry standards, by demanding that systems are documented and are portable to other hardware and software platforms, and by making contractual arrangements that oblige their supplier to facilitate and cooperate if they change to another supplier.
- *Absorbing uncertainty;* the power derived by IS suppliers from their ability to absorb uncertainty can be reduced by keeping enough knowledge and skills within the client organization to assess the possibilities provided by and the limitations of information technology, and to evaluate prices, lead times and quality of IS products and services.
- *Selective use of information* by the IS supplier can be reduced by demanding quality and progress reports, and conducting audits; or by demanding that the supplier uses a quality system the client organization can inspect.

3.7 Conclusions

In this chapter, several established organizational theories have been analyzed and elements of the theories have been adapted to IS outsourcing decision making. The conclusions with regard to IS outsourcing are summarized in this section, organized according to the categories of variables that were introduced in Chapter 2. The names of the theoretical perspectives are abbreviated using the acronyms listed in Table 3.4.

3.7.1 Situational factors

Some of the situational factors have appeared in a number of theories, sometimes under a different name. Some factors have been renamed for clarity or brevity. The names of the situational factors, the theories they are derived from and their original names are listed in Table 3.5. A short interpretation of the situational factors is given below. For further descriptions of the factors, the reader is referred to the descriptions of the pertinent theoretical perspectives given in this chapter.

The factor *scale* refers to the scale on which the client organization wants an activity to be performed, compared to the scale on which the average or potential supplier performs this activity. *Scale advantages* is the degree to which the pertinent activities have inherent possibilities of economies of scale. *Barriers for re-use* are present if client organizations need exclusive use of components, staff or resources.

The *number of suppliers* in a certain market segment is the number of adequate IS suppliers that have the skills, experience and resources to provide the pertinent IS products or services to the client organization. The *barriers to entry and exit* in the IS market segment determine whether IS suppliers can enter and exit the IS market segment easily. *Standardization* is the degree to which IS products or services are homogeneous and standardized. *Market information* is the availability of information on IS suppliers, IS products and services, and prices and lead times.

Measurability is whether the output of the IS activities can be measured easily and objectively by the client organizations. Uncertainty is the lack of information on requirements and future contingencies, and depends on volume uncertainty, technical uncertainty and

Acronym	Theoretical perspective	Section
DLC	Division of Labour and Coordination	3.2
TCT	Transaction Cost Theory	3.3
ACT	Agency Cost Theory	3.4
CF	Theories on Competitive Forces	3.5.1
CC	Core Competence paradigm	3.5.2
PP	Theories on Power and Politics	3.6

Table 3.4 Acronyms for theoretical perspectives

Situational factor	Source	Original name (if different)
scale	DLC	
scale advantages	DLC	inherent possibilities for economies of scale
barriers for re-use	DLC	number of suppliers
	DLC	number of sellers
	TCT	ex ante number of suppliers
barriers to entry and exit	DLC	
standardization	DLC	homogeneous standardised products or services
market information	DLC	availability of market information
measurability	DLC	output measurability
	ACT	output measurability
uncertainty	DLC	uncertainty or lack of information required for tasks
	TCT	uncertainty about future contingencies
	ACT	outcome uncertainty
specificity	TCT	asset specificity
	DLC	similarity (negated)
frequency	TCT	
switching costs of client	TCT	ex post number of suppliers
	CF	switching costs of buyer
	PP	substitutability
complexity	TCT	
IS maturity	TCT	degree of bounded rationality
risk aversion of supplier	ACT	risk aversion of agent
programmability	ACT	
length of relationship	ACT	length of agency relationship
switching costs of supplier	CF	
supplier concentration	CF	
importance of volume supplier	CF	importance of buyer for supplier's for business volume
buyer concentration	CF	
importance of volume for client	CF	importance of supplier for buyers buying volume
competitive use of IS	CF	impact of inputs on cost and differentiation
	CC	core competence, distinguishing buyer from competitors
IS use by competitors	CF	competitive use of IS by competitors
IS outsourcing by competitors	CF	barriers to entry by vertical integration
resource acquisition	PP	
absorbing uncertainty	PP	
selective use of information	PP	

Table 3.5 Name and source of situational factors

functional uncertainty.

Specificity is the degree of customization of IS products or services to the idiosyncratic needs of the client organization. Three types of specificity are distinguished: site specificity, resource specificity and human asset specificity. If the specificity of the client organization's requirements is high, then the similarity between activities for multiple clients is low. *Frequency* is the number of times a client organization needs a specific IS activity. The *switching costs of the client* are the costs the client organisation must make to transfer an IS activity to another IS supplier. The switching costs of the client determine whether an ex post small number of suppliers situation arises. *Complexity* of the information systems and IS activities is distinguished by the technical complexity of the systems and components and the functional complexity of the requirements.

IS maturity indicates the client organization's awareness and knowledge of information systems and its ability to specify requirements and manage IS activities. IS maturity determines the extent to which bounded rationality applies.

Supplier aversion of risk is the degree to which IS suppliers are willing to take part of the risk of IS activities and the amount of risk compensation the supplier demands for taking a certain risk. *Programmability* is the extent to which the working procedures for the IS activities can be specified. The length of the outsourcing relationship determines whether the client organization can learn to monitor the IS supplier.

The *switching costs* of the supplier are the costs entailed by the IS supplier when switching to working for another client organisation. The *supplier concentration* is the number and size distribution of the IS suppliers in the pertinent IS market segment. The importance of the percentage of *volume for the supplier* is the part of the IS supplier's business volume the client organization represents.

Buyer concentration is the number and size distribution of the client organizations in the pertinent IS market segment. The importance of the percentage of volume for the client is the part of the volume of IS products and services the client organization buys from the supplier. Competitive use of IS is the extent to which the pertinent systems or IS activities distinguish the client organization from the competitors in the client's market. IS use by competitors is the degree to which the client's competitors use IS for competitive advantage. IS outsourcing by competitors is the degree of IS outsourcing among competitors in the client's market segment.

Resource acquisition is the degree to which the client organisation controls resources that IS suppliers have a need for, such as follow-up projects, publicity, a good reference for additional work or an entry into a new client segment. Absorbing uncertainty is the degree to which IS suppliers have knowledge and experience that client organizations have a need for. Selective use of information is the degree to which suppliers withhold or misrepresent information with regard to the IS activity.

3.7.2 Intermediate variables

The intermediate variables that were derived from the theoretical perspectives are listed in Table 3.6. Some variables appeared in a number of theories, sometimes under a different name. The names of the situational factors, the theories they are derived from and their original names are listed in Table 3.6 and the relationship of each intermediate variable to attractiveness for outsourcing is shown. If for example, economies of scale is high, then the attractiveness for outsourcing is high, because a positive relationship is assumed between economies of scale and the attractiveness of outsourcing. The intermediate variables are described below, with the arguments for the relationship to outsourcing and the situational factors that influence the intermediate variables.

Economies of scale refers to the phenomenon that production efficiency increases when the volume of production increases. DLC explains why economies of scale arise and gives a number of factors that determine the presence of economies of scale. TCT presumes that outsourcing leads to lower production costs, but does not give arguments or factors for it. If external IS suppliers have more economies of scale than client organizations, then IS outsourcing is attractive to client organizations. Economies of scale arise if the supplier performs the pertinent activities on a larger scale, if the activities have scale advantages, if there are no barriers for re-use and if specificity is low.

Market pressure is a notion from DLC and refers to the pressure on IS suppliers to provide high quality at low cost to survive market competition. Market pressure on IS suppliers in a particular market segment is high if there is a large number of adequate IS suppliers, if there are few barriers for entry and exit, and if standardization and

Intermediate variable	Source	Original name (if different)	Attractiveness to outsourcing
economies of scale	DLC		
	TCT		+
market pressure	DLC	conditions for perfect competition	+
control	DLC		+
opportunism	TCT		-
information asymmetry	DLC		
	ACT		-
power	PP	power	+
	CF	bargaining power of buyer/supplier	
strategicness	CC	core competence	-

Table 3.6 Name and source of intermediate variables

availability of market information is high. Outsourcing is sensible only if market pressure is high, because otherwise there is no real competition and suppliers are not stimulated to deploy their best efforts and resources.

Control refers to whether the client organization can keep control over IS function and IS suppliers after outsourcing. A client organization retains control if measurability is high and uncertainty is low. Outsourcing is not advised if this leads to a situation in which the client organization can not control the IS supplier.

Opportunism is low if the uncertainty, the specificity, the frequency, the switching costs of the client and the complexity are low and if the IS maturity and the number of adequate suppliers are high. If the probability of opportunism is high, then outsourcing is not advised, because this will put the client organization at risk of suffering from the possible opportunistic behavior of suppliers.

Information asymmetry is low if measurability and supplier aversion to risk are high, if uncertainty and programmability are minimal, and the relationship is short. If information asymmetry is high, outsourcing is not attractive, because monitoring the IS supplier becomes very difficult.

Power refers to the power of the client organization with regard to an IS supplier. The bargaining power of the IS supplier and the bargaining power of the client organization, as mentioned in CF, are included in this intermediate variable. The power of a client organization with regard to an IS supplier is high if the switching costs of the supplier and importance of volume for supplier are high, and if switching costs of client, supplier concentration and competitiveness are low. Outsourcing is not advised if this would lead to a situation in which the supplier has more power than the client organisation.

Strategicness involves the importance of the information systems or IS activities to the client organization's competitive position and continuity. *Strategicness* is high if the competitive use of IS and IS use by competitors is high and if the degree of IS outsourcing by competitors is low. If strategicness is high, then outsourcing is not advised, because outsourcing would make the competitive advantage available to competitors and make the client organization highly dependent on the IS supplier.

The relationships between the situational factors and the intermediate variables are summarized in Table 3.7

3.7.3 Decision variables

The main decision variable found implicitly or explicitly in most theories is outsourcing versus insourcing. The attractiveness of outsourcing is determined by the values of the intermediate variables, that are influenced by the situational factors, as described in the

Situational factor	economies of scale	market pressure	control	opportunism	information asymmetry	power	strategicness
information systems and IS function							
scale	+						
scale advantages	+						
barriers to re-use	-						
standardization		+					
measurability			+		-		
uncertainty			-	+	+		
specificity	-			+			
frequency				-			
switching costs of client				+			
complexity				+			
programmability					-		
length of relationship					-		
competitive use of IS							+
client organisation and environment							
IS maturity					-		
buyer concentration						+	
importance of volume for client						-	
resource acquisition						+	
IS use by competitors							+
IS outsourcing by competitors							-
IS market and IS suppliers							
number of suppliers		+	-				
barriers to entry and exit		-					
market information		+					
risk aversion of supplier					+		
switching costs of supplier						+	
supplier concentration						-	
importance of volume for IS supplier		+					
absorbing uncertainty						-	
selective use of information						-	

+ = positive relationship   - = negative relationship

Table 3.7 Relationships between situational factors and intermediate variables

previous section. A number of other decision variables that have also been derived from the theories are summarized below.

Coordination mechanisms

Coordination mechanisms are the mechanisms that DLC distinguishes to coordinate activities. If IS activities are outsourced, the client organization can coordinate the IS supplier mainly by standardization of skills and output. The other coordination mechanisms can however also be applied to some extent (see section 3.2.5).

Strategies for reducing uncertainty

Uncertainty can be reduced by a number of strategies distinguished in DLC. If the uncertainty of IS activities is high and there is considerable information asymmetry between a client organisation and an IS supplier, then the strategies described in section 3.2.5 may reduce this uncertainty and information asymmetry.

Governance modes

TCT distinguishes four modes for governing transactions (see section 3.3.1). The attractiveness of these modes is determined by the degree of specificity and the frequency of the IS activities. Market governance using a contract equivalent to sale is the most attractive for non-specific IS activities. Market governance using trilateral contracts, including for example external audits and data centre benchmarks, are most appropriate for occasional mixed or idiosyncratic IS activities. Market governance using bilateral contracts is advised for recurrent mixed IS activities, while hierarchical governance should be chosen for recurrent idiosyncratic IS activities.

Types of contract

TCT also distinguishes a number of contract types (see section 3.3.1), determined by the specificity and frequency of the transactions. Classical contracting is appropriate for exchanging discrete and relatively homogeneous IS products or services, such as hardware or system software, and for non-specific IS activities. Neo-classical contracting, in which not all future contingencies are spelled out, is advised for occasional mixed or idiosyncratic IS activities, such as information planning. Relational contracts, that are based on a relationship between the client organization and the supplier, should be chosen for recurrent mixed or idiosyncratic IS activities, such as software maintenance.

Strategies for sharing risk between client and supplier

Sharing risk with the supplier reduces the risk for the client organization and is an incentive for the IS supplier to lower production costs, according to ACT. If the supplier is risk averse, then the client must pay a risk premium to have the supplier accept the risk (see section 3.4.2).

The following price mechanisms transfer the risk of IS activities increasingly to the supplier: a fixed annual fee, a price depending on the time and materials spent for the activity, a price per unit of work, a fixed price for a fixed portion of work, or a price depending on the benefits to the client. The risk of uncontrollable lead times for IS activities can be reduced by agreeing a fixed lead time.

Tactics to increase the client organization's power

Client organizations can maximize their power of resource acquisition by withholding part of the resources from the supplier, for example by splitting a project in phases and only awarding the first phase to the supplier, or by postponing a percentage of payments for a development project until the system has been proven to be error-free (see section 3.6). Client organizations can minimize their dependency on suppliers by choosing technical components that confirm to industry standards, by demanding that systems are documented and are portable to other hardware and software platforms, and by making contractual arrangements that oblige their supplier to facilitate and cooperate if the client changes to another supplier. The power that an IS supplier derives from their ability to absorb uncertainty can be reduced by keeping enough knowledge and skills within the client organization to assess the possibilities and limitations of information technology and to evaluate prices, lead times and quality of IS products and services. Selective use of information by the IS supplier can be reduced by demanding quality and progress reports, and by conducting audits, or by demanding that the supplier uses a quality system that the client organisation can inspect.

CHAPTER 4

Case Studies

IS outsourcing is a phenomenon with many practical implications. Most empirical research undertaken by other researchers has focused on the expectations and opinions of stakeholders before or shortly after an outsourcing decision. The pilot study for this book revealed that most consequences of outsourcing only arise one or a few years after the implementation of outsourcing decisions. In this research, the consequences of 23 sourcing decisions were investigated, retrospectively for up to 10 years back, and longitudinally, over a period of two years after the sourcing decision.

This chapter starts with the considerations for choosing the case study method and with the research design. The sourcing decision processes, design of the outsourcing relationships, selection of the suppliers and implementation, management and termination of the relationships are described in sections 4.2 to 4.5. The actual consequences of the sourcing decisions are evaluated, followed by analysis of the situational factors and the decision variables that may have caused the positive or negative consequences, in sections 4.6 to 4.8. Conclusions are drawn in the final section with regard to the variables and guidelines given in chapters 2 and 3.

4.1 Case study design

In this section, the choice for conducting case study research is explained, the research design is elaborated, the methods of data collection and analysis are given, and the organizations and cases are described.

4.1.1 Research method

The research methods used most in information systems research are (Nissen, Klein and Hirschheim, 1991):

- *case studies,* where one or a small number of entities is examined with regard to a large number of, not necessarily pre-determined, variables, and no experimental control is used,
- *experiments,* where the phenomenon is isolated from its context and the independent variables can be manipulated,
- *surveys,* where a large number of entities is examined with regard to a limited number of pre-determined variables.

For each research project the most appropriate research method has to be determined and justified. Authors on research methods have different views on the criteria that determine appropriate research methods. The different viewpoints are given below.

Criteria for choosing a method

Several authors, such as Van der Zwaan (1990) and De Leeuw (1990), posit that the research method should be determined by the phase of the study: exploratory, descriptive, explanatory or testing. They state that case study research is particularly appropriate for the exploratory phases of research in new areas and that experiments or surveys are the only way to do explanatory or testing inquiries.

Yin (1984) and Ryan et al. (1992) however state that each method is applicable for each phase of research. Experiments often have an exploratory motive (Hacking, 1989) and case studies can be used for testing (Yin, 1984). A more appropriate view is therefore a pluralistic one. Each method can be used in all phases and the choice should be determined by the specific characteristics of the research project. Yin (1984) gives three criteria:

1. *Type of research question:* does the research question focus on "why" and "how" a certain phenomenon arises or merely on "what" the phenomenon comprises and to what extent it occurs?
2. *Extent of control* over behavioral events: is the phenomenon inter-twined with the context or can it be isolated and controlled without losing relevance?
3. *Degree of focus* on contemporary events: is the focus on historical events that are documented comprehensively, or on contemporary events?

Four criteria can be added, which are described more extensively in De Looff and Berghout (1993):

4. Are the *terminology* and corresponding concepts in the area under

investigation consistent and unequivocal?

5. Is a *sufficient number of entities* available and accessible to obtain statistically significant results? Are entities easily accessible or does it take a lot of time and persuasion to find and engage research entities?

6. Is *measuring* relevant variables *complex* and *labor-intensive*? Are unequivocal constructs available for all variables and is the required data readily available?

7. Does the phenomenon evolve over time, or is it static?

Surveys are not very appropriate for "why" and "how" questions, because these questions deal with operational links that must be traced over time, rather than mere frequencies or incidence (Yin, 1984) and require interpretation. Case study research has a distinct advantage when a "how" or "why" question is asked about a contemporary set of events, over which the investigator has little or no control (Yin, 1984).

An experimental approach can be chosen if an investigator can manipulate behavior directly, precisely and systematically. Experiments and surveys are not appropriate if the context of a phenomenon is essential for its comprehension. The effect of a management information system can, for example, be measured in a laboratory situation. Control over the events is then good, but the phenomenon is isolated from its context. One may question whether the latter situation is a genuine representation of the environment in which a manager takes decisions (Galliers, 1987). Information systems are usually very much interconnected with their context. They influence or control, directly or indirectly, almost all processes in an organization. Changing the information systems changes the organization, which in turn may influence the information systems (Harrington, 1991). The context is therefore essential and it is hard to separate the context from the phenomenon (Benbasat et al., 1987; Galliers, 1987; Kaplan and Duchon, 1988).

The variables in information systems research can usually not be manipulated and replicated. It is for example, not realistic to ask an organization to apply three different methods for taking IT investment decisions and it is impossible to do this with the same starting conditions.

Contemporary phenomena are usually not documented comprehensively enough to allow for historical research and archival study. Information technology is a contemporary and rapidly changing phenomenon. The rare historical material that is available is often unfit for use due to a lack of accuracy.

Using questionnaires is debatable if the terminology in the research area is inconsistent and equivocal. It is not certain that all respondents will use the same interpretation of terms used in the questionnaire. With interviews, the interviewer can check how the interviewee interprets the terms, while in large-scale surveys, this is not possible. One may doubt whether a respondent to a questionnaire reads a list of definitions and whether the respondent is willing and able to adapt their framework in the short time spent filling out a questionnaire. In the IS area, terminology is seldom consistent. Trends and buzz words make it very hard to describe phenomena unequivocally. If in a survey, for example, respondents are asked about fourth generation programming languages, one may doubt whether a respondent can distinguish these sufficiently from second, third and fifth generation languages to justify conclusions.

If the number of entities available is small or if entities are hard to find and engage, then surveys are not feasible. If measuring relevant variables is complex and labor-intensive, and unequivocal constructs are unavailable, then written questionnaires are not appropriate. If phenomena evolve over time, then longitudinal research on the same entities is required, which is usually not possible with surveys if respondents participate anonymously and can not be traced through time.

Choice of research method

All the above conditions indicate that the case study method is most appropriate for research on IS outsourcing decision making, thus it was chosen for this research. The topic requires that "why" and "how" questions are answered. The variables in IS outsourcing can not be manipulated, because no client organization would be willing to change their IS sourcing for a research project. IS outsourcing in its current forms is relatively new. Terminology in IS outsourcing is unclear and new terms for different types of outsourcing appear regularly. The number of actual IS outsourcing decisions available for research is not large enough to obtain statistically valid results. IS outsourcing arrangements are not easily accessible due to the confidential and strategic nature of the decisions involved. It takes a lot of time and persuasion to find and engage organizations. Measuring variables, such as the costs of internal and external provision of certain IS activities, is very complex and labor-intensive and this data is not unequivocally and readily available. The consequences of IS outsourcing decisions only appear after some time, for example at the time of contract renewal, so longitudinal research is required.

Case studies have been used to investigate IS outsourcing by Lacity and Hirschheim (1993) and by Willcocks and Fitzgerald (1993). Other researchers have sometimes used surveys, often in conjunction with case studies. Some of these surveys were aimed at getting quantitative and indicative information (Arnett and Jones, 1994; Willcocks and Fitzgerald, 1993), such as information on the size and growth of the market for IS outsourcing, opinions on outsourcing, indications of reasons and dangers of outsourcing. Other surveys have been aimed at measuring statistical relationships between theoretical variables, such as asset specificity and uncertainty and the degree of outsourcing (Aubert, Rivard and Patry, 1994; Loh and Venkatraman, 1993a).

Validity of the case study method

Case study research has a number of traditional prejudices against it and is sometimes treated with disdain. Yin (1984) notes that cases studies are often presumed to have a lack of rigor, little basis for scientific generalization, and that case studies take too long and result in massive, unreadable documents. Lee (1989) and Kennedy (1979) describe presumed problems in making controlled observations and deductions and in allowing for replicability and generalizability.

The assumed lack of rigor can be explained by some apparently sloppy case studies, but is not inherent to case study research (Yin, 1984). Equivocality and bias also appears in the conduct of experiments and in designing questionnaires.

The *generalizability* of case study results is often questioned: how can conclusions drawn from one or a few entities be generalized? The number of entities in a case study is indeed typically too small for statistically justified generalization; however, with regard to generalizability, case study research can better be compared to experiments (Ryan et al., 1992). "... case studies, like experiments, are generalizable to theoretical propositions and not to populations or universes. In this sense, the case study, like the experiment, does not represent a "sample," and the investigator's goal is to expand and generalize theories (analytic generalization) and not to enumerate frequencies (statistical generalization)" (Yin, 1984). Case study results are not generalized to a population from which a sample was taken, but to other situations that are believed or assumed to be sufficiently similar to the study sample that findings also apply there (Kennedy, 1979).

Kennedy (1979) distinguishes between the *range* of generalization and the *strength* of confidence one has in generalization. "Whether or not statistics are used, inferences of generalization are always tentative. Data might offer confirming or disconfirming evidence, but never conclusive evidence. ... Furthermore, the strength of evidence is a matter of judgment, .. rather than a binary decision. ... generalization is not simply a function of the number of units one has observed. More important are the kinds of units observed, that is, the range of characteristics of the units investigated and the range of conditions under which observation occurred" (Kennedy, 1979).

Making controlled observations is difficult with case studies. If scientists want to test relationships that are expected to exist between factors, they observe the influence of one factor on another factor, and remove or control potentially confounding influences. Laboratory experiments accomplish this through the use of control groups and treatment groups in social or medical sciences or by controlling all environmental conditions in natural sciences. Statistical studies control confounding influences by using statistical controls and by choosing a number of entities sufficiently large to reduce those influences to stochastic errors.

With case study research in a natural environment, influences cannot be removed and the number of entities is usually not large enough to use statistical controls. Influences can however, be measured and case sites can be chosen to obtain the necessary values and variety in the relevant variables. Cases can also be investigated before and after a certain change, assuming other variables remain the same. Similar cases in different situations can be compared.

Controlled deductions in case study research do not follow the rules of mathematics, but are based on the rules of logic (Yin, 1984). Deductions from qualitative data are made by reasoning instead of calculation, but should be equally traceable.

Allowing for replicability is not possible by observing exactly the same set of events more than once. One can however, apply the same theory to a different set of initial conditions, resulting in different predictions. Another option is to maintain all raw data, such as interview notes and case reports, and record all procedures for data analysis. Another investigator can analyze the same data and should be able to draw the same conclusions from the data.

4.1.2 Research design

Research questions
The research questions for the case study were:

1. How do organizations make IS sourcing decisions (see sections 4.2 to 4.5)?
2. What are the actual consequences of IS sourcing decisions, in the short and long term (see section 4.6)?
3. How can these positive or negative consequences be related to the specific type of sourcing and the specific circumstances (see sections 4.7 and 4.8)?

The research was not aimed at determining the opinions of stakeholders towards outsourcing in general, but at determining the consequences of actual outsourcing decisions, and at relating these consequences to the situation and to the decisions taken. The research questions are descriptive and explanatory: what are the consequences and how can they be explained?

Units of analysis

The units of analysis may be individuals, such as patients or employees, events, such as decisions, programs or implementation processes, or entities, such as groups, neighborhoods, organizations, or societies. It is important to determine the boundary of a case. If cases are groups, which persons are included? If cases are have geographical boundaries, how should boundary problems be treated? In what time frame are cases going to be examined?

In this research, the units of analysis were IS sourcing decision processes and the consecutive outsourcing arrangements. Stakeholders included all groups within the client organization as well as the supplier organization and if possible the external advisors or auditors who were involved, actively or passively, in the sourcing decision process. The emphasis was however on higher management and on the client organization. The cases were investigated before and directly after the sourcing decision was made and one or two years after the decision, in 1993 and 1994.

Tactics to meet quality criteria

Each research design should comply to certain quality criteria. Yin gives four criteria and suggests tactics to make case studies meet these criteria (see Table 4.1). Most of these tactics were used in this case study, and their use is described in the following sections.

Construct validity

In the case studies, multiple sources of evidence were used, namely interviews with different stakeholders and documentary evidence on the sourcing decision and on the outsourced activities.

A chain of evidence was established in chapter 3, by deriving intermediate variables and situational factors from established organizational theories.

Criteria	Requirements	Case study tactics
Construct validity	operational measures are correct use representations of concepts studied	multiple sources of evidence establish chain of evidence have informants review draft case study report
Internal validity	relationships between concepts are causal	do pattern matching do explanation building do time-series analysis
External validity	findings can be generalized to certain domain	use replication logic
Reliability	study can be repeated, with the same results.	use case study protocol evelop case study data base

Table 4.1 Case study tactics for four design tests (Yin, 1984)

Reviewing draft case study report by informants was not performed, because of time constraints. Moreover, the case study reports were constructed from multiple interview reports and relevant documentation. The format of the case study report was established after all interviews were held, so there was considerable time between the interview and the time the case study report was written.

Internal validity

Internal validity concerns establishing a causal relationship, whereby certain conditions are shown to lead to certain consequences.

Pattern matching compares an empirically based pattern with a predicted one (Yin, 1984). This was performed in this research by comparing cases to see if similar decisions in different situations or different decisions in similar situations lead to different consequences.

Explanation building was established by asking explicitly whether certain positive or negative consequences of outsourcing were caused by certain circumstances and decisions. Interviewees were asked to clarify this presumed relationship.

A form of *time-series analysis* was used by investigating the situation before and immediately after the implementation of an outsourcing decision and the situation some time after the implementation.

Other researchers who have conducted empirical studies in IS outsourcing have often determined relationships between variables by measuring situational factors and sourcing decisions and analyzing whether certain situational factors coincided with certain sourcing decisions. (e.g. Aubert, Patry and Rivard, 1994; Loh and Venkatraman, 1994a). The implicit assumption of these researchers is that decision makers in practice generally choose the sourcing option that is best in their specific situation, or that firms taking the wrong sourcing decision will disappear. This approach may be valid for strategic decisions with an immediate and decisive impact on the continuity of organizations, but it does not hold for IS outsourcing. Many client organizations that admit having taken adverse outsourcing decisions still exist, and many injudicious decisions may even go unnoticed. In this research, the success and the consequences of the sourcing decisions are therefore investigated explicitly. Decisions that were taken in specific situations are given as advice for other decision makers only if the decisions led to successful sourcing, and dissuaded if the consequences were adverse.

Measuring the success of sourcing decisions was however not straightforward. Sourcing decisions were often successful in certain respects but less successful in other respects. Stakeholders had different opinions with regard to the success of the sourcing decisions they were involved in, and their opinions varied over time. The measurement of success depended on the choice of the standard against which success was measured. A sourcing decision may, for example, yield some improvements compared to the initial situation, but be far from optimum compared to how other organizations are performing.

External validity

The domain to which a case study's findings can be generalized depends on the selection of the cases. Case study findings can be generalized to situations that are sufficiently similar to the cases investigated with regard to relevant variables.

The aim of this research is to support different types of outsourcing by different types of organizations. The cases were therefore selected as to obtain variety in all relevant variables, especially in type of organization, type of outsourcing arrangement and successes as well as failures.

The majority of the cases in this research were in the Dutch public sector, mainly within central government organizations. The variety of business processes and sourcing decisions found was as large as that found in the private sector and all types of processes and systems were included. Apart from a few differences, which are described explicitly in this chapter, no indications were found to assume that sourcing decisions made by private sector organizations are different and require different decision support. The variables that appear in the literature on IS outsourcing could all be applied to the public sector. A number of additional variables were found in this research, but these variables are not specific to the public sector and no indication was found that the variables do not apply to IS outsourcing by private sector organizations. The research results can therefore be considered for use in both public and private sector organizations.

Reliability

A case study is called reliable when it is possible for another researcher to repeat the operations of the case study, such as the data collection procedures, with the same results (Yin, 1984).

All procedures for this case study research were written down in a case study protocol. The protocol covers case selection procedures, procedures for obtaining participation by case organizations and interviewees, and procedures for data collection and analysis.

All the data collected is held in a case study data base. The following items have been provided for each case study: name of the organization; name and position of interviewees, interview reports, references to documentation, summaries of documents and a case study report.

Qualitative versus quantitative research

The distinction between qualitative and quantitative research can refer to the nature of the variables investigated and to the method of data analysis. Quantitative variables are variables that can be measured on a cardinal scale; examples include lead times of projects, number of employees, and number of errors in software. Qualitative variables can not be measured on a cardinal scale, but can often be measured using an ordinal scale, such as a five-point scale from "totally agree" to "totally disagree" or "low", "medium", and "high".

Quantitative data analysis means that the quantitative or qualitative variables are represented by numbers and that the analysis is performed by calculation, including calculating occurrences, mean values, variations and correlations. Qualitative analysis is based on reasoning and explanation.

This research includes both quantitative and qualitative variables, and the data analysis is largely qualitative, though occurrences of specific situations have been counted.

Passive or active researcher

The role of the researcher can be passive or active, which refers to whether the researcher is part of the phenomenon under investigation. A researcher can for example, be a participant in a decision process in an organization or be the subject of a psychological experiment.

Action research is a type of active research and implies that a researcher has an active role in solving a problem or taking decisions and at the same time investigates the problem. Action research may provide insights that can not be gained by an outsider. The action goals and the research goals may however conflict and it is not always possible for researchers to observe their own behavior objectively. Van Waes (1991) has performed action research, and found that a participant researcher does not necessarily harm the objectivity of the research.

In the case study research described in this chapter, the re-

Organization	Employees	Primary process
Ministry of Social Affairs and Employment (SZW)	2,400	developing and maintaining policies for social security, employment and labor conditions
Directorate General of Public Works and Water Management (RWS)	10,000	managing public works and water management
Dutch Railways (NS)	29,000	transporting passengers and freight
Central Bureau of Statistics (CBS)	2,500	providing social and economic statistics
Municipality of Eindhoven	2,100	maintaining the local infrastructure
DSM (former Dutch State Mines)	21,000	producing chemicals for the global market

Table 4.2 Organizations participating in the case study research (situation in 1994)

1 Development of a system to predict air pollution by road traffic on proposed routes of motorways.
2 Development, implementation, maintenance and operation of a system for planning and managing maintenance of buildings and installations.
3 Selection, implementation and operation of a software package for calculating and paying social security benefits.
4 Development, implementation, maintenance and operation of a system for the public land registry. The system has strong connections to the system for taxes on real estate, and the new system has speeded the collection of taxes considerably.
5 Privatization of an IS department, involving the transfer of 200 employee, mainframes and other resources. The department was sold to a consortium of IS suppliers and spending was guaranteed for a period of five years. After these five years, the consortium sold the company to an outsourcing company.
6 Development of a system for managing the maintenance of railways.
7 Privatization of an internal IS department. The department was sold to a supplier that consisted mainly of outsourced departments taken over from other organizations.
8 Operation of network hardware and software for over 1,000 workstations. Internalized two years later.
9 Development of a system for storage and retrieval of all collective labor agreements in the Netherlands. Entering the collective labor agreements in the system was also outsourced.
10 Operation of a large network. A contract with a network supplier to provide personnel if the work load was high or one of the four internal network specialists was not available. After a year, the internal specialists had been trained to be able to replace one another and the contract was terminated.
11 Information planning for an information-intensive user department. A consultant was hired to take interviews and write the information plan.
12 Development, implementation and maintenance of a system for storing and processing a large volume of measurements of water-levels and water quality.
13 Development, implementation and maintenance of a system for the granting and monitoring of licenses for discharging effluent water.
14 Selection and lease of a human resources information system for a ministry. At the time, very few packages were available for human resources management in government organizations.
15 Development, implementation and maintenance of a system for managing the flow of large ships passing locks, weirs, bridges, and traffic posts.
16 Transforming a central IS department into an independent subsidiary, but retaining full ownership.
17 Implementation of two software packages for the management and retrieval of all documentation of a ministry. The packages were selected by a team with members drawn from several ministries.
18 Development of a system for planning and recording inspections of high pressure manufacturing installations.
19 Outsourcing of a data gathering process was considered, but rejected, among other reasons because of the importance of the process and its interconnectedness with the data processing. Instead, some internal improvements were made.
20 Outsourcing of the IS department to a large organization with an IS department that offered services to external clients.
21 Cooperation between several municipalities in a region, to provide all IS activities the municipalities needed. The joint venture was owned by two municipalities, and served over 100 other municipalities. The joint venture was privatized and sold to a holding. Two years later the holding went bankrupt, and the joint venture was sold to another IS supplier.
22 Hiring an external consultant to assist with information planning.
23 Development, implementation, maintenance and operation of a financial information system comprising all financial aspects of the organization. Cooperation with other similar organizations was abandoned, because of differences in requirements.

Table 4.3 Summary of cases

searcher took a passive role. The outsourcing decisions were investigated during the decision making process and after the decision had been taken, but the outcome of the decision was not influenced by the researcher.

4.1.3 Organizations and cases

A total of 23 IS sourcing decisions within six organizations was investigated in this research project over a period of two years, 1993 and 1994. The case organizations were identified from personal networks and selected on their inclination and willingness to take part in the research project. The organizations that participated are listed in Table 4.2. Detailed findings with regard to the Central Bureau of Statistics and the former Dutch State Mines can be found in Stevens (1994) and Winkels (1995).

Cases were selected within the case study organizations so as to obtain the requisite variety of cases with regard to the variables. The cases are summarized in Table 4.3. The cases are not presented with reference to the corresponding organization, to preserve confidentiality.

The IS activities, IS components and information systems in the cases are summarized in Table 4.4 and Table 4.5 (see Chapter 2 for definitions of these distinctions). Most of the 23 cases involved several IS activities and IS components. All categories are fairly evenly

IS activities	IS Components				
	Software	Hardware	Data	People	Procedures
Planning	2	2	2	2	2
Development	17	13	12	12	15
Implementation	15	12	10	11	13
Maintenance	16	13	10	11	13
Operation	11	11	9	8	8

Table 4.4 Number of cases of outsourcing IS activities with regard to IS components

IS activities	Information systems		
	Primary systems	Primary supp. systems	Secondary systems
Planning	2	2	2
Development	4	7	15
Implementation	4	8	12
Maintenance	5	9	13
Operation	6	9	11

Table 4.5 Number of cases of outsourcing IS activities with regard to information systems

represented, though outsourcing of planning was investigated in only two cases. The size of the outsourcing operations varied from $30,000 for a project of three months to $150 million over four years.

4.1.4 Data collection and analysis

Data can be collected from documents, archival records, interviews, direct observation, participant-observation and physical artifacts (Yin, 1984). Data collection methods can be divided in:

* *direct observation* of social or physical processes or objects,
* *indirect observation* by interviewing the people involved or by studying documents or archival records.

Initially, it was planned to do indirect as well as direct observation, by attending meetings on outsourcing decisions; however, decision makers at the case study sites considered it inappropriate to let a researcher attend these, often confidential, meetings. When making outsourcing decisions or negotiating with potential suppliers, participants often had no time available to be interviewed. Finally, it was almost impossible to make the research coincide with the timing of the decisions and meetings. The research was therefore confined to indirect observation.

Interviews
The information needed for the research was obtained from the IS management and the general management of the participating client organizations, both at the top and the user department level. Table 4.6 summarizes the positions of the interviewees. Most of the interviewees were staff of the central IS department or an IS manager of a user department. These functionaries were well informed and available for interviewing.
The interviews were semi-structured using a list of subjects. Each

Position	Number of interviewees
Top	
• General manager	3
• IS manager	5
• IS staff	19
User departments	
• General manager	3
• IS manager	27
• IS staff	4

Table 4.6 Positions of interviewees

subject was discussed at each interview, though not necessarily in same order. The questions followed the general pattern of the phases in IS outsourcing decision making processes, as described in the sections 4.2 to 4.5. Interviewees were free to elaborate on each subject, within time constraints. Additional questions were asked, if necessary, to obtain the required information per subject. The interviews took between one and two hours. No tape recorder was used but notes were taken.

Documents
The data gathered from interviews were compared to documentation provided by the interviewees. Interviewees suggested both formal and informal documents, related to different phases of the outsourcing decision and the implementation. Documents included internal memoranda from parties involved in the outsourcing decisions, external assessments of internal IS services and IS suppliers, project documentation, (requests for) proposals, contracts, bills and correspondence. Many of these documents had a confidential character.

Analysis
The notes of each interview were transcribed into an interview

Description	Development of a system to predict air pollution by road traffic on proposed routes of motorways.
System	Primary system
Components	Software and procedures
Activities	Development
Motives	No internal capacity available and against organization's policy to build capacity.
Legal relationship	None. Independent IS supplier
Transactional relationship	Cooperation agreement. Tariffs, conditions and standard contract.
Economic relationship	Percentage of client organizations IS spending: >50% Percentage of IS supplier's revenues: <10%
Location	Supplier's staff worked at supplier's premises. Client organization had no office space available and no hardware and system software for development.
Ownership	Software and procedures: client organization
Exclusiveness	Software and procedures were exclusively for client organization. Cooperation with a similar organization was tried, but failed because of divergent needs, different urgency and budget avail ability.

Table 4.7 Example of part of a case study report

report, and each document was summarized. A case study report was compiled for each case, based on data obtained from the interviews and documents. Part of one of the case study reports is summarized in Table 4.7.

Each case study report was given a standardized structure, following the structure of the framework described in chapter 2, and the value of all the variables was determined for each case. If interviewees expanded on a subject, their explanation was added to the report. In cases where interviewees and/or documents disagreed, the interviewees were requested to clarify the situation.

Both quantitative and qualitative analysis was performed. The quantitative analysis consisted of counting how many cases fell into each of the categories of the variables described in chapters 2 and 3, while the qualitative analysis consisted of analyzing the explanations of the interviewees.

Presentation of results

The presentation of the case study results in this book is restricted to the cross-case analysis. Confidentiality and space constraints impede describing individual cases. Descriptions of individual cases are used only as typical examples of, or exceptions to the findings. Qualitative data, explanations and background information are added, if applicable. The numbers in the tables in this chapter do not always add up to the total number of cases or interviewees, because the questions did not always apply to all of the cases and some cases fell into more than one category.

Phases

A number of phases are distinguished in the sourcing decision process. The phases, and the number of cases in which the phases were performed, are listed in Table 4.8.

The order in which the phases were performed differed between the cases. The selection of the IS supplier and the design of the outsourcing relationship were often performed in conjunction. The call for tender sometimes contained demands as to the preferred relation-

Phase	Number of cases
1 Initial sourcing decision	22
2 Designing the outsourcing arrangement	22
3 Selecting the IS supplier	21
4 Implementation of the outsourcing decision	20
5 Management of the outsourcing relationship	20
6 Termination of the outsourcing relationship	12

Table 4.8 Phases of outsourcing decision processes

ship, pricing mechanism, and so on. The details of the design were part of the tender responses and were elaborated during the contract negotiation or even after the implementation of the outsourcing decision. In none of the cases was the initial sourcing decision taken or changed after the tendering phase, not even in the cases where none of the responses were satisfactory.

4.2 Initial sourcing decision

The decision making processes differed among the cases investigated. In this section, the triggers, decision processes, alternatives, goals and expectations in the initial sourcing decision are described. An analysis of the initial situation and the results of the sourcing decisions are given.

4.2.1 Triggers for sourcing evaluations

The triggers that gave rise to sourcing evaluations were extremely diverse. The subject was sometimes brought up by users or business unit managers if they were dissatisfied with the products and services they received. IS management considered the outsourcing of parts of the organization's IS function for which the internal IS department had insufficient capacity or expertise. They hired external staff to solve a temporary shortage of staff, or outsourced the operation of old systems to free capacity for developing new systems. Some IS managers evaluated outsourcing proactively, before top management did it for them, to prove that the internal IS department was competitive and did not need to be outsourced. The triggers found in the case studies are summarized in Table 4.9.

The regular information planning and strategy cycle was the trigger in only one case. The large-scale outsourcing operations were all treated as one-off isolated decisions, with little or no connection to

Trigger	Number of cases
dissatisfaction with IS function	2
back to the core business	17
privatization trend	11
staffing level reduction program	5
new systems or activities	13
(temporary) shortage of capacity	11
media attention for outsourcing	2
offer by supplier	2
information planning	1
major business changes	7
excess capacity internal IS function	3

Table 4.9 Triggers for starting outsourcing evaluation

Functionaries	Number of cases
Top	
• General management	14
• IS management	6
• IS staff	2
Business units	
• General management	6
• IS management	3
• IS staff	3

Table 4.10 Functionaries triggering outsourcing evaluation

information planning and without using the information available in the information plan, other than for drawing up the final contract. The outsourcing decisions for individual activities were mostly taken implicitly or ad hoc, without a clear relationship to the information plan.

Major technological or functional changes were another trigger for considering outsourcing. In one of the cases, the organization relocated from over twenty separate offices to one large head office. This required a new network, the development and operation of which was outsourced.

Most often, IS outsourcing discussions were initiated by the general or financial top management. To general managers, the IS function was often an uncontrollable cost and a peripheral function they felt incapable of understanding, let alone managing. IS suppliers often approached top managers instead of IS managers, because they are considered to be more susceptible to a supplier's claims of being able to relieve them of a headache, to hire their IS staff, to give the organization a cash infusion and to be a strategic partner with the organization's interests at heart.

Triggers in the public sector

In the public sector, the most prominent trigger was the privatization trend. Privatization is more fundamental than outsourcing by private corporations, as it implies transferring activities and resources from the public sector to the private sector. Privatization was and still is an issue of considerable political and ideological debate. In the 1980s there was a strong trend towards privatization, to reduce government involvement and to decrease the size of the public sector in favor of free market enterprises. The UK Prime Minister Margaret Thatcher and the US President Ronald Reagan were strong proponents of privatization. In the Netherlands, the second Cabinet of Lubbers followed this trend and privatized many public bodies. The privatization trend was based upon implicit ideological assumptions that markets are inherently more efficient and that decreasing the staffing levels of government organizations would lead to a cheaper and more flexible public sector. Dutch government officials were expected to follow the trend and look for ways to reduce the staffing levels in the public sector; the IS function was an obvious candidate for privatization, as it was considered to be a support function and not a core activity. A number of Dutch government IS departments were privatized for this reason, some almost regardless of the consequences.

A factor that contributed to the privatization trend was that the Dutch public sector accounting system differs from what is common in the private sector. It is very attractive to public sector organizations to sell IT assets, as public sector accounting systems prescribe that assets are depreciated in the year they are bought, and assets therefore have no balance sheet value when they are sold. A strict division between budgets for personnel expenses and for material expenses impeded rational evaluation of the costs of hiring internal personnel versus contracting personnel from external IS suppliers. In some of the cases investigated, the personnel budget was not sufficient to recruit employees, but the material budget allowed the hiring of external IS staff at considerably higher costs, sometimes for several years. In 1992, the strict separation between the personnel and material budget was removed and the restrictions on transferring budgets from one year to another were alleviated.

Value Added Tax (VAT) makes outsourcing less attractive to public sector organizations. In the Netherlands, suppliers have to charge 17.5% VAT on their tariffs, and public sector organizations are generally not compensated for these extra costs. The Dutch ministry of Finance has issued transition measures in which public sector organizations are compensated for the extra VAT paid in the first years after they privatize part of their organization.

Trends in IS management

A number of other developments in IS management coincided with outsourcing during the period of the case study research. In most of the case organizations, there was an overall trend towards decentralization from the holding or top level to business unit or middle management level. Support functions, that had often been performed by large centralized staff units, were decentralized to business units. These units were empowered by giving them control over all the functions and resources needed for their business. Large centralized staff units were reduced and many organizations' head offices were cut back severely.

The *awareness* of line management for the role, possibilities and limitations of information systems was increased by awareness programs. Users and line managers have become increasingly knowledgeable about information technology and more critical towards the IS function.

After the period of extensive decentralization, line managers realized that there were information relationships between business units and that efficiency gains could be achieved by cooperation. Top management noted that corporate information needs were not met and that suboptimization and redundant work were present. In many organizations, this insight led to the establishment of *IS steering committees*, joined by the line managers or the IS managers of the business units. These steering committees define their common needs and identified opportunities to coordinate information needs between the units and produce savings by cooperating. An operational unit at the holding level was commonly (re)established, often called *common services* or *facility center* instead of central department. These units treat the business units as internal customers and charge for services delivered. The strategic unit at the holding level can act as an advisor to top management on the corporate information strategy and act as an internal consultancy firm that assisted business units with information planning and project management.

Total *IS expenses*, which in the past often had a steady annual growth, no longer increased as fast as before or were forcibly reduced. The role of large concentrated hardware, mainly mainframes, was reduced, in favor of smaller deconcentrated hardware, mini computers and personal computers. These developments are called downsizing and client/server architecture.

4.2.2 Initial sourcing decision process

Functionaries involved in decision process

The positions of the functionaries involved officially in the IS outsourcing decisions, and their attitude towards the outsourcing decision is summarized in Table 4.11. Most of the top IS managers were against outsourcing. The top general managers involved in outsourcing were all in favor and took the lead in the decision process, with little

	In favor	Against
Top		
• General manager	9	0
• IS manager	2	6
• IS staff	0	4
User departments		
• General manager	5	2
• IS manager	13	2
• IS staff	1	0

Table 4.11 Functionaries in decision process and outsourcing attitude

or no involvement of IS managers.

Sourcing decisions require expertise and experience in information systems, the IS market, outsourcing and negotiating. This expertise was not always present in the decision teams. Knowledge of information technology and of the IS market was lacking in many cases. Most decision teams had no experience with IS sourcing decision making, because most organizations only take large sourcing decisions once or a few times. In some cases, external experts were hired to advise on outsourcing. The impression of the IS staff however, was that these experts were hired mainly to defend the decision already taken by top management.

Activities in decision process

The actual sourcing decision was often taken in a short time and without clear distinction into several steps. Analysis of the current situation was often only performed at the time the current activities and resources had to be described in the final contract. Future changes in the business processes, information systems, IS activities or advancements in information technology were seldom taken into account. Analysis of quantitative and qualitative requirements for IS staff and resources was lacking in most cases. The capacity that was available at the time of the decision was usually taken as a starting point, without further analysis of slack resources, shortages, or activities that were superfluous.

The position of the decision processes in relation to the information planning and strategy process was not always clear. Individual development projects often followed from information plans, but the fact that the projects were outsourced was an implicit consequence of earlier outsourcing decisions and not part of an overall outsourcing strategy formulated in the information plan.

Structuredness of decision process

No formal method for IS sourcing decisions was used in any of the cases. Interviewees indicated that such methods were not available, and that they believed IS sourcing decisions were too strategic or political to be captured by formal analysis. Decisions were based mainly on ideology, trends, and personal expectations. Staff level reduction programs were another common trigger that was often not analyzed further. Decision makers relied on general reasoning about economies of scale, specialization, focus on core business, and market efficiency, without analyzing whether these advantages applied to their organizations and the type of outsourcing they were considering.

Little analysis was made of the current situation and possibility for internal improvements. Very few decision makers compared all internal and external options and the expected consequences in a structured process. The triggers and perceptions that initiated the outsourcing discussion often remained the only aspects considered in the evaluation and the perceptions were not investigated as to their correctness.

Four of the cases involved privatization of government IS departments and were discussed briefly in the Parliament. In only one case, a member of Parliament asked critical and specific questions about a privatization. These questions were answered by ideological reasoning about the general advantages of free enterprises.

Time scope of decision process

The time scope considered was seldom longer than the duration of the resulting contract, and usually less. Developments in the client organization, in the information systems needed and in the information technology available were not taken into account or only for the near future.

Costs and lead time of decision process

The lead time of the decision process was on average 13% of the length of the resulting contract. In most cases involving the transfer of people or resources to a supplier, the decision process took significantly more time. In one extreme case, it took three years to outsource the IS department, with a subsequent contract for three years. The actual decision to outsource however, was often made at a very early stage and by very few people, usually top or financial management, at a level where no detailed knowledge of the IS function and the IS market was present.

As few of the decision processes involved external experts, the costs of the decision process consisted mostly of time spent by internal personnel. These costs were not administered as such, but estimates varied between 2 and 5% of the value of the resulting contract. The large-scale outsourcing operations involving the transfer of IS staff put a high demand on top management's time.

Side-effects of outsourcing decision process

The fact that outsourcing was considered had in itself significant positive and negative consequences, regardless of whether outsourcing was actually chosen. Interviewees mentioned that the sourcing evaluation resulted in an increased awareness of the role of IT and the IS function among users and managers, a valuable evaluation of the current situation, a full description of all products and services the IS function provided, more insight into the costs of IS, a comparison with outside suppliers, and suggestions for improvement. In some cases, the threat that the possibility of outsourcing posed to the IS department and to the users created a momentum for changes that were not achievable before.

Negative consequences of the outsourcing evaluation included a loss of productivity and a loss of motivation because of uncertainty and fear among the IS staff. As a consequence, users sometimes lost trust in the IS department and some of the best employees left the organization. In one case, the uncertainty and the lack of openness of the decision makers led to strikes and demonstrations by the IS staff. The price the supplier was willing to pay for the department dropped by 35% during the year of decision making and negotiation. In another case, the central IS department complained that during the decision process, which took over two years, the revenues of the department decreased rapidly, even though the user departments had increasing IS work loads. The users appeared to have started outsourcing to other suppliers or performing activities themselves.

Decision makers had difficulty determining the appropriate timing and amount of information to be issued during the decision process. They realized the need for openness at an early stage, but they did not want to inform the users and IS staff before they had taken a decision. They also did not want to endanger the negotiation results by giving names of potential suppliers.

4.2.3 Alternatives and constraints

The number of alternatives considered was in most cases no more than two or three. In 13 cases, total outsourcing was the only alternative considered. Many interviewees indicated afterwards that the analysis of problems, causes, possible improvements and internal and external alternatives was inadequate. As can be seen from Table 4.12, maintaining internal provision, possibly with internal improvements, was seldom considered in the decision process. Even if internal provision was considered, the comparison was often inadequate and not based on systematic analysis. Cooperation with other organizations in the same industry was considered in 7 cases, but chosen in no more than 2 cases. In the other 5 cases, cooperation was rejected or

Alternatives	Number of cases
internal provision	3
internal provision with improvements:	
• consolidation	3
• internal transfer pricing	4
• free choice of provider	1
• internal contracts	1
• external service provision	2
cooperation with organizations in same industry	7

Table 4.12 Alternatives for outsourcing considered in the decision process

Constraints	Number of cases
shortage of staff and not allowed to hire personnel	13
outsourcing is company policy	4
obliged to take services from internal provider	1

Table 4.13 Constraints in decision process

failed, because the pertinent organizations could not agree on requirements or strategy.

Decision makers were in doubt whether to try to improve the IS
department before outsourcing or to outsource the department and
have the IS supplier conduct improvements. The advantage of improving the IS department before outsourcing was that the price that IS
suppliers would be willing to pay would be higher. The disadvantages
they perceived were that it would take too much time and effort to
improve the department and that an external supplier would probably
be better suited for it. In all cases, improvement was left to the IS
supplier.

Internal alternatives, including maintaining the current situation, were often evaluated on an unequal basis. The internal situation
was compared to external proposals in which the supplier would
provide less services, or at a lower quality, or take measures that the
internal IS department was not allowed to take.

Many outsourcing decisions were forced by constraints from
higher authorities (see Table 4.13). After most of the large-scale
outsourcing operations, subsequent IS activities had to be outsourced,
often to the supplier to which the IS department was outsourced,
because of a shortage of staff and other resources, or because of
contractual obligations, even when interviewees believed a particular
activity would be performed better internally or by another IS supplier.
Interviewees considered it detrimental that outsourcing was enforced
by pressure on staffing levels, because this led to the outsourcing of
activities that should not have been outsourced.

	General management			IS management		
	low	med	high	low	med	high
costs	2	3	18	4	8	11
lead time	4	12	7	3	14	6
staffing levels	3	2	18	4	7	12
quality	9	6	8	3	4	16
flexibility	7	11	5	5	11	7
controllability	5	12	6	3	13	7
continuity	10	10	3	5	13	5

*Table 4.14 Importance of criteria for outsourcing as perceived by general and IS
management*

	no improvement	some improvement	high improvement
lower costs	0	15	8
shorter lead times	1	18	4
reduction of staffing levels	9	6	8
higher quality	1	11	11
higher flexibility	1	15	7
higher controllability	4	12	7
higher continuity	6	10	7

Table 4.15 Improvements expected by decision makers

4.2.4 Goal variables and expectations

The goal variables the decision makers used in their decisions are given in Table 4.14, together with the importance the general management and the IS management attached to each of the criteria.

Top managers put a strong and often one-sided emphasis on cost reduction or a reduction in staffing levels, almost irrespective of the consequences. Other criteria, such as quality and flexibility, were hardly ever valued by general management. The improvements decision makers expected from outsourcing are summarized in Table 4.15.

The core business argument was pervasive. Top managers often followed a strategy of focusing on the organizations core business. Many decision makers chose outsourcing using the argument that the IS function was not part of their core business. Very few of them could however give an operational criterion for what they considered part of their core business. When asked, they described their core business in terms of the organization's mission statement. One of the interviewees stated: "we are a manufacturer of [product X], not a software house, why should we have an in-house IS department?"

The alternative notion of core competencies, as proposed in chapter 3, was not used in any of the cases. Providing IS products and services is the core business only for IS suppliers. Client organizations should investigate whether their IS function distinguishes them from their competitors. These considerations were not found in the cases. Decision makers acknowledged some disadvantages and foresaw some dangers, but these were generally seen as relatively unimportant.

All client organizations that transferred their IS department to an IS supplier had the expectation, stimulated by fluent presentations from the suppliers' sales staff, that the supplier would keep the department as a separate unit with an autonomous culture and growth, and use the knowledge and services of its other units to improve the department taken over. The supplier would use its marketing knowledge and network to find other clients for the department beside the client organization, and thereby achieve economies of scale and extend the departments view. The department would be transformed from a bureaucratic internal staff department to an innovative market oriented and flexible and customer friendly IS supplier. The supplier would be a strategic partner doing more than just performing the activities requested, but keeping up to date with the client's business processes and initiating strategic opportunities for applying IT for competitive advantage.

Public versus private sector goals

The public sector is distinguished from the private sector by the fact that making profit and maximizing shareholders value is not the main objective of public sector organizations, and that the continuity of public sector organizations does not depend upon outperforming competitors. The existence and continuity of most public sector organizations is, however, not self-evident. Though they do not depend on profit or shareholder value for their survival, public sector organizations can be reorganized, reduced or even discontinued by higher authorities if their legitimacy or necessity is no longer valid, or if their performance has become unacceptable. Public sector organizations therefore also face a strong pressure to minimize their costs and to maximize the quality of their services.

Additionally, public sector organizations have to meet demands that most private corporations do not face. Public administration involves political and legal factors that have a value-laden component. Public bodies have as an objective the performance of a socially desirable function, which is not a means to generate income, but an end in itself. A citizen's legal security and equality of rights must be guaranteed.

IT outsourcing decisions by public sector organizations are therefore not based upon the consequences for the organizations competitive position, but upon the effects on the cost and the quality of their services, and on achieving the political objectives and strategies.

One of the elements of the Government Agreement of the Second Lubbers Cabinet agreed in 1986 was the reduction of the central government by 20,000 full time employees, 4,000 of which should be achieved in 1987. Savings of 1,000 million guilders were projected in the budgets, 50,000 per full time employee. The agreement stated that privatization would be included in this reduction only if the employees ceased to be civil servants and the costs of the privatized unit were not paid fully by the government. If a privatization did not lead to the projected savings of 50,000 guilders per employee, then the department had to compensate for the difference by additional cuts. Remarkably, in the same Government Agreement, improvement of the quality of government was striven for, and the Agreement suggests improving the IS functions and information systems of government organizations as one of the means to achieve these quality improvements.

4.2.5 Analysis of initial situation

Analysis process

The analysis of the initial situation before outsourcing often focused on the total costs of the IS function, 'as compared to (expected) offers from IS suppliers. The current products and services were seldom evaluated, and no analysis was made of the problems that had triggered the sourcing evaluation, or the causes of and possible solutions to these problems.

The evaluation of the current costs often was not based on an integral allocation of all internal and external costs. In most cases, only the direct external expenses were analyzed and the costs of personnel and overheads were not allocated to the pertinent IS activities.

Determining the costs retrospectively for the research was very difficult, as most financial administrations appeared unsuited for outsourcing analysis. IS costs were often dispersed among several budgets, such as the personnel budget, and the budget for office supplies. IS expenses for specific projects were often paid directly from the project budgets. Interviewees estimated that the actual IS costs were up to two times the amount registered as such. Costs were not allocated to individual information systems, IS components and IS activities, which is necessary to take decisions on separate parts of the IS function.

Decision makers regarded mainly (their perception of) the absolute total costs, instead of the costs relative to the IS activities performed. Managers often perceived the total costs and the staffing levels of the IS function as high and uncontrollable and had doubts about the legitimacy of these costs. Reduction of total costs or comparing total costs to other organizations or benchmarking databases is useless without regarding the products and services provided, but was a goal variable in many of the cases. Hourly tariffs of internal and external personnel were compared without regarding productivity or learning time. Improvements in efficiency, by reducing costs of specified products or services without reducing quality and lead time, was seldom a goal variable.

From the fact that increased flexibility was one of the major reasons for outsourcing, one would expect that organizations would take the opportunity to evaluate the usefulness and necessity of all information systems and activities before outsourcing. This was often not the case and many contracts were based on all the activities the IS function performed at the time of outsourcing, necessary or not. If components and systems were listed, only the technical quality, the maintainability, the programming language and the documentation were analyzed. None of the client organizations evaluated the functional quality, the costs, the benefits and the necessity of the systems in use, to the extent that they actually terminated part of the systems.

Analysis results

The evaluation of the internal central IS departments prior to their outsourcing was in most cases negative. The departments were recognized for their technical expertise and high technical quality of their products; however, the attitude of the department's staff was not customer oriented enough, or business-like and flexible. The technology in use and the staff's skills were outdated and the staff was not innovative and flexible enough to deploy new technology and working methods.

Many activities were performed that none of the user departments had asked for. The technical quality of the systems was often too high for the intended use, because the internal IS staff wanted to provide the best possible performance and budgets were often sufficient to do so. Some of the IS departments relied heavily on staff hired from external suppliers, especially for the development of new systems. The management of the department had often not become used to the decentralization of IS budgets and the authorities to user departments and still acted as if the central department was there to determine what the users needed. They viewed the users as laymen and considered themselves to be specialists who were better able to determine what the users really needed. The IS staff had little knowledge of the business processes.

The back log of systems that needed to be developed was often so high that it sometimes took over a year before development of a requested system actually started. The IS resources, especially the large central hardware and the networks, were often not fully utilized and had excess capacity. The total IS budget of the client organizations had increased annually by 5 to 10% in the years prior to this research, but general management perceived no increase in the activities performed.

The line managers and IS staff at the user departments admitted a number of faults on their side. Most user departments did not have a proper information planning process and did not use information systems in a structured and planned way. Costs were not measured and allocated correctly and were not planned a few years ahead. Project management was not strict enough and user department's project managers were often not skilled enough. Requirements for activities were rarely specified in advance and were often changed during execution. The central IS department was thereby judged unfairly according to implicit and changing criteria.

4.2.6 Results of sourcing decisions

The results of the initial sourcing decisions are summarized in Table 4.16. Cell A represents the cases in which outsourcing was considered but rejected. In 6 cases, internal activities were outsourced

Initial situation	Sourcing decision	
	Insource	Outsource
Internal	(A) 2	(B) 6
External	(C) 2	(D) 2
New activity	(E) 0	(F) 15

Table 4.16 Summary of initial sourcing decisions

(cell B). Re-internalization after outsourcing appeared twice (cell C). In 2 cases, an already outsourced situation remained outsourced (cell D). The research included no cases of new activities that were insourced (cell E). The remaining 15 cases involved new IS activities that were outsourced (cell F).

4.3 Designing the outsourcing relationship

The process of designing the outsourcing relationship is described in this section. The resulting values of the decision variables in the cases are described in section 4.8.

Designing the outsourcing relationship often got much less attention than the initial sourcing decision. With large-scale outsourcing operations, selling the IS department to an IS supplier had a much higher priority than designing the consecutive service provision.

The actual design of the outsourcing relationship, such as the type of supplier and the management structure, determined to a large extent whether the improvements expected were realized. Improvements in flexibility, for example, were only achieved if the outsourcing relationship was designed to be flexible.

The objectives and expectations of the initial sourcing decision were often disregarded during the design of the outsourcing relationship. Decision makers assumed that improvements would be achieved automatically. Economies of scale were, for example, often expected, but seldom incorporated in the design. In most cases, the organization demanded that the IS department sold to an external supplier would remain a separate unit, thus impairing most of the supplier's opportunities for economies of scale. Economies of scale can only be realized if a supplier is allowed and forced to integrate units performing similar activities. This was impaired if a client organization demanded exclusive use of IS staff and resources or put no pressure on the supplier to integrate and utilize the increases in scale.

4.4 Selecting the IS supplier

Selecting a supplier comprises determining which suppliers might be appropriate for certain IS activities, requesting a proposal, and evaluating the proposals.

4.4.1 Selection process

Functionaries

The functionaries involved in the selection process are listed in Table 4.17. Almost all decision makers consulted the internal legal department. The legal departments often had suggestions and warnings that exceeded pure legal affairs and were later regarded as having been very useful. During the outsourcing, however, their advice was often not followed. The same holds for procurement departments; these were often not involved at all or only in the final stages of contracting, even though these departments had extensive experience with many types of outsourcing. Rules and procedures for procurement were not followed by the IS outsourcing decision makers, not even in the organizations that outsourced large parts of their primary processes.

Three of the case study organizations hired an external expert to select the IS supplier and negotiate a contract. In one of these cases, the loyalty of the expert to the client organization was later doubted seriously. This expert reduced the number of potential suppliers to one in a very short time, based on unclear requirements. He negotiated an agreement that was clearly in favor of the supplier and was not very critical towards the future supplier. Some time after the implementation, the supplier appointed him head of the outsourced department. In the other cases, the external expert contributed much to the structeredness and thoroughness of the selection procedures.

In one case, internal IS staff and external experts were involved in many parts of the outsourcing decision process, but not in the actual selling and negotiation process. Negotiations were conducted by top management, without detailed knowledge of IS, the IS market and procurement, assisted only by legal and financial experts. The IS staff and the organization's procurement department were involved only in drafting the contract. The actual deal, however, was not beneficial from

	Number of cases
Top	
• General manager	5
• IS manager	4
• IS staff	2
User departments	
• General manager	5
• IS manager	9
• IS staff	3

Table 4.17 Functionaries involved in selection process

an IS and procurement point of view. The choice of supplier appeared to be adverse and the conditions of the deal were unfavorable.

Structuredness

Formal criteria for the selection of a supplier were found in only 9 out of the 23 cases. In the other 14 cases, selection was based on general impressions of the appropriateness of the supplier, and a formal method to evaluate suppliers was used in only 3 of the 9 cases in which formal criteria were used. The methods that were used included assessment of the value of the criteria by more than one functionary, using objective measures to assess the value of the criteria, and deriving the choice of the supplier from the scores in a formalized way. In other cases, criteria were assessed by one functionary, based on personal impressions or data provided by the suppliers. Even in the cases where formal criteria or evaluation methods were used, the actual choice was sometimes determined by personal impressions and preferences, and the method was used mainly to rationalize and justify the choice.

Costs and lead time

The selection of an appropriate IS supplier took more time than most decision makers expected. The average lead time was 4 months, which was 20% of the average duration of the resulting contract. The client organizations that performed a thorough analysis of the initial situation needed significantly less time for this phase.

The total selection procedures often took a significant period of time, up to a year. In some cases, negotiations with a supplier took months and then failed. In these cases, the uncertainty among IS staff and users led to many problems. The costs of supplier selection consisted mainly of time spent by internal staff and was not administered. Estimates of the total selection costs varied between 1 and 4% of the costs of the resulting contract.

4.4.2 Call for tender

The client organizations that issued a detailed and specific call for tender received more adequate and to-the-point responses and the prices offered were in a significantly smaller range than the broad calls for tender. Some clients made their own estimates of reasonable prices and lead times, based on previous experience or expert assessments. These clients were better able to determine whether the responses were reasonable.

The procedures for tendering and selection were not always made clear to the suppliers. In some cases, the suppliers were not given enough time to draw up a thorough tender response. Some client organizations spent over a year planning a new system, and then gave the suppliers two weeks to draw up a tender response.

The quality of the tender responses varied heavily with the amount of information and time given to the suppliers. Request for tender couched in broad terms and leaving little time for reply yielded tender responses where the highest price was up to three times as high as the lowest offer, and the lead times varied by a factor two. These responses as a result of this were unrealistic. Client organizations choosing the cheapest of these responses often experienced many problems, as the supplier had underestimated the effort needed.

4.4.3 Selection of potential suppliers

Some client organizations used pre-selection to select a short-list of suppliers to be invited to tender. In the other cases, suppliers were mostly selected based on previous experiences, personal contacts and impressions. Some decision makers did extensive market research, particularly if a ready-made package was selected.

The internal IS department was invited to give a tender response in only 4 of the cases, and these were all cases of partial outsourcing of specific activities. In none of the six cases of outsourcing the entire department, was the internal department invited to submit a bid. The bids of the external suppliers were simply compared to the perceptions of the internal situation, without giving the internal department the opportunity to propose an improved situation.

4.4.4 Evaluation of tender responses

The criteria for selection included characteristics of the suppliers and of their proposals (see Table 4.18). A number of these criteria are described below. The 6 clients that bought ready-made software packages paid little attention to the characteristics of the supplier, even though this was found to be important for the continuity of the support and the release of new versions.

The *business record* of an IS supplier is a retrospective evaluation of the development of the supplier. Suppliers that showed consistent steady, autonomous, growth based on a satisfied customer base appeared to be more coherent and integrated than suppliers that had grown extremely fast by taking over many other firms and IS departments. A good business record was, however, not a guarantee for continuity, as in the early 1990s, a number of Dutch IS suppliers that were considered to be very healthy and prosperous experienced serious problems, and were taken over or even went bankrupt.

Whether the client valued the supplier's specialism and experience in the client's business process and industry, in the pertinent technology, activity and type of outsourcing, depended upon the specificity of the outsourced activity. For the outsourcing of firm-specific systems, it is more important that the supplier knows the

Criteria	Importance			
	none	low	medium	high
size				
• people	3	13	3	4
• revenue	3	13	3	4
financial position	3	11	6	3
business record	1	11	7	4
specialism				
• pertinent technology	3	9	5	6
• pertinent activity	1	6	10	6
• pertinent business process	1	7	3	12
• pertinent type of outsourcing	1	8	9	5
• industry of client	1	8	2	12
type of supplier	1	10	8	4
geographical coverage	8	12	1	2
portfolio of products and services	0	11	11	1
costs	0	5	5	13
lead time	0	5	13	5
quality	0	1	8	14
willingness to take risk	0	13	8	2
consequences for personnel	13	3	1	6
personal impressions	0	8	4	11

Table 4.18 Importance of criteria for selection of IS supplier

business process and industry, than for outsourcing non-specific systems or infrastructural components such as the client's network.

During the research period, a trend was noticed that suppliers were specializing increasingly on business processes. Small suppliers focused on specific customer groups and large suppliers reorganized from being structured along technical functions and disciplines to business units that focused on specific market segments.

A distinction of types of suppliers is made between suppliers that had as their core business providing IS products and services and suppliers that had IS as a by-product, for example to utilize excess capacity of their internal IS department. Outsourcing to suppliers for which IS was not core business led to problems with quality and continuity. The IS department of the supplier was not always used to working for external client organizations and had little knowledge of the client's business processes. Problems also arose with priorities if the IS department had to divide their attention between serving the parent company and serving external clients. Continuity was endangered, because top management could at any time decide to stop providing IS services to external clients.

Another distinction between types of suppliers observed later was between suppliers taking over IS departments only as a financial investment, and suppliers taking over IS departments with complementary staff, resources, products and services to integrate the departments with other units and extend the business portfolio. Suppliers that took over IS departments as a financial investment often did little to improve the departments and did not invest money, bring in their own staff, or provide contacts and clients. One client organization outsourced the IS department to a consortium of three organizations, two of which had little interest in IS. The partners in the consortium benefited from the guaranteed spending agreement but made little effort to improve the IS department.

Geographical coverage was asked mainly for activities or systems with multinational coverage. Clients demanded that the supplier had at least the same geographical coverage as their own business.

The supplier's portfolio of products and services was especially relevant to clients who wanted total solutions providers that could provide all products and services the organization needed.

The supplier's willingness to take risk was shown by making commitments instead of holding back, such as offering to take over all staff, instead of offering that taking over some of the staff might become part of the deal. Other suppliers offered fixed price and fixed lead time agreements for software development, and invested considerable effort in the tendering procedure.

The consequences for the IS personnel were valued as very important in all of the 5 cases that involved the transfer of personnel to the supplier. Decision makers mainly looked at whether the staff would get comparable employment conditions.

Personal impressions and qualitative judgment of the IS suppliers and their intentions played a major role in supplier selection, either as an explicit criterion or implicitly. The decision makers who decided to outsource their organization's IS department were influenced highly by their impressions of the trustworthiness of the supplier's top managers and their persuasive presentations.

The relative importance decision makers gave to the selection criteria differed. Different stakeholders often had other priorities. IS managers valued quality over costs, while general management was sometimes willing to make concessions with regard to quality if the costs or lead time were considerably better. A number of client organizations first determined which tender responses met the technical and functional requirements, and then chose the offer with the lowest price or lead time. One decision maker demanded that suppliers send two envelopes, one with the actual tender response and one with the price offered. He then evaluated all the tender responses and selected the proposals that met the criteria. The envelopes containing the prices of the proposals that did not meet the requirements were returned unopened, and out of the other proposals, the cheapest was selected.

Suppliers of ready-made packages and other components were evaluated mainly with regard to the characteristics of their products and services. With tailor-made products and services, the client organization put more emphasis on the characteristics of the supplier's staff, resources, experience, references and working methods. The client often wanted to assess the quality of the individual employees the supplier wanted to deploy for activities that depended heavily on the quality of the staff, such as consultancy, information planning and initial system design.

A criterion that was remarkable for its absence was the power of the supplier with respect to the client, measured by, for example, the relative size of the supplier and the percentage of the work load the client represented.

The motives of the suppliers for taking over a client organization's IS department varied: entering a new market segment, obtaining new clients, using the excess capacity of the department taken over, enjoying the financial benefits of high guaranteed spending, having the continuity of guaranteed revenues for a longer period, solving a shortage of staff, using unique knowledge and skills of the department, or creating new business opportunities. The willingness of suppliers to take over a client organization's IS department varied with market developments. If the IS market in general was prosperous and suppliers had more work than they had staff and resources to do, they were more willing to take over IS staff and resources and offered a higher price than at times when they had trouble deploying their existing staff.

4.4.5 Negotiations

Negotiations for outsourcing of IS departments were often based on some estimation of the value of an internal IS department. Accountants investigating one of the government IS departments in this case study research noted that determining the value of the IS department was difficult and required many arbitrary assumptions. The financial administrations were often not designed to determine the economic value of the department. Debts and claims were not always registered and the assets had no book value. Overhead costs, such as costs of office space and human resource management, were not always allocated to the department. Expected revenues after outsourcing are difficult to determine if no internal transfer pricing is used. Prices for takeovers are often determined by multiplying the annual profit by a certain factor, but internal IS departments that do not charge for their services do not make any profit, which meant this method could not be used. During negotiations, decision makers noticed that their estimates were not very relevant anyway, as an estimation of the internal value is hardly an indicator for the market value or the price suppliers are willing to pay.

Common negotiation practices were often disregarded. Many client organizations announced their choice of a supplier before negotiations had ended, and often even before a final price was settled. Many IS suppliers demanded exclusive negotiations at a very early

money

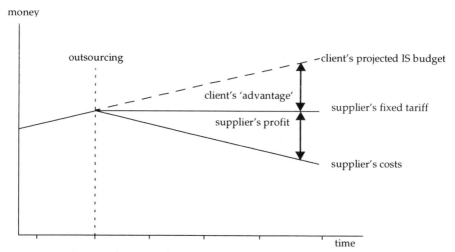

Figure 4.1 Supposed 'win-win' scenario

stage. The client organizations that postponed the final choice of supplier and negotiated with at least two suppliers until agreements were finalized, achieved far better results.

Client organizations often did not determine the expected price and lead times of the activities they were outsourcing, and therefore could not assess whether the proposals they received were reasonable. In only one case of outsourcing of software development did the decision makers perform their own estimates, using function point analysis. This information was then used in their negotiations with the suppliers.

One negotiation strategy often used by suppliers was to propose a 'win-win' scenario. The suppliers noted that the IS budgets of the client organizations were usually increasing and proposed to take over the IS department and activities for a fixed tariff equal to the initial costs of the internal IS department. The client organization would no longer have to face increases in the IS budget and the supplier would make a profit by increasing the efficiency over time because of economies of scale (see Figure 4.1).

This 'win-win' scenario appeared to be deceptive. IS budgets increased mostly because client organizations deployed IT in more functions and updated to newer technology. Existing activities with existing technology usually got cheaper over time, regardless of who performed the activities. Therefore, if the supplier provided the existing activities for a tariff equal to the initial costs, the client organization missed the savings from the decreasing prices of the hardware and the increasing quality of tools, and still had to pay for new systems and new technologies.

Contract element	Missing in cases
detailed specification of requirements	10
methods for measuring compliance	14
measures for non-compliance	18
arrangements for the implementation or transition phase	7
arrangements for the management of the outsourcing relationship	5
arrangements for intermediate changes in requirements	17
arrangements for early and regular termination	15

Table 4.19 Missing contract elements

4.4.6 Contracts

Considerable time was spent writing and negotiating contracts. This step often took significantly longer than the initial outsourcing decision, and much effort and expertise was devoted to writing the contract. Many elements that appeared to be essential were however, missing (see Table 4.19).

A detailed specification of requirements was missing mainly in the contracts governing outsourcing of IS departments. The services were often specified by a clause such as "supplier will provide the services currently provided by the internal department", usually followed by a list of the names of the information systems in use and a short description of the services. No detailed functional or technical requirements were specified.

In contracts for operating information systems, requirements often included only the availability of the system, response time, mean time between failures and mean time between repairs, but no functional specification of the actual operation services, or degree of connectivity, interoperability, ease of adaptation, and so on.

Many clients that had specified the requirements failed to include methods for measuring compliance. Measuring availability and response time of a system, for example, appeared to be very difficult and required specialized monitoring tools. If no methods for measuring compliance were included in the contract, then agreeing methods that are accepted by both parties was very difficult. Many clients however did not make the effort to measure compliance or relied on the supplier's reports. Measuring compliance to functional and technical requirements for system development requires specialized skills and tools. Extensive testing appeared to require significantly more effort than clients expected.

Measures for non-compliance were missing in many cases. Other clients had agreed measures such as penalty clauses for non-performance and agreements for solving the non-performance. Suppliers were often opposed to accepting full liability clauses. Liability clauses were often limited to direct liability and the total amount was restricted. Some clients however managed to negotiate full acceptance of liability by the supplier, including indirect damages, such as loss of business volume.

Outsourcing the entire IS department was always covered by two separate contracts: (1) a contract for the transfer of activa and passiva: the hardware, software, the obligations from leases and rents, licenses and the administration of the department, the transfer of the IS staff, their employment conditions, and an employment guarantee for the same term as the guaranteed spending; and (2) a contract for the cooperation between the client organization and the IS supplier, containing the conditions governing IS activities that the supplier would perform for the client, and the amount of spending that was guaranteed for a certain period. Some clauses appeared not to be legally enforceable, such as the quality measures the supplier was obliged to take to improve the department taken over. These measures implied no specific performance with regard to the client organization and could therefore not be enforced by law, and the measures were paid for at the time the department was transferred.

Many contracts contained index clauses that gave the supplier the option to increase the tariffs according to market development. These index clauses often referred to 'market developments' instead of to objective cost of living standards. Deals based on guaranteeing a certain capacity in person years did not specify the number of person hours contained in a person year. One supplier had an agreement to provide a number of person hours that was determined by multiplying the number of employees transferred by the number of regular work hours of a full time employee, but had two third of the IS staff work excessive overtime and deployed the remaining third for other clients.

Four client organizations used framework contracts with specific suppliers, that stipulated all conditions applying to all transactions with each supplier. The framework contracts also contained agreements on tariffs and volume discounts. Contracts for individual activities only needed descriptions of the requirements needed and if necessary, deviations from the conditions of the framework contract.

Standard contracts, designed by third parties, were used in 6 cases. In the Netherlands, many public sector organizations use the standard contracts issued by the Dutch Ministry of Internal Affairs. These standard contracts were often adapted to the specific needs and insights of the client organization. Standard contracts saved significantly on contracting costs and resulted in more solid contracts. Client organizations found the standard contracts issued by the COSSO, a Dutch organization of IT suppliers, to be too much in favor of the supplier. In these contracts, the liability of the supplier was very restricted and no penalty clauses were included. A few client organizations also included the standard conditions of the AVOA, a Dutch organization of independent advisors.

Some client organizations experienced problems with determining the legal entity to sign the contract, especially when the contract was agreed with a legal entity that had yet to be established. In at least one case, the legal entity with which the client had agreed the contract was never even established. Other client organizations signed a contract with the parent company of the IS supplier they were actually doing business with, to ensure the continuity of the service and make the contract more enforceable.

4.5 Implementation, management and termination

4.5.1 Implementation of the outsourcing decision

The lead time of the implementation of the outsourcing decision was on average 8% of the length of the contract. The costs of the implementation were, on average, 12% of the total costs of the outsourced activities over the contract period. The implementation costs included the initial costs of relocating people and hardware, and the estimated cost of productivity loss during the transition period.

The initial costs and the lead time were significantly higher if the outsourcing included the transfer of people and hardware (13% versus 6%) and were almost always higher than expected by the interviewees. The efforts to transfer software, hardware and data depended to a large extent on the quality of the systems and documentation, on the degree of standardization and on whether the components had been transferred before.

Suppliers often pressed to start with the activities as soon as possible and to finish writing the contract during execution. Client organizations that agreed to this found that their negotiation position was considerably less than before the start of the activity and they had great difficulty finishing the contract in short time and to their advantage.

One of the advantages of outsourcing mentioned by some interviewees is that it gives the client organization a one-time opportunity to reorganize and rationalize the IS function in a way that is not possible in a stable situation. This opportunity was however seldom used, and the IS departments were all transferred in their initial state, without major changes or rationalizations.

Client organizations that had outsourced their IS department experienced that it took up to a year for the user departments and the remaining IS staff to get used to cooperating with the external supplier. Procedures and communication had to be established and become customary. The working relationship became more business-like and each product or service had to be negotiated and charged.

The IS staff taken over by the supplier had to get used to working for a commercial organization, accounting for their work time and charging for their services to their former colleagues. Some employees did not take employment with the supplier or resigned after a short time, because they could not get used to the new way of working or the culture and management style of the IS supplier.

4.5.2 Management of the outsourcing relationship

In 12 cases, unforeseen changes in requirements, volume or technology arose. These changes led to major problems or were not possible in 9 of these cases. These and other consequences of outsourcing are described more extensively in section 4.6.

Suppliers had often negotiated for a possibility to increase the tariffs, and used this option, even when market developments were contrary. One supplier increased the tariffs by 5%, because of increased salary costs, while market tariffs for the pertinent services were all decreasing.

The improvements and measures promised by the suppliers were not always realized. Oral assurances were not always met and could not be enforced. The only reliable source of the motivation and intentions of the suppliers appeared to be the contractual agreements, and published sources, such as the board of directors' plans as published in the annual report.

4.5.3 Termination of the outsourcing relationship

Outsourcing relationships terminated because the product was finished or the contract had ended, but also because parties had major disagreements and wanted to end the relationship before the end of the contract.

A total of 5 outsourcing relationships were ended to the satisfaction of both parties after the product was finished or the contract had ended and the activity was no longer needed. In 7 other cases, the contract ended, but the activity was still needed. In 2 of these cases, the contract renewal was awarded to the same supplier. In the other 5 cases, a new tender process was started, in 3 cases because the client organization was dissatisfied with the supplier and in the other 2 cases to compare the supplier to proposals from other suppliers and to stimulate the supplier to offer a competitive price. The remaining 11 outsourcing relationships were still operational at the end of the research period.

After termination of outsourcing arrangements involving the transfer of staff, some clients had an option to take back some of the staff if they wanted. In 3 cases, the staff used this option and went back to their former employer. This preserved valuable knowledge and skills for the client organization.

4.6 Consequences of sourcing decisions

All phases of the sourcing decision processes in the cases investigated were described in the previous sections. The actual consequences of the sourcing decisions are analyzed in this section. General conclusions are drawn about whether outsourcing leads to higher or lower values for the goal variables. In the sections following this section, these consequences are related to the situational factors and to the decision variables.

The consequences of sourcing decisions are described in terms of the goal variables mentioned in Chapter 2. The absolute values of the goal variables are not very meaningful unless they are compared to values in similar situations. The consequences of each of the sourcing decisions were compared to one or more of the following sources of reference:

- the initial situation before the implementation of the sourcing decision,
- the situation that would have emerged if the sourcing decision had not been taken or if a different decision was taken,
- the goals and expectations the decision makers had when taking the sourcing decision,
- similar situations within the client organization, for example similar IS activities outsourced previously or to other suppliers, or similar activities performed by the internal IS department,
- similar situations in similar other organizations.

The consequences of the IS outsourcing decisions in the cases investigated are summarized in Table 4.20.

4.6.1 Overall satisfaction

The sourcing decisions led to mixed results and the overall satisfaction of decision makers ranged widely and was often below their expectations. Many improvements were not achieved and problems and disadvantages arose that were not anticipated. Many decision makers were not able to make a good comparison between the initial situation and the situation after the implementation of the sourcing decision, because of the lack of analysis of the initial situation.

The best indication for the overall satisfaction is whether the client organization wanted to continue the outsourcing relationship after the contract or the pertinent activity had ended. In 5 of the 12 cases where the contract had ended within the research period, the client organization did not renew the contract or strongly reduced the amount of work outsourced to the supplier. In the 11 cases where the contract

Consequence	Category Number of cases			
Overall satisfaction	low	medium	high	
	7	9	7	
Costs (actual compared to initial or expected costs)	>110%	100-110%	90-100%	<90%
	13	4	6	0
Lead time (actual compared to initial or expected costs)	>110%	100-110%	90-100%	<90%
	13	5	5	0
Staffing levels (reduction in full time equivalents)	0 fte	1-200 fte	>200 fte	
	17	3	3	
Quality (meeting requirements)	low	medium	high	
	6	12	5	
Flexibility (ease of changing activities and requirements)	low	medium	high	
	7	5	11	
Controllability (ease of measuring and enforcing compliance)	low	medium	high	
	14	6	3	
Continuity (continuity of products and services)	low	medium	high	
	6	13	4	

Table 4.20 Number of cases in each category of consequences of IS outsourcing

had not ended at the end of the research period, interviewees in 4 cases stated that they would have changed to another supplier or performed the activities internally if they were not restricted by the contract. Some of the dissatisfied interviewees stated that the situation would probably have been even worse if the initial situation had continued.

Another sign of dissatisfaction was that many business units within client organizations that had outsourced the central IS department re-internalized activities and established small IS units that performed IS activities or outsourced to other suppliers. Most client organizations that were dissatisfied did not re-internalize the IS activities, but changed to another supplier, and often changed the design of the outsourcing relationship.

Three of the client organizations that had transferred their IS department to an IS supplier were very disappointed about the IS suppliers' promises to be a strategic partner. The fact that the department remained a separate unit implied that the client organization was still served by the same staff as before the outsourcing operation. It also impaired most of the supplier's options to achieve economies of scale, because the supplier could not integrate the unit with the other units. The unit did not grow, but remained the same, only due to the guaranteed spending. As soon as the guaranteed spending had finished, the revenues dropped to 80, 50 and 10% of the initial revenues and only 80, 60, and 8% of the staff transferred was still employed after the guaranteed spending agreement ended. The remaining revenues came mainly from operating existing systems and components the client was not yet able to transfer to another supplier.

The supplier had not used the knowledge and services of its other units to improve the quality and responsiveness of the unit. The supplier had also not used its marketing knowledge and network to find other clients. The unit's revenues from clients other than the former parent company were only 10, 5 and 4%. The major barrier for transforming the department from a bureaucratic internal staff department to an innovative and customer oriented IS supplier were the IS employees, who were often not able to change from technical and operational experts to commercial and customer friendly advisors.

None of the suppliers turned out to be a real strategic partner. The suppliers made no effort to or were unable to keep up to date with the client's business processes and initiate strategic opportunities to apply IT for competitive advantage. The suppliers were more interested in short term revenues during the guaranteed spending period than in being a long term business partner.

Three client organizations had more positive experiences with their IS supplier. In one case, the client organization was very dissatisfied with the initial supplier that had taken over the client's IS department. Two years after the transfer, the supplier went bankrupt, and the former department was sold to a smaller holding that did act as a strategic partner, reinstalled the cooperative culture, and used its marketing channels and the expertise and services of its other units. Interviewees explained the difference between the first and the second supplier by the fact that the first supplier was a large holding of separate IS units taken over from different client organizations, with little synergy or commonalities, and focused very much on short term revenues. The second supplier was chosen more carefully, using a better negotiation strategy and with more involvement of the IS staff and the user departments, and the supplier was much more dedicated and cooperative.

The most important factor that appeared to determine the satisfaction of the client organization was the intentions the supplier had with taking over the IS department: obtaining the highest possible short term revenues during the period of the guaranteed spending, or establishing a long term relationship based on good service and customer satisfaction. This criterion determined almost all other consequences. None of the client organizations was however able to predict the supplier's intentions in advance, because all suppliers presented their intentions as aimed at a long term relationship, and it was impossible to predict who was sincere and who was not.

Some suppliers did not meet their promises and simply did not perform certain activities agreed in the contract. In one case, part of the agreement was that the supplier would implement certain improvements within the department taken over. The supplier was compensated for these efforts by an increase in the amount paid for taking over the department. The supplier did not implement the improvements, and stated that the amount paid was the result of negotiations and had no relationship with the assured quality improvements.

4.6.2 Costs

It appeared impossible to determine whether outsourcing is generally cheaper or more expensive than internal provision. Both the initial situation and the situation after implementation were not administered systematically enough to evaluate costs, and the situation had often changed so much that comparison was not useful.

Increased cost awareness was sometimes achieved if the organization had stricter rules for external expenses than for internal commissions. The increase was often not as high as expected, especially if outsourcing was not accompanied by decentralization of budgets and tighter budget control. As long as users were not faced with the costs of their requirements, cost awareness did not increase. Guaranteed spendings were sometimes paid from a central budget. This led to a lack of cost/benefit analysis, no strict contracts and project management and no capacity planning. The business units were not aware that they spent more than the guaranteed spending and had no budget reserved for the excess amounts.

Another reason for disappointing cost reductions was that the decision makers had not always anticipated that lower costs would not necessarily mean a lower price for the client organization. A lower price was only achieved if the client organization had conducted good negotiation and contracting, had a knowledge of market prices, and had the power and means to enforce that part of the savings gained were transferred to the client organization.

This research was not focused on how much the suppliers have earned from taking over the IS departments and activities, but the impression of some of the interviewees is that the supplier had decreased the cost significantly, while charging the same price or more than the initial internal costs.

Many agreements contained a clause that the prices the supplier charged must conform market tariffs. Most of the client organizations never tried to validate the supplier's tariffs, for example by issuing a tender or by having an external audit performed.

4.6.3 Lead time

No general conclusions could be drawn on whether outsourcing leads to higher or lower lead times for the execution of activities, for much the same reasons as those for costs. The lead times for the preparation for execution did however show large differences. The major disappointment to client organizations was that the lead time of the activities other than the actual production time was underestimated. Requirement specification, market research, tendering, negotiation, contracting and acquainting the supplier and testing the result took significantly more time than most decision makers expected.

4.6.4 Flexibility

Flexibility was distinguished into portfolio flexibility, the ability to start new activities at any time, and activity flexibility, the ability to change requirements or terminate activities during execution. Portfolio flexibility generally increased, while activity flexibility was decreased by outsourcing.

Portfolio flexibility increased because client organizations could start any activity they needed almost at any time, provided that there were suppliers offering these services. They did not have to recruit or retrain staff or wait until the internal IS department had capacity available.

Activity flexibility often decreased, because each change in requirements had to be discussed with the supplier and often required adaptation of the contract. This usually took some time and suppliers sometimes took advantage of the fact that the activity was already on its way and demanded excessive fees for extra work. Most interviewees considered this a disadvantage, because it delayed and hampered making changes to requirements. Other interviewees appreciated the formality and considered it an advantage that requirements could not be adjusted continuously, considering that many problems with previous internal projects had been caused by the fact that user departments could and often did adjust their requirements.

The flexibility of small adjustments to software decreased with outsourcing, mainly because each request had to be approved and go through a tendering procedure. This is especially problematic in public sector organizations, where information systems have to be adjusted to changes in the law almost instantaneously. Other organizations had however established long term agreements for the maintenance of information systems that obliged the supplier to process an urgent request within an agreed time.

4.6.5 Controllability

Controllability depended on monitoring and reporting costs, lead time, progress and quality, and on the ability to enforce compliance if the performance of the supplier did not meet the requirements.

Monitoring and reporting was often impaired by factors on both the supplier's side and the client's side. The supplier did not report adequately, providing either too much detail, such as large overviews of all resource usage, or being too general, such as providing only the total costs of that month's resource usage. Development project reports often included descriptions of intermediate products and a summary of resource usage, but no indication of quality or progress, such as the percentage of work done. Many suppliers did not give adequate predictions of delays or expected repair times. Many disputes arose from unclear or incorrect bills. Client organizations often did not demand reports. The skills and knowledge needed to interpret reports were not always present. Some users simply trusted the supplier and did not try to ask for or understand a supplier's report. Sometimes the client's budget and planning were unrealistic, or clients changed or added to the requirements after the activities had started.

Clients often did not use the measures they had at hand to enforce compliance. They were sometimes not able to prove that non-compliance could be blamed on the supplier, especially if their requirements had been defined ambiguously. In other cases, clients did not want to burden the relationship or were reluctant to face the high costs and effort of legal action.

Many interviewees had expected that outsourcing would lead to a more business-like relationship and higher controllability, because performance could be enforced by a contract instead of by internal agreements. Contracts however appeared to be an essential but far from sufficient condition for controllability. Requirements could almost never be specified completely and it was seldom enough if the suppliers confined their efforts to the absolute minimum of the contractual requirements. The supplier sometimes had so much power over the client organization that the client could not afford to break with the supplier. If the supplier went bankrupt, the contract had no value. The costs and time required to take legal action would have been very high and the eventual result would probably not have been satisfactory. Therefore, none of the client organizations that were dissatisfied with their supplier actually went to court.

4.6.6 Continuity

The cases with low or medium continuity included suppliers that went bankrupt, but also cases where the supplier was taken over. In other cases, the supplier stopped releasing new versions of software packages or no longer supported old versions. The turnover of IS personnel provided by some suppliers was very high. Some client organizations therefore selected the external staff the supplier would deploy and obliged the supplier not to change the personnel during the activity. This was done especially with information planning and the initial phases of system design, because these activities relied heavily on the personal qualities of the staff deployed.

One client organization improved continuity at first by hiring external staff if internal staff were not available, but later by retraining staff to be more generalized. The client organization first hired a backup service of external experts for a critical function for which the organization had a department of four specialists. These specialists had different tasks and were not able to replace one another. An external supplier provided specialists if one of the employees was ill or if the work load was high. The costs of this backup service for 50 days a year were more than twice the costs of a full time employee. After a year, the client organization terminated the contract and retrained the internal specialists so they were able to replace one another, thereby solving the continuity problem.

4.6.7 Consequences for the IS staff

The higher management of the department taken over was almost always replaced by employees of the supplier. The new managers were assigned mainly to guard the supplier's financial interests.

The unions and the *ondernemingsraden* (works councils) and dienstcommissies (idem in public sector organizations) emphasized formal employment guarantees, employment conditions and keeping the department together as a separate and recognizable unit. The most important factor however that appeared to influence the employment of the staff transferred was the intentions and qualities of the supplier and the satisfaction of the client organization. Formal employment conditions can not be enforced if the employer is not viable, and if an employer's business runs well, employment is guaranteed automatically.

It appeared difficult to determine whether the IS staff's employment conditions with the supplier were really the same as those of the client organization, especially if the client was a public sector organization. Pension rights and early retirement arrangements had to be transferred, job descriptions and ratings had to be transposed, education allowances, days off, health insurance, number of years in service, and so on, had to be compared.

Some of the employees taken over by suppliers resigned shortly after the outsourcing operation, because they could not get used to the supplier's culture, management style or working hours. The work pressure often increased and the culture was more business-like and sometimes more authoritarian. At the end of the guaranteed spending agreements, the suppliers often laid off a major part of the staff, because they had not managed to obtain enough additional revenues for the unit to remain viable.

Other employees were very satisfied with the transfer and enjoyed working for a commercial organization. They were now valued for their contribution to the core business of the supplier instead of being viewed as an unavoidable staff function that only caused increasing and uncontrollable costs. Their career opportunities were often enhanced and they received more education and motivation.

The client organizations reduced their staffing levels by transferring staff to an external IS supplier, but business unit managers that were not satisfied with the supplier's performance often outsourced IS activities to other suppliers or hired or retrained new IS staff.

4.6.8 Short term versus long term consequences

The numbers in Table 4.20 are averaged over the period of the investigation. In general, the positive consequences appeared just after the implementation of the outsourcing decision, while the negative consequences appeared later.

If attestable cost savings arose, they were often achieved immediately, as suppliers usually paid an amount of money for taking over an IS department. High and long guaranteed spendings however made the deal less attractive in later years, when the costs of hardware and software had dropped and the demand for the supplier's services had decreased, but the tariffs of the supplier remained the same or even increased.

Quality and lead times sometimes deteriorated when the supplier deployed the best personnel for new clients and left the client organization with low skilled personnel. Controllability often decreased, as the IS knowledge of the internal staff decreased and became outdated, or turnover of the remaining internal staff was high due to decreased career opportunities.

Barriers to flexibility were not discovered until major changes were needed. The change that created most problems was the general trend of a decreased need for mainframe capacity because of the move towards downsizing and client/server systems, using mini computers and personal computers.

Problems with continuity became apparent when the guaranteed spending period was over and the IS supplier had not acquired enough other clients to ensure the viability of the outsourced unit. The suppliers often made little effort to save the units, because their investments had already paid off. The former parent company of the outsourced IS departments depended on their former IS department and felt responsible for their former staff, and therefore mediated in selling the IS department to another supplier or in one case even bought the department back temporarily.

After the outsourcing implementation, decision makers became more aware of the importance of other factors than short term reductions of costs and staffing levels. The decision makers realized afterwards that other goals and long term improvements were also important.

4.6.9 Privatization goals

The four motives for privatization in the late 1980s and early 1990s, described in section 4.2.4, were not fully achieved in the cases of privatization of government IS departments. Budget reductions were not achieved, and in most cases, the total IS budget even increased. Streamlining the central government was only achieved in terms of a reduction in the number of civil servants. This did not lead to a more flexible and alert government. The quality of services barely increased, mainly because the services were provided by the same staff and the suppliers made little effort to improve the quality. Stimulating the private sector only led to providing a number of supplier with an easy profit.

Though it is not possible to determine exactly whether the privatizations increased or decreased the costs of the IS activities, it is certain that the savings were much less than the 50,000 guilders per full time employee that the Government Agreement demanded and that no additional savings were demanded to compensate for this.

Today it has been realized that the assumptions made about the privatization trend are not always valid and that privatization should not be an end in itself. The Dutch Public Accounts Committee, de Algemene Rekenkamer, has criticized several privatizations, including the privatization of a large government data center. A government commission, the commissie-Sint, concluded that pure privatization, i.e., transferring all activities, staff and resources to private corporations, is often not the best option. The commission has proposed the use of less rigorous forms of privatization and a search for other ways of increasing the flexibility and independency of government organizations. Budgeting and accounting rules have been changed, to allow for tradeoffs between personnel and material expenses and for making reservations and depreciations. The Dutch Ministry of Finance currently compensates public sector organizations for VAT paid in the first few years after a privatization.

While negotiating, some public sector organizations did not take into account the 17.5% Value Added Tax (VAT) they already paid on their external expenses. The supplier often offered to take over IS activities at a price equal to the initial internal costs including VAT, and charged the full VAT above this price, even though the supplier was allowed to compensate VAT received with VAT paid. Since the external expenses in the initial situation amounted for from 30 to 40% of the total expenses, these client organizations overpaid by 5 to 7%.

4.7 Situational factors

In chapter 3, a number of the situational factors were derived from established organizational theories. All of these situational factors appeared to be relevant in one or more of the cases investigated, and relationships between situational factors and consequences of outsourcing were found in particular cases. A number of additional situational factors emerged from the case studies. The intermediate variables were not included in the case studies.

This case study research was not aimed at determining statistical relationships between situational factors and consequences of outsourcing, for reasons given in section 4.1. The case studies focused on whether the factors could be determined in practice, whether they were used by decision makers, and whether examples and explanations of specific relationships between the factors and the consequences of outsourcing could be found.

The situational factors are listed in Table 4.21. An indication of the relationships between the situational factors and the consequences of outsourcing is given by listing the number of cases with a specific value for the situational factor and a specific value for overall satisfaction. This table should be considered with great care and it is not pretended that the numbers listed in the table give any evidence in favor of or against the relationships derived in chapter 3. For the purpose of constructing this table, the values of the situational factors are simplified to a classification of low, medium and high. Overall satisfaction with the sourcing decision is an aggregate of the satisfaction of the different stakeholders in the decision process and the results of the goal variables in the particular case.

A specific situational factor is said to have a positive relationship with the consequences of outsourcing, if most cases have either a low value for the factor and a low degree of satisfaction or a high value for the factor and a high degree of satisfaction. A negative relationship is present if many cases have opposite values for the pertinent factor and the degree of satisfaction. The scale of the supplier, compared to the scale at which the client organization performed the activities, was for example, high in 12 (1+5+6) cases. In 6 of these 12 cases, the overall satisfaction with the sourcing decision was high, while in 1 case satisfaction was low. This suggests that the positive relationship between scale and the consequences of outsourcing that was derived in chapter 3 can also be found in practice. Most of the assumed relationships are however not very apparent from the table. It should be noted again that the numbers listed in Table 4.21 are only an indication of the presumed relationships. Some of the results are described below.

4.7.1 Information systems and IS function

The supplier performed the outsourced activities on the same scale as the client in 8 cases. Economies of scale were not achieved in these cases, even though that was often cited as an advantage of outsourcing. *Scale advantages* were present mainly with mainframe and network operation. The need for mainframe capacity decreased, though a firm role remained for large-scale and critical systems and as a backbone of an organizations IS infrastructure.

The highly interconnected cases included outsourcing of the client's network or other parts of the technical infrastructure. If the

Situational factor				Number of cases					
value of factor:	low			medium			high		
overall satisfaction:	low	med	high	low	med	high	low	med	high
scale	2	2	1	4	2	0	1	5	6
scale advantages	2	2	1	4	4	3	1	3	3
barriers for reuse	3	0	0	2	4	1	3	5	5
standardization	3	3	2	4	5	4	0	1	1
interconnectedness*	1	2	3	4	2	1	2	5	3
measurability	3	3	2	3	3	3	1	3	2
volume uncertainty	3	2	3	1	5	3	3	2	1
technical uncertainty	0	0	0	4	5	5	3	4	0
functional uncertainty	3	2	2	3	4	1	1	3	4
distribution*	2	1	4	1	0	2	4	8	1
heterogeneity*	2	2	5	0	4	2	4	4	0
specifiability*	2	4	1	3	4	4	1	2	3
human asset specificity	2	0	2	3	4	0	2	5	5
physical asset specificity	3	3	6	2	2	0	1	5	1
site specificity	4	3	6	1	0	0	2	6	1
frequency	4	5	5	3	2	1	1	1	1
switching costs of client	1	1	2	1	0	2	6	7	3
complexity	1	0	0	1	3	2	5	6	5
innovativeness*	3	4	1	3	4	4	1	1	2
variability*	2	4	3	3	4	3	2	1	1
infrastructure*	3	3	5	7	2	0	2	4	2
programmability	3	4	3	3	5	2	1	0	2
length of relationship	3	5	5	2	2	2	2	2	0
competitive use of IS	6	5	6	1	4	1	0	0	0
exactingness of technical requirements*	4	3	1	3	3	5	1	3	1
criticality of systems*	1	1	4	3	5	1	3	3	2
confidentiality of software or data*	3	6	4	1	1	2	3	2	1

Table 4.21 Situational factors versus overall satisfaction

Situational factor	Number of cases								
value of factor:	low			medium			high		
overall satisfaction:	low	med	high	low	med	high	low	med	high

client organization and environment

	low	med	high	low	med	high	low	med	high
IS maturity	6	6	1	1	5	3	0	0	3
uncertainty of business processes*	2	3	5	3	5	1	2	1	1
complexity of business processes*	0	0	0	3	6	4	4	3	3
structuredness of business processes*	0	0	0	5	6	3	2	3	4
variability of business processes*	2	4	5	2	3	2	3	1	1
information intensity of processes*	0	1	0	2	4	1	5	4	6
heterogeneity of user community*	1	1	2	3	5	3	3	3	2
buyer concentration	2	1	1	2	3	3	3	5	3
importance of volume for client	1	1	2	1	0	1	5	8	4
resource acquisition	2	2	4	5	5	2	0	2	1
IS use by competitors	6	4	5	1	4	1	0	1	1
IS outsourcing by competitors	3	2	2	1	6	2	3	3	1

IS market and suppliers

	low	med	high	low	med	high	low	med	high
number of adequate suppliers	2	5	3	3	3	2	2	1	2
barriers to entry and exit	1	0	1	3	5	2	3	4	4
availability of market information	4	5	1	3	4	4	0	0	2
risk aversion of supplier	0	0	0	0	4	5	7	5	2
switching costs of supplier	1	1	3	5	2	2	1	6	2
degree of subcontracting	2	3	6	5	4	0	0	2	1
supplier concentration	2	1	1	3	3	4	2	5	2
importance of volume for IS supplier	2	1	4	5	5	2	0	3	1
absorbing uncertainty	2	0	3	3	6	3	2	3	1
selective use of information	3	6	4	1	2	3	3	1	0

* = a situational factor not derived from organizational theories but from the case studies.

Table 4.21 Situational factors versus overall satisfaction (continued)

quality of service in these cases was low, disagreements often arose as to who was responsible for solving the problem: the provider of the network services, or the provider of the systems using the network.

Infrastructure refers to whether components are used by many information systems. Infrastructure components, such as hardware, systems software and programming tools, were often less specific and commonly available. The interconnectedness of infrastructure components was however often higher, because these components had many relationships with other systems.

The *human asset specificity* of most of the information systems investigated was high, because the systems were unique and tailor-made for the client organization. Outsourcing of unique systems requires that the supplier's staff becomes familiar with the client organization and the business processes. In most of these cases, there was only one or a few suppliers with the business knowledge to develop and maintain these systems. The client organizations were all very dependent on their supplier, because they could not obtain the services from other suppliers and often lost the knowledge and capacity to internalize the activities. *Physical asset specificity* and *site specificity* were not as high, unless the client organization had very specific requirements with regard to the tools and resources to be used or the users were very dispersed or bound to specific locations.

The *criticality* of many of the systems investigated was high and these systems were often very important for the client organizations business processes and continuity. Criticality and competitive use did not in itself appear to speak against outsourcing. If systems were important, sourcing decisions had to be taken with even more care. The emphasis was usually more on quality, continuity and flexibility and less on costs than with less strategic systems. Outsourcing of critical systems put the client organization at a higher risk if the continuity of the supplier was at danger; however, continuity of internal services was also not always guaranteed. Outsourcing of critical systems gave the supplier more power, because the client was more dependent on the system. Outsourcing of competitive systems may make competitive advantage available to competitors. Only a few of the cases were in a competitive environment, and the interviewees did not consider the systems distinguished them from their competitors.

The *exactingness* of the technical requirements were high for large time-critical systems or systems transferring large amounts of money or supporting important decisions. These systems had to be developed and operated more professionally and had to withstand external audits, be highly secure and to be certified. This needed investments that only large internal or external suppliers could afford.

Confidentiality was an issue if confidential business information about the client organization or personal information about employees, clients or citizens was stored in the information system. None of the interviewees considered confidentiality a reason for not choosing outsourcing. They did however take measures to ensure confidentiality after outsourcing. In one case, the data stored in the system was not confidential, but the client organization had obtained the data from firms and unions as a result of legal obligations, and they did not want the supplier to make a profit selling data that had been obtained for free.

4.7.2 Client organization and environment

The *IS maturity* of the users and line managers was relatively low in 12 of the 23 cases. Managers were not always aware of the possibilities and the influence of IS and IT on the business processes. They had insufficient knowledge of the IS market and of designing and managing relationships with external IS suppliers. They underestimated the complexity and the effort needed to manage IS activities. This led to outsourcing decisions and assignments that were not thought through and were not well designed. Requirements were not specified in enough detail and not all consequences were considered. Suppliers indicated that they also appreciated if the client organization was an equal partner and was able to determine their requirements and specify these requirements unambiguously. If the client's IS maturity was low, the supplier had to make a considerable effort to determine the exact requirements and the final result was often not what the client actually needed. During the research period, a general increase in the IS maturity of the users was observed.

Most of the operational business processes in the cases investigated were very information-intense or consisted of information processing. This was not of concern to any of the interviewees and had no noticeable influence on the outsourcing decisions, even though the importance and the strategic impact of their systems was higher and the risk of dependence and discontinuity, loss of innovative power and competitive advantage was larger.

High variability and uncertainty of business processes posed problems, especially if sourcing decisions coincided with or preceded reorganizations and if it was not clear whether the company planned to move into a new market or face potential changes in their existing market. These problems would also have occurred if the projects were performed internally, but became more serious in outsourcing situations, because with outsourcing it is more difficult to change requirements during activities. One of the case study organizations was planning to change to another logistics concept and to make major changes to the locations of production and the transport of products. The IS staff that remained after an outsourcing operation had just enough capacity to sustain the existing systems and few arrangements were made to enable the major changes in the information systems that would be needed in the new situation.

The cases differed in the amount of resource acquisition the clients controlled, and thus the power the clients had over the IS suppliers. Some clients used the power they derived from the prospect of additional business for the supplier. They postponed payments until the results were satisfactory, and they used the fact that they would provide a good reference and publicity for the supplier entering a new market segment or obtaining new business opportunities. One client organization was a large and well-known organization that received a lot of publicity. The supplier was aware of the fact that their performance would be highlighted in the trade press and the interviewees at the client organizations had the impression that this had motivated the supplier considerably to deploy their best efforts. In another case, the supplier developed, sold and operated ready-made packages, which were developed in cooperation with their largest client and former parent company. The supplier depended on the client for obtaining business knowledge and specification of requirements. The client had indicated the intention to buy the package if it met requirements, but gave no guarantee. The supplier needed the client to buy the package, as this was a necessary reference for selling the package to other clients. This gave the client considerable power and motivated the supplier to develop systems in the client's best interests.

High heterogeneity of the user community was often present with regard to the IS maturity, the degree of automation, the number of internal IS staff, and the degree of outsourcing. This led to the business units having different needs for support from central staff units and increased the occurrence of unclear or changing requirements for joint IS activities, due to different working procedures, cultures and sometimes to some rivalry between the business units.

4.7.3 IS market and suppliers

The market for IS products and services appeared to be not as open and competitive as decision makers expected. Supply is concentrated in a relatively small number of suppliers, who are connected in many ways, through joint ventures, strategic relationships and commercial interests. Client organizations were often affiliated with one or a few suppliers, for example by a guaranteed spending agreement or a preferred supplier relationship. This impaired true competition and caused many problems.

Comparing products, services, prices, lead times and quality of suppliers was very difficult, due to the abstract nature of IS and the lack of uniform terminology and units of measurement. IS services are not a homogeneous good that can be measured by unidimensional characteristics. The products or services often had to be made at the time the relationship started, for example with making an information plan or developing tailor-made software.

Decision makers often had insufficient information about the IS market. Many decision makers knew only a few suppliers and were swayed by personal contacts with employees of suppliers. They had insufficient insight into the specialties and qualities of suppliers and into reasonable cost prices and lead times. Thus they could not always assess whether the prices and lead times offered were reasonable and competitive. High measurability of IS activities is useful only if a client can judge whether the costs and lead time measured are reasonable and within common market margins.

The supplier's willingness to take risks determined how much risk the client could transfer to the supplier and the price the supplier asked for taking the risk. Suppliers that were willing to take risks made a considerable investment in the tendering process and were willing to perform a feasibility study at their own cost. Others were willing to develop or adapt software packages for a client organization and to take the risk of selling the package. In one case, involving the development of a large financial information system that would take over 100 person years, no supplier appeared willing to take the risk of offering a fixed price to develop the system. During the research period, it was observed that suppliers became increasingly willing to take responsibility for the activities they perform for clients.

A high degree of subcontracting did not lead to problems if it was a well-considered and deliberate strategy of the supplier, if the strategy was clear to the clients and if the supplier had a steady long-term relationship with its subcontractors. It did pose problems if the supplier was forced to subcontract or subcontracted on an ad hoc basis, or if the supplier depended on staff hired from other suppliers.

4.7.4 Public or private sector

Whether an organization is part of the public or the private sector is actually not a situational factor in itself, but a distinction that yields a certain general pattern of situational factors. One should be careful with these generalizations, because individual public sector organizations can be different.

The primary processes of most public sector organizations are very information intensive or only contain information processing. Handling requests for social security benefits, maintaining the land registry, and even political decision making, for example, are essentially information processes. All of the five (former) public sector organizations investigated have highly information intensive primary processes. The Dutch Railway company (NS) and the Dutch Directorate General of Public Works and Water Management (RWS) have physical primary processes, namely transport of passengers and freight, and public works and water management, but the planning and controlling of these processes is very information intensive. The processes of the Central Bureau of Statistics (CBS) contain only information processing, namely collecting, processing and disseminating social and economic information. Public sector organizations are therefore strongly dependent upon their information systems.

The primary processes are almost always unique and are not found in the private sector. Ready-made software packages were not available for most public sector processes and IS suppliers could not use their experience and knowledge from other client organizations for services to public sector organizations, which made outsourcing less favorable to public sector organizations.

The complexity of information systems in the public sector is often very high, mainly because of the complexity of the legislation that underlies the organizations' processes. There are many stakeholders in the policies of public bodies, who may have very different, conflicting and morally justifiable perspectives. Political decision makers give more consideration to fairness and justifiableness than to the practicability of their decisions and the consequences for information systems. Information systems need to be changed frequently, because of the large number of reorganizations and changes in legislation that public sector organizations face. Most changes have to be implemented instantaneously, sometimes retrospectively. Flexibility and a thorough knowledge of the processes are needed, thus some organizations retained an internal IS department.

Most primary processes in the public sector are unique; however they are often performed repetitively by a number of similar public sector organizations. Social security benefits are for example, provided by all municipalities, and all hospitals have similar information needs, as do schools and environmental inspection units. Secondary processes, such as human resources management and book keeping, are similar across ministries, provinces and municipalities. Different processes sometimes need similar information; municipal social security departments and land registry departments, for example, both need information on inhabitants. Many public sector organizations could therefore benefit from using the same information systems or information and achieve considerable economies of scale. Cooperation can be more easily achieved in the public sector than in the private sector, as public sector organizations do not compete.

Surprisingly, very few examples of cooperation were found, and many projects that were outsourced by more than one client organization did not succeed. Attempts by ministries to develop joint information systems for financial management, human resources management and measurement of air pollution failed or led to only one or a few ministries adopting the system. One of the few successful examples found in this research was the cooperation between several ministries in selecting and adapting a library management system. Interviewees explained this success by the fact that there were already information relationships between the ministries, because many documents were lent between the ministries, and that this increased the benefits and motivation to use a common system. Apparently, efficiency considerations are not enough to stimulate cooperation, and only actual interconnectedness motivates autonomous organizations to cooperate.

In the 1970s, regional IT centers were created to serve municipalities and other public sector organizations in their region. The IS departments of the three largest Dutch municipalities are the only regional centers that still exist and also serve smaller municipalities in their region. A fourth regional center, which originated from the IS department of the municipality of Eindhoven, is now very successful, despite problems in the initial phase. The center sells software packages for various functions to over a hundred municipalities and other public sector organizations and operates these packages for a few dozen of their clients.

Interviewees explained this lack of cooperation by the fact that the Dutch public sector is highly decentralized and organizations operate autonomously, especially with regard to support functions. Central government has decentralized many responsibilities to the provinces and municipalities, and within ministries, many tasks are decentralized to directorates. The Dutch Ministry of Internal Affairs has a coordinating role in central government's IS management, but no single ministry or government organization has the authority to enforce cooperation.

In the past, public sector organizations were not always attractive to IS specialists; the compensation rules did not offer many possibilities to pay personnel according to their market value and for differentiated rewards based on performance, which made it difficult to recruit and retain good IS staff. The possibilities for differences in payment based on market value and performance are however improving.

Internal IS staff of public sector organizations have often objected to being outsourced, because they would cease to be civil servants. In the Netherlands, there are significant differences in legal and employment conditions between the public and private sector, and employees sometimes choose to be civil servants for ideological reasons.

4.8 Decision variables

The decision variables are grouped into variables that describe the relationship between the client organization and an IS supplier, variables that describe the way transactions are divided among suppliers and contracts, variables that describe the management and operational structure of individual transactions and variables that describe the internal organization of the outsourcing coordination.

4.8.1 Outsourcing relationship

The variables that describe the relationship between the client organization and an IS supplier, and the values of the variables in the cases, are summarized in Table 4.22.

Legal relationship

Two client organizations chose to transform the internal IS department to an independent subsidiary with profit responsibility, but fully owned by the client organization. This approach yielded the result that many of the advantages of outsourcing were achieved, such as a more business-like relationship and clear cost allocation, but the client organization retained the ultimate authority to appoint top managers and determine the supplier's overall strategy. If the subsidiary charged excessive tariffs, the profits would flow back to the client as a dividend. The relationship was however not as business-like as it would be with an independent IS supplier. Responsibilities were demarcated less sharply, requirements were not always specified in advance and bills were not always clear. The profit motive of the IS subsidiary was sometimes crossed by the hierarchical orders of top management, such as the adoption of a specific new technology, without sufficient financial compensation.

Joint ventures or cooperation with other client organizations were successful if the requirements of the organizations were comparable and if the organizations were at the same stage in their decision making processes. If one organization needed a system fast and the other organizations had not yet even decided whether and when they would

Variable	Values				
Legal relationship	same entity	subsidiary	joint venture with clients	joint venture with supplier	independent supplier
	1	3	3	0	16
Economic relationship					
• Supplier revenues	<20%	20-80%	>80%		
	10	5	8		
• Client IS spendings	<20%	20-80%	>80%		
	3	17	3		
Transactional relationship	none	working relationship	cooperation agreement	guaranteed spending	
	9	12	11	12	
Choice of partners					
• Client	free	limited	one		
	12	4	7		
• Supplier	free	limited	one		
	21	2	0		

Table 4.22 Number of cases in each type of outsourcing

need such a system, then the most appropriate solution appeared to be that the first organization developed the system and that the other organizations would see if the system met their needs, and buy the system later, sharing in the development costs. A breakpoint that appeared in cooperation arrangements was that the participating organizations put too much emphasis on their unique needs instead of considering the overwhelming similarities. Many divergent requirements led to a system that was either too large and complicated and took too much time and money to develop, or to a compromise that satisfied none of the partners. Another problem was that the activities were usually managed by a group with representatives from all the partners, but without sufficient authority to take major decisions. The representatives had to consult their superiors for each decision, which led to a lack of power and considerable delay.

Transactional relationship

Relationships spanning multiple transactions were found in over half of the number of cases, mainly between clients and their former internal IS departments.

The major advantage of a working relationship was that the IS supplier became acquainted with the client organization and its information systems and that the client organization got to know the IS supplier's qualities and weaknesses.

A guaranteed spending agreement was established in all cases where the IS staff was transferred. The suppliers demanded the guaranteed spending in return for the employment guarantee they gave to the staff they took over. The guaranteed spending agreements varied between 3 and 5 years. The amount of guaranteed spending was between 120% and 90% of the former internal costs in the first year and was between 110% and 60% in the last year. The supplier often demanded that the client organization would undertake not to reestablish a comparable internal IS unit or to hire additional IS staff.

In one case, the guaranteed spending was further divided into separate amounts for three categories of services and into monthly amounts. Underspending in one category or one month could not be compensated by surpluses in other categories or months. During the first year, 10% of the annual costs were paid without receiving services, because in particular months not all guarantees for all services were met, while at the same time 12% was spent above the guaranteed spending, at a much higher tariff than the base line, for services above the guaranteed spending. At the end of the first year, the client organization installed a steering committee to predict capacity requirements and level the demands to exactly the guaranteed spending per category per month. Despite this, the agreement had adverse effects on the cost/benefit analysis and on the planning of IS activities.

In another case of guaranteed spending, the supplier also had a preferred position for all IS activities. The client was obliged to invite the supplier to tender for each IS activity, and the client organization was obliged to award the tender if the price was not higher than the highest of three other tender responses. The client organization was not allowed to outsource to another supplier without consulting their preferred supplier, ostensibly because applications had to interface with the infrastructure operated by the preferred supplier.

Economic relationship

Clients chose a supplier that was partially or totally dependent upon the client for their business volume in 13 cases. For most of these 13 cases, this was explained by the fact that the supplier was the former internal IS department of the client, and the outsourced department had not (yet) managed to engage a significant number of other clients. Clients outsourced the major part of their IS activities to one supplier in 3 cases. This gave the supplier considerable power over the clients.

Choice of business partners

Freedom of client organization. If there was a guaranteed spending agreement in place, business units were often obliged to outsource to the IS supplier that had taken over the former internal IS department. In some cases, exceptions were made for activities that were outside the supplier's specialism. In other cases, the central contract authority had trouble meeting the guaranteed spending and obliged the business units to spend part of the guaranteed spending, proportional to the business unit's former IS costs or to the size of the unit.

The client organizations that allowed their business units to chose any supplier often obliged the units to take certain services from specific suppliers. If there was a central internal IS department, business units were often obliged to use the central processing hardware and the wide area network provided by the department. This avoided underuse of the capacity of the internal IS department, such as the mainframe capacity, which would lead to higher costs for the activities that were performed by the department. In general, infrastructural components and activities were often more restricted than application software, because a common infrastructure facilitates information exchange and efficiency is increased by common use. Top management of one client organization obliged the business units to request proposals from the former internal IS department and at least two external suppliers. If business units wanted to outsource to an external supplier, they had to give a business motivation for why they did not choose the former internal department.

Freedom of internal IS department. Internal IS departments were sometimes allowed to offer services to other clients outside the parent organization. This gave these departments the opportunity to deploy possible excess capacity, for example of the network or the central processing hardware. It was also a test of the performance and competitiveness of the department's quality and tariffs, and yielded valuable insights from other organizations.

Problems arose when priorities had to be determined between internal and external clients. External clients were often given priority, because they were more critical and because they yielded "real" money instead of internal transfer money. Obtaining and working with external clients also required different management methods and a marketing and order department had to be installed. The conflicts between managing activities for internal versus external clients increased if the share of external clients increased. A share of about 10% external revenue appeared sufficient to provide a market test and yet to not give too many problems with management and priorities.

4.8.2 Division among suppliers and contracts

The grouping of transactions and the division among suppliers and contracts is summarized in Table 4.23.

Number of IS suppliers

The clients organization that outsourced to multiple suppliers were better able to compare suppliers, which gave them more insight into the performance and competitiveness of the supplier. The client organizations could choose for any activity the supplier specialized in that particular area. It allowed the clients to transfer activities to another supplier more easily, if one supplier did not perform well. These facts helped the client avoid becoming dependent on one supplier and stimulated the suppliers to deploy their best efforts and resources. One client organization, for example, outsourced the maintenance of over 100 small and large applications split into two groups to two suppliers. Another client organization even hired staff from

Division among suppliers					
number of suppliers	1	2	3	4	>4
	2	4	5	3	2
way of separating	systems	components	activities		
	3	5	7		
Division among contracts					
number of contracts	1	2	3	4	>4
	2	4	5	3	2
way of separating	systems	components	activities		
	3	5	7		

Table 4.23 Grouping of transactions

three different suppliers simultaneously to develop one large information system.

Dividing activities among multiple suppliers however did increase the effort needed to coordinate activities and their interfaces. The client organization had to communicate with a number of suppliers and to make sure that the activities performed by different suppliers interfaced with each other. If problems arose, it was not always clear which supplier could be held responsible. In one case, eight suppliers had to be consulted to determine and fix a problem with response times: the developer of the application, the data base administrator, the operator of the central hardware, the operator of the wide area network, the operator of the local area networks and the personal computers, and the supplier of the operating system and the database management system. The contracts were not clear on responsibilities, the cause of the problem was difficult to determine and the suppliers were not cooperative. Another reason for client organizations to outsource to one supplier was that they had outsourced their IS department to a supplier and had guaranteed to outsource a large part of their IS activities to the supplier, in exchange for an employment guarantee for the staff taken over.

Generally, however, the advantages of flexibility and competition outweighed the costs of extra coordination between multiple suppliers. Three of the guaranteed spending agreements ended within the research period. All three client organizations immediately changed their outsourcing strategy, and started outsourcing separate well-defined pieces of work to multiple suppliers with separate and enforceable contracts. They maintained some long term relationships with a limited number of suppliers, but these relationships were not based on any obligations and were continued only for as long as the client was satisfied with the supplier's performance.

Way of separating

Separate transactions with separate contracts were established for consecutive IS activities or for different subsystems. This improved controllability, because estimates of costs and lead time became more accurate with the completion of earlier projects, and because the client had the option to switch to another supplier for other transactions. Separate transactions, however, led to some coordination problems, if they were outsourced to different suppliers.

Outsourcing activities to different suppliers. Different IS activities require diverse skills and specialties, but also have many interrelationships. This posed a number of dilemma's about whether or not to outsource activities to different suppliers.

Some client organizations outsourced planning, consultancy and feasibility studies to the supplier that was to execute the activities that arose from the planning and feasibility studies. Some interviewees expected that a supplier that performs operational IS activities is better able to perform executable and realistic planning than a consultancy firm that specializes in planning and advice but never performs operational IS activities. Other interviewees however, chose to outsource planning to a specialized firm, because they believed planning required different skills that were often not be found in firms that performed operational activities. They also believed that such a supplier would not be objective, as they had an interest in planning as many new activities as possible and in planning activities their own firm was best able to provide and make the most profit from.

The consecutive phases of system development were often outsourced to different suppliers. The initial phases, up to and sometimes including functional design, were often performed internally, sometimes assisted by external staff on a time and materials basis. The following phases, up to construction, were often outsourced on a fixed price and fixed date basis. This approach was chosen for several reasons: the phases needed a different type of outsourcing management structure; the first phases often ended with a go-no go decision or with a choice of several principal solutions; and the supplier was more motivated to deploy its best efforts, employees and resources. In most cases, the next phase was awarded to the same supplier, but the interviewees were convinced that the supplier had made a better offer because of the competition than if they had just asked the supplier to continue. The client organization had to ensure that the result of the initial phases were documented in a way that they could easily be understood by and transferred to another supplier. Problems sometimes arose with this separation, because there was often no sharp distinction between the phases, iterations were needed, either planned, for example with prototyping, or unplanned, if requirements changed during the project. Some technical decisions had to be made in the design phase and functional details often had to be elaborated in the construction phase.

Some client organizations outsourced all consecutive phases to the same supplier, to avoid the costs and quality losses of transfer of knowledge and intermediate results. Most large suppliers however had specialized staff and departments for each phase, and transferred the intermediate results from one department to another.

The maintenance of systems was outsourced to the supplier that had developed the system in 13 cases. The advantage of this choice was that the supplier already knew the system and that the developers took extra effort to increase the system's maintainability. In 5 cases, the maintenance was outsourced to the supplier that operated the system. The advantage of this approach was that it was not necessary to determine which supplier was responsible for problems with the systems and that the adjustment of the system to the infrastructure was done by one supplier. The disadvantage was that maintenance and operation requires very different skills and resources, and the suppliers operating the systems were not always the best for maintenance and vice versa. Maintenance was outsourced separately in 3 cases. In one case, the maintenance in the first year after the development of a new system was outsourced to the developing supplier, to ensure that the supplier would develop a maintainable system, and a new tender was issued for maintenance in the following years.

Outsourcing components to different suppliers. A separation that yielded many problems was the one between the central processing hardware and the wide area network (WAN) and the personal computers and the local area networks (LANs). If these activities were outsourced to separate suppliers, conflicts often arose about the separation between the two groups of components and about who was responsible for solving certain problems with availability and connectivity.

Another common area of interface problems was between operation of the infrastructure, which usually included hardware and systems software, and the development and maintenance of application software. As these two groups of components require very different skills and resources, they were often outsourced to different suppliers. Application software should however, be suited to being operated using the client organization's infrastructure. The supplier operating the infrastructure was often involved in the development process too late or not at all, yielding an application that could not be operated using the existing infrastructure. These problems arose mostly if operating the infrastructure was outsourced by a central staff unit and developing the applications was outsourced by the business units. One client organization obliged all business units to consult the central unit that coordinated the infrastructure from the start of any development project for software that was to be operated using the client's infrastructure or connected to the infrastructure.

Outsourcing systems to different suppliers. Outsourcing the development of different systems to different suppliers was common practice in most client organizations. Problems arose sometimes with systems that interacted with each other or that shared the same infrastructure. These problems were usually avoided by defining the interfaces between the systems clearly.

Number of contracts and separation
Some client organizations governed the activities outsourced to a supplier by one all-encompassing contract, while other organizations established separate contracts for each activity. Most of the consider-

ations for dividing activities among suppliers also applied to separating contracts.

4.8.3 Management structure

The management structure of the outsourcing relationships investigated are summarized in Table 4.24.

Requirements definition

Many client organizations described the requirements for the activities they outsourced in broad and functional terms. This often posed problems with interpreting and enforcing compliance to these requirements and led to disputes about the exact content of the requirements.

Pricing mechanism

Decision makers that outsourced on a fixed price basis often expected to have maximum controllability. It appeared however, that this was only the case if the requirements could be specified in advance and in enough detail to be enforced. In the cases where requirements were not specified in detail, it was difficult to determine whether the supplier had performed all of the work the fixed price was based on. Requirements often changed, and the supplier charged the client for the extra work. The client often did not know what price would be reasonable for a certain portion of work. Suppliers had no trouble

Variable	Values				
Requirements definition	broad	detailed	functional	technical	
	14	9	16	7	
Pricing mechanism	none	time & materials	fixed fee	work load client	benefits to
	1	16	8	6	0
Lead time mechanism	fixed	variable			
	5	19			
Quality control mechanism	intermediate	only final	by client	by supplier	by third party
	9	14	17	4	3
Coordination mechanisms	mutual adjustment	direct supervision	work process	output	skills
	13	8	5	20	15
Conflict resolution mechanism	hierarchy	escalation procedures	third party arbitration	Legal action	
	4	10	2	14	

Table 4.24 Management structure

meeting a fixed price that was 50% above the expected costs. If the budget was used and the product had not been finished, the client had the option of paying more or demanding compliance. In the latter case, the supplier often scrambled through the work or even went bankrupt. Suppliers only agreed to a fixed price mechanism if the activity was relatively predictable and straight-forward, while client organizations wanted the mechanism for innovative and uncertain activities.

Payment based on time and materials was used mostly for planning and for development of innovative information systems, because specifying requirements for these activities is difficult.

A number of clients agreed a pricing mechanism based on work load. The units of workload were sometimes defined in technical terms, such as the number of function points or lines of code developed, the number of central processing unit (CPU) seconds or million instructions per second (MIPS), or the number of megabytes of data stored, and sometimes in functional terms, such as the number of documents entered, the number of loans in a library, or the number of citizens in a municipality.

Software development was sometimes paid for on a basis of a price per function point. The function point method is very clear to users, because the consequences of their requirements and change requests can be translated to the corresponding costs easily. The reliability and the accuracy of the method however, appeared to be disappointing. A reliable and accurate function point analysis appeared possible only after the detailed design had been finished. The method was not suited for calculating the costs of a feasibility study or of the initial design. The price per function point also varied widely. In one case, a client requested proposals with function point analysis for software development based on a finished initial design. The number of function points that the suppliers calculated varied between 2000 and 2500 and the price per function point varied by a factor 2.

Contracts in which payment was based on some benefits that accrued to the client company were not found in this research. This type of contract is perhaps not yet accepted widely, at least in the Netherlands. Some interviewees replied that it would be very difficult to use this type of payment, because many other factors besides the performance of the supplier influence the benefits.

Lead time mechanism
In 9 cases, a fixed lead time was agreed. In most of these cases, no agreement was made on what would happen if the deadline was not met. A fixed lead time did not increase the controllability of the lead time as much as decision makers expected, for the same reasons as mentioned above regarding the fixed price mechanism.

Quality control mechanism
Quality was measured proactively or reactively. Proactive quality

control included demanding that a supplier used quality procedures that were written down and could be checked. Reactive quality control included demanding progress and quality reports, and testing or inspecting intermediate and final products or services. Proactive quality control was applied in no more than 5 cases, and the actual use of the quality procedures was not checked by the client organizations.

In 4 cases, external quality audits were performed. These audits almost always led to considerable adjustments by the supplier and always yielded more savings than the costs of the audits.

Testing was performed by the supplier, by the client organization or by a third party. Testing intermediate products was only performed with software development using the prototyping method. Reports often only included the use of resources and the hours spent by the supplier's staff, and seldom a statement concerning the actual progress made and the degree to which the requirements had been met.

Coordination

Coordination by mutual adjustment was found in the case study of former internal IS departments, between employees that used to be colleagues before the IS department was outsourced. In these cases, the relationship was not that business-like, contracts were not relied on, and most contracts were too informal for reliability.

Direct supervision of IS supplier's staff implies that the client organization buys the right to use the IS supplier's staff under it's command, which is often called body shopping. This mechanism was used in 8 cases and was often combined with a time and materials pricing mechanism. The option was chosen in both cases of outsourcing of information planning, because the client organization wanted full control over how the process was performed.

Communication between client and suppliers varied considerably: some clients wanted to supervise the supplier very closely and had daily contact at various levels, while other clients wanted to keep the relationship as business-like as possible and wanted only a small number of formal meetings. The latter organizations also wanted to be able to 'summon' a high level manager from the supplier in the case of serious problems, and this would not make much impression if there was regular informal communication at all levels.

No distinction was made between progress meetings, dealing with progress of work, time and money spent, and design or functional meetings, dealing with functional decisions about the information systems to be developed or operated. These meetings have very different aims and require a different frequency, different decisions are made, different information is required and involvement of different decision makers.

Many IS suppliers had account managers who acted as intermediaries between the client organization and the IS suppliers' operational units. Interviewees valued the fact that they could contact one person for all services and questions. They disliked the fact that the account manager was an extra layer between the client and the supplier's operational staff, which sometimes made communicating requirements more difficult and yielded considerable delay when requesting minor changes. Some of the account managers had insufficient IS knowledge, were seldom available and focused more on maximizing the supplier's profit than on providing a good service to the clients. Turnover among the account managers was sometimes very high, which yielded considerable delays and annoyance for the client. One business unit manager had dealt with five consecutive account managers in two years.

Conflict resolution mechanism

A joint hierarchical superior was present in the cases where the supplier was part of the same legal entity as the client organization. Resolving disputes by third party arbitration appeared just twice. Escalation procedures appeared to be quite common, especially between parties with a long term relationship. In none of the 14 cases that relied on litigation were disagreements actually brought to court.

4.8.4 Operational structure

The operational structure is described by the location, ownership, employment and exclusiveness of the IS components. The values of the variables in the cases are summarized in Table 4.25

Location

The IS components were located at the supplier's site in one-third of the cases. In almost all cases, the IS personnel was located at the supplier's site. Some clients preferred to have the IS personnel at their site and under their control. This also facilitated knowledge transfer to the internal IS staff. The availability of office space was an important

		Hardware	Software	Data	Staff	Procedures
Location	Client's site	15	15	15	5	n/a
	Supplier's site	8	8	8	18	
Ownership/	Client	15	16	23	3	17
employment	Supplier	8	7	0	20	6
Exclusiveness	Dedicated	16	17	23	2	18
	Shared	7	6	0	21	5

Table 4.25 Operational structure

consideration for clients not to have the supplier's staff at their office. Other clients wanted to keep the relationship business-like and did not want the daily bother of minor questions from the supplier's staff. If an internal IS department was taken over by an external supplier, then economies of scale were only achieved if the department was moved to the supplier's office.

Ownership

Tailor-made software, procedures and data were always owned by the client, unless the client organization planned explicitly to have the IS supplier sell the components to other clients. One client organization asked for a number of tailor-made adaptations to a ready-made package. The client did not want to own the adaptations and the supplier planned to sell the extra features to other clients. The client only had to pay an extra license fee that was approximately one-third of the development costs of the adaptations.

Hardware was owned by the supplier in 8 cases. This gave the supplier the opportunity to sell excess capacity to other clients and saved the client the initial investments of buying the hardware.

Employment

The IS staff was employed by the client in 3 cases and by the supplier in the remaining 20 cases. The costs of hiring staff from a supplier were much higher than the costs of internal staff, even if overhead costs were allocated to the costs of the internal staff. The tariff of external staff was 50-80% higher than the integral costs of comparable internal staff. The main advantage of hiring staff was however, that staff could be hired for as long as needed and the client did not have to pay or lay off the staff if they were no longer needed. One of the reasons for the external staff's higher tariff was the fact that external staff was not deployed every day. Suppliers therefore often gave volume discounts if a client hired staff for a longer period.

Some client organizations hired external staff full time for a year or more. Suppliers often gave volume discounts, but the costs were still considerably higher than employing internal staff. These clients were often obliged to outsource and were not allowed to employ new staff, or they were not able to attract or manage the staff needed. Other clients stated that, even for a period of a year known in advance, employing internal staff was too inflexible and would still have left them with staff they had no need for after that year. Hiring external staff was not always as flexible as expected, because clients became dependent on the staff.

Client organizations also hired external staff because of their fresh and unbiased view and their experience in other organizations. External staff did not have to account for political and personal sensitivities as much as internal staff, and could thereby defend difficult or unpopular decisions. Sometimes external staff were hired because an 'objective expert opinion' was valued higher above that of the advice of internal staff.

Public sector organizations faced a strict division between budgets for personnel and for material expenses. Due to cuts in the personnel budget, they were often not allowed to employ new staff, and had to hire expensive external staff paid for from the material budget, even if that was clearly much more expensive.

Exclusiveness

Some client organizations demanded exclusive use of a supplier' hardware, mainly for security reasons, while in other cases the supplier was allowed to use the hardware for other clients.

If ready-made software packages were available that met the client's requirements, then these packages were considerably cheaper than having tailor-made system developed. No development time was needed and the packages had been tested and corrected for previous clients.

Ready-made packages were only available for relatively common functions for which the information requirements were more or less the same among many organizations. If a client organization performed a business process in an innovative way, then often no suitable packages were available. During the research period, ready-made packages became available for more business functions. In two cases, market research yielded no suitable packages, but by the time the tailor-made system was implemented, suitable packages had appeared.

If ready-made packages did not completely meet the requirements, either the requirements or the package had to be adapted. Having a ready-made package adapted yielded many problems, mainly because this approach has all the disadvantages of developing tailor-made software, such as a long lead time and high costs, but none of the advantages, such as flexibility and ownership. If the supplier wanted to release a new version of the package, the tailor-made options had to be incorporated or updated separately. Very few suppliers had configuration management that was able to support client-specific adaptations to ready-made packages adequately and at reasonable costs.

Some ready-made packages could be configured to the specific needs of the client organization. The danger of a package with many features and configuration options appeared to be that configuring the package took almost as much time and effort as developing tailor-made software, and that users started experimenting with the options and using features that the decision makers had not planned to be used. If a configurable package was used by several user departments, the departments often made different configurations, which made the package less uniform and interchangeable.

Most client organizations underestimated the importance of continuity of the supplier of ready-made packages, system software, hardware and other shared components. Client organizations faced many problems if the supplier of a standard component went bankrupt, stopped releasing new versions or stopped supporting existing versions. One large software development project faced the bankruptcy of the supplier of the database management system. The technical design was finished, but the project had to start almost from the beginning, because the design was based heavily on the idiosyncrasies of the database management system.

4.8.5 Internal organization of outsourcing coordination

Internal activities and skills
In each of the cases, the following activities were necessary to coordinate the IS function and the IS activities that were outsourced:

- determining the organization's IS strategy,
- determining and specifying requirements for IS activities,
- coordinating the interfaces between the separate IS activities,
- conducting market research,
- issuing a call for tender and selecting a supplier,
- negotiating and writing a contract,
- monitoring and evaluating the performance of the supplier and the products and services delivered.

Many top managers assumed that after outsourcing they would no longer need a knowledge of IT and the IS market, that they only had to tell the supplier their information needs, in 'business terms,' and the supplier would determine the best technical solution and implement that for a reasonable price. En passant, the supplier would, as a strategic partner, assist in determining the information strategy and come up with new useful applications of IT for the client's business processes.

In practice, it appeared insufficient to define requirements in broad functional terms, because IT is not yet well enough standardized that no technical choices have to be made, and the new systems had to fit into the existing technical architecture. Furthermore, a client needs a knowledge of IT and the IS market to evaluate whether the price and lead time offered by a supplier are reasonable.

The supplier was often not able or willing to assist the client with their information strategy. Determining an information strategy requires knowledge of new products, markets and the strategies of the client, from formal and informal channels. The supplier had insufficient knowledge of the business processes and most client organizations did not want to share this information with their supplier. It is not sensible to ask advice from a supplier who has an interest in the client organization investing in IT. Client organizations that had outsourced, appeared to need the following knowledge and skills:

- knowledge of the possibilities and limitations of information technology,
- skills to determine useful applications of IT for the business processes,
- skills to translate these ideas into measurable requirement specifications,
- knowledge of the IS market and the qualities and specialties of IS suppliers,
- skills in conducting marketing research and tendering procedures,
- skills in negotiating and writing a contract,
- skills in evaluating supplier's performance and testing products and services delivered.

This knowledge and the skills were often available shortly after the outsourcing operation, but disappeared if the remaining internal IS staff did not keep up to date with operational activities or found employment elsewhere. The client organizations that continued to employ part of the IS staff internally and also had them perform a small part of the operational activities were better able to retain these skills and knowledge. Operational staff who had performed the IS activities before outsourcing were not always capable of coordinating the same activities performed by suppliers. Managing external relationships appeared to require fundamentally different skills from actually performing the activities.

Centralization
A number of the skills needed after outsourcing appeared to be rather specialized and were used infrequently by individual business units. Business unit managers often made the same elementary mistakes in specifying requirements, tendering, negotiating and contracting. Requirement specification, market research, feasibility studies and coordinating the outsourcing often put very high demands on the business unit's staff and resources. Some of the client organizations therefore centralized these activities and skills in a staff unit that assisted the business units with specifying their requirements, with the tendering process and with writing and negotiating the contract. These units sometimes also established framework agreements with a small number of suppliers and managed the contracts for the organization's common infrastructure. This was much more efficient and decreased the number of errors in negotiating and contracting. These units did not charge for their services, to avoid business units

failing to consult the internal advisors for cost reasons. The staff members acted as external advisors, but had inside knowledge of the business processes and the informal channels, were more loyal to the organization and were better accepted by the users and managers.

A problem that sometimes appeared with a central unit coordinating outsourcing was that the unit sometimes got blamed by the user departments for shortcomings of the supplier. In general, the problem arose that the unit sometimes acted more as a client instead of an advisor of the actual client, namely the business unit, and that the business unit no longer felt committed to the outsourcing.

If IS budgets were decentralized but a guaranteed spending was agreed for the entire organization, the spending by the business units had to be coordinated, to avoid (temporary) over or underspending.

If the user community was very dispersed and decentralized, many problems arose that impeded unified requirement specification and management of the outsourcing relationship. In some cases, a steering committee coordinated the user requests and specified the requirements.

User involvement

A number of problems arose from a lack of user involvement in software development activities. User involvement is necessary for the supplier to obtain a knowledge of the business processes and the information needs of a client. This took considerable time from the users and some users could not free themselves from their daily work or were not allowed to participate by their managers. In at least one case, the client's project manager reacted to a lack of user involvement by hiring more external staff. This resulted in a system that did not meet the (implicit) user requirements. It was remarkable that the users apparently had no time to be involved in the system development but did have enough time to criticize the resulting system extensively. Suppliers sometimes asked the client organization to commit to a certain amount of user involvement.

IS maturity appeared to be essential for coordinating outsourcing. If users and business unit managers were not able to determine their requirements and had unrealistic expectations with regard to costs and lead times, then they were often disappointed by the results.

Outsourcing of outsourcing coordination

Outsourcing coordination can itself be outsourced, for example by hiring an external expert to assist with developing an outsourcing strategy, with managing and controlling the external suppliers, and with testing and quality assurance. Some external experts hired by client organizations had an interest in being overly compassionate to or severe with the supplier. If outsourcing coordination or project management was outsourced to the supplier to which the activities themselves were outsourced, the advisor was often not very critical towards the supplier and stimulated the client organization for example to increase the number of functions of a system to be developed. If the client organization had a number of preferred suppliers, and coordinating the activities of one preferred supplier was outsourced to an advisor of one of the other preferred suppliers, the advisor was overly critical to the competitor.

4.9 Conclusions

Many decision makers at client organizations had overly high expectations of outsourcing, often stimulated by positive media and political attention, and by the persuasive presentations of IS suppliers.

The case study research described in this chapter has shown that client organizations should be critical towards these high expectations. Outsourcing led to improvements in a number of cases, but not in all situations. The improvements were never established automatically, but had to be enforced by the client organization, by making measurable agreements and by keeping and sustaining enough knowledge and sufficient skills to remain an alert client.

4.9.1 Outsourcing decision making

Large outsourcing decisions tended to be taken mainly by top or financial management and involved different stakeholders with different interests and perceptions with regard to the IS function. Many decisions were taken based on ideology, trends and personal expectations.

A lack of systematic analysis was observed in the early stages of most outsourcing decisions. Information systems outsourcing decisions did not start with analyzing the current situation thoroughly, examining the problems that gave rise to considering outsourcing and evaluating all available internal and external alternatives. Outsourcing decisions appeared to have long term impacts but were not based on a long term IS strategy. Very few decision makers performed a thorough analysis of the IS activities to be performed, evaluated the internal IS services and the possibilities for internal improvement, or examined all the expected effects of IS outsourcing.

Decision makers often did not realize that the goals and improvements expected would only be achieved if the outsourcing arrangement was designed to allow for and enforce these improvements. The selection of an IS supplier was often influenced largely by personal impressions of decision makers and the persuasive presentations of the suppliers. Negotiations were restricted to one supplier at a very early stage and before conditions were agreed.

4.9.2 Consequences of IS outsourcing

Cost savings and other improvements through economies of scale were only achieved in the cases where the supplier actually performed similar activities on a considerably larger scale and the outsourcing relationship was organized in a way that permitted and forced the supplier to reuse staff, skills and resources for multiple clients. Economies of scale could sometimes be achieved internally, for example by consolidating IS units and resources.

The expectations of cost reductions and other improvements were not met in the cases where the IS department was outsourced to a supplier that maintained the department as a separate business unit, without integrating the unit with the other units of the supplier and without having the unit work for other clients.

Improvements in individual activities were achieved when a client organization outsourced activities that needed staff, skills and resources not present with the client organization, to a supplier that had these resources available and had extensive experience with the pertinent technology, activity and business process.

Managers that outsourced IS to get rid of a function they found hard to manage, and to free time for "more important" functions, showed a lack of awareness of the importance of IS. Information technology and information systems were essential to all the client organizations and not only needed attention, but this attention paid off. The most common complaint among IS staff being outsourced was the lack of IS awareness among top management. Top managers often emphasized short term reductions of costs and staffing levels. They compared the IS function to catering, the post service and security, while the IS function is fundamentally different from those functions, as it can not be bought as a commodity and is essential to almost all business processes.

Moreover, the demands on management time were not always reduced by and sometimes even increased with outsourcing. Uncontrollable costs often had more to do with uncontrollable user requirements and inadequate allocation and budget mechanisms than with inefficiency of the IS department. Problems with finding and keeping adequate IS staff and managing the IS department were replaced by problems with choosing the right IS supplier, interpreting contracts, reviewing the supplier's bill, measuring the supplier's performance, and taking (legal) action to enforce compliance. Outsourcing does not mean less management involvement, but a change from managing an internal department to managing outsourcing contracts

Outsourcing was often chosen to solve problems with the internal IS department, such as uncontrollable costs and insufficient quality and flexibility. Many problems were however, not inherent to internal IS departments and were not solved automatically by outsourcing. Problems such as unclear or changing user requirements or insufficient cost awareness were not weaknesses of the internal or external supplier but of the users and line managers of the client organization. Problems that the IS function could be held accountable for were sometimes solved by an external supplier, but that supplier charged the costs of solving the problems to the client. Above that, some suppliers took advantage of the problems and the lack of control, and charged excessive fees. Some client organizations solved problems with the IS function themselves, by improving the management of the IS function and retraining and motivating the IS staff.

IS suppliers were often not subject to market pressure, because in many situations there was no real competition. For most parts of the IS function, there was only one or a few adequate suppliers, no homogeneous and specified products, no uniform terminology and not enough information on prices, lead times, and on the specialties of supplier. Many client organizations could not assess the quality and efficiency of their supplier. Significant switching costs often impaired the client organization to chose another supplier.

The goals and expectations of the privatization trend in the public sector were not completely met. Staffing levels and the number of civil servants were reduced, but the corresponding budget savings were not achieved, because the tariffs of the external IS suppliers were not lower and were sometimes higher than the internal costs of the IS activities. Increased control and flexibility of the public sector was achieved to some extent, but the high and long term guaranteed spending agreements that suppliers demanded in exchange for employment guarantees for the transferred staff were very inflexible and led to less thorough cost/benefit analyses and less strict project management. The third goal of the privatization trend, to stimulate the private sector, was achieved to some extent, because the privatizations gave a number of suppliers a higher business volume and higher profits.

4.9.3 Situational factors for outsourcing

Outsourcing appeared to be beneficial only if there were attestable reasons why an external supplier could achieve improvements.

Information systems supporting business processes that contained information processing only, or were otherwise heavily dependent on unique and specific information systems, required an IS supplier with specific knowledge of the client's business processes. If client organizations outsourced these systems to an IS supplier over which they had no ultimate control, they risked losing control over their organizational strategy or at least faced increased costs and decreased continuity of their business processes.

The case studies showed that outsourcing is advisable only in situations where the advantages of scale could be ascertained, sufficient adequate suppliers were available, the requirements for services could be specified in advance and measured afterwards, and activities were not highly interconnected.

The only differences found between sourcing decisions in the public and the private sector were that most primary processes in the public sector are unique, complex and information-intense. The fact that public sector organizations operate in low-competitive environments allows for cooperation among these organizations if they have similar or complementary information needs, but due to the high autonomy of Dutch public sector organizations, these joint projects seldom arose and even less often succeeded. A number of restrictions in the public sector accounting systems impaired rational economic decision processes, but these restrictions have recently been alleviated.

4.9.4 Decision variables

The potential improvements of outsourcing were never achieved automatically but had to be enforced by the client organization. Strategies that were successful in managing outsourcing relationships to the advantage of the client retained flexibility and control by preserving competition, being independent and retaining enough knowledge and skills to be a critical client.

Essential element in contracts appear to be: detailed requirements specifications, methods for measuring compliance and measures for non-compliance, and arrangements for implementation, management, change and termination of the outsourcing relationship. Good contracts appeared to be a very essential, but far from sufficient condition for high controllability. The value of contracts is limited if client organizations do not have the actual power and ability to determine whether the supplier complies to the contract and to enforce compliance.

Successful client organizations outsourced separate, measurable, IS activities to multiple suppliers, using short term enforceable contracts with provisions for changing circumstances. They retained an internal IS department that had the knowledge and skills to determine useful applications of IT in their business processes, to translate these into measurable specifications, to conduct market research, to select an adequate supplier, to negotiate a solid contract and to assess the supplier's performance. The IS departments retained skilled employees and kept their knowledge up to date by performing part of the operational IS activities, which also increased the client's independence.

4.9.5 Developing a decision model for client organizations

A prescriptive decision model is presented in the next chapter, that is intended to support those who are involved in IS sourcing decision processes. The decision model is based largely on the conclusions drawn from the case studies described in this chapter. The structure of the decision model is based on the phases of IS outsourcing decision making that were encountered during the case study research.

Elements from decision models of other authors are also included in the decision model. In chapter 1 it was argued that none of the decision models available currently complied to all demands. Certain elements of the models are however useful. The guidelines of the CCOI (1990) were largely confirmed by the case study research and are included in the decision model. Most of the factors proposed by Beulen (1994) are also included. The basic approach of Lacity, Willcocks and Feeney (1995) and Lacity and Hirschheim (1995) is adopted, i.e., that client organizations should maintain flexibility and control by selective outsourcing of well-defined IS activities to multiple suppliers. Other practical suggestions from these authors have also been taken into account.

CHAPTER 5

A Model for
IS Outsourcing
Decision Making

Information systems outsourcing has both positive and negative consequences on the short and long term development of the organization. The model presented in this chapter is the result of the research described in the previous chapters, and it is based on established organizational theories and on empirical research. The model is intended to support those who are involved in IS outsourcing decision processes. When using this model, decision makers will benefit from the lessons learned from previous outsourcing operations by other organizations. A structured method increases the probability that all aspects and all stakeholders are incorporated in the decision process and that common pitfalls are avoided.

This chapter can be read and used independently from the other chapters of this book. A few tables and paragraphs are duplicated in this chapter for ease of reference. It is useful to read the introduction to this book (chapter 1), to gain an overall impression of IS outsourcing and the research this model is based upon, and the framework for IS outsourcing (chapter 2), to understand the terminology that is used. The model is based upon established organizational theories (chapter 3) and case study research (chapter 4). The phases and variables of the model correspond to the structure of the framework for IS outsourcing. The underpinning of the guidelines presented in this chapter can be found in chapters 3 and 4 in the corresponding sections.

Coverage and target audience

The model covers all phases of IS outsourcing decision making, from the initial sourcing decision to managing and terminating the outsourcing relationship. All parts of the IS function are covered, and differences between information systems, IS activities and IS components are incorporated. Guidelines are given for the actual decisions and for the process of decision making.

The model is designed to be used by functionaries of client organizations taking decisions on the sourcing of IS activities. This may be general management, IS management or outsourcing consultants.

Principles

The decision model is based on the following principles, that underlay all steps and guidelines:

- The outcome of outsourcing decisions is situation-dependent. An outsourcing arrangement that is best for one organization may be inappropriate for other organizations in other circumstances. Outsourcing decision making should include an analysis of situational factors.
- The decision process itself is situation-dependent. The steps to be taken and the role of the variables and the functionaries involved depend upon the specific situation. Decision makers may chose to combine or leave out steps suggested in this model or to perform them in a different order. The decision process should start with determining the part of the IS function that is under consideration, the variables that the decision makers are authorized to change, and the factors that must be taken as they are.
- There is a strong relationship between outsourcing and information planning and strategy. Outsourcing decisions must be based upon the quantitative and qualitative capacity requirements of the information systems that need to be developed and operated. At the same time, outsourcing decisions influence the number and nature of IS activities that can be performed.
- Outsourcing should not be a one-off isolated decision. Outsourcing is only one of a number of organizational measures that can improve the IS function. All internal and external options for improving the IS function must be considered equally and on a regular basis, for example as part of the information planning and strategy formulation process.
- Outsourcing decisions should consider all goal variables. Variables can be given different weight depending on the specific situation, but putting a one-sided emphasis on, for example, short term reductions in costs or staffing levels may result in unacceptable decay in other variables, such as the organization's competitive position, and the quality, responsiveness, flexibility, and controllability of the IS function.

Phase	Section
1 Initial sourcing decision	5.1
2 Designing the outsourcing arrangement	5.2
3 Selecting the IS supplier	5.3
4 Implementation of the outsourcing decision	5.4
5 Management of the outsourcing relationship	5.5
6 Termination of the outsourcing relationship	5.6

Table 5.1 Phases of the model for IS outsourcing decision making

Structure and presentation

The decision model is structured along the phases of outsourcing decision making. The phases that are distinguished are listed in Table 5.1.

These phases do not arise necessarily in the order they are presented. In specific situations, some phases may not be relevant or additional phases may be needed, and phases may be executed in a different order and more than once. Figure 5.1 can be used to determine which phases are relevant in a specific situation.

The initial sourcing decision may for example be taken after the reactions to a call for tender are received. Client organizations may include in the call for tender how they want to organize the outsourcing relationship. If the actual sourcing decision is already made or enforced by the organization's policies, the decision process can start with tendering or with organizing the outsourcing relationship. If a client organization has a transactional relationship with an IS supplier that enforces outsourcing to that supplier, most of the tendering activities can be omitted. The initial sourcing decision may depend on the availability of adequate suppliers, which can sometimes only be determined by issuing a tendering procedure.

Each phase is described in one of the following sections. Each section starts with a table containing the purpose, triggers, activities and results of that phase. The description continues with a subsection for each of the activities to be found in that phase.

The first two phases are described in the most detail, because the research for this book was aimed mainly at the initial decision and the design of the outsourcing relationship. Another reason for this emphasis is that after a good initial sourcing decision and a well-designed outsourcing relationship, many decisions with regard to the consecutive phases have already been taken and these phases will pose less problems.

Readers with a general interest in IS outsourcing can if they wish confine themselves to reading the general statements at the beginning of each subsection. Each activity is then described for those readers who are involved in outsourcing evaluations or have a deeper interest. Detailed descriptions of the guidelines, tables and diagrams are

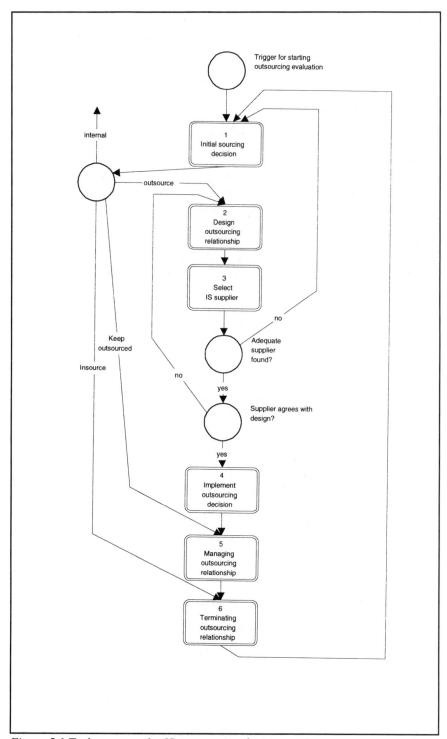

Figure 5.1 Task structure for IS outsourcing decision making

included for decision makers who want to use the model in practice. The description is completed with examples and a review of common problems and pitfalls.

The theoretical and empirical underpinning of the model presented here has been given in chapters 3 and 4. The underpinning is not repeated in this chapter, to retain a clear distinction between descriptive and prescriptive conclusions, and to make the model relatively concise and appropriate for practical use. No explicit references are included in this chapter to chapters 3 and 4, but the model is structured along the same phases and variables as the previous chapters. The underpinning of each guideline can be found in the corresponding sections of the previous chapters.

The phases and guidelines should be used with care. For clarity of presentation, most guidelines are described in diagrams, tables or if-then rules. This might suggest that sourcing decisions can be formalized using deterministic algorithms. Outsourcing decisions are however, strategic managerial decisions, which can not be structured totally and require creativity and common sense in equal doses.

5.1 Initial sourcing decision

Phase 1	Initial sourcing decision
Purpose	The aim of this phase is to decide whether specific parts of the IS function should be outsourced or be performed internally
Trigger	• a new IS activity is started • an internal IS activity might be better outsourced • an outsourced IS activity might be better internalized • an outsourced IS activity might be outsourced better. • the information plan is made/revised
Activities	5.1.1 Decide whether to initiate sourcing evaluation 5.1.2 Set up initial sourcing decision process 5.1.3 Determine goal variables 5.1.4 Assess current situation and changes planned 5.1.5 Assess situational factors 5.1.6 Determine attractiveness of outsourcing 5.1.7 Chose sourcing option
Results	An initial decision for each group of IS activities that is considered. The decision can be to keep the initial situation, to change from internal to external or vice versa, or to keep the initial sourcing but reorganize.
Proceed with	• if new activity is insourced: organize internally (not included in this model) • if new activity is outsourced: Phase 2, Designing the outsourcing arrangement • if currently internal activity kept internal: organize internally (not included) • if currently internal activity is outsourced: Phase 2, Designing the arrangement • if currently external activity is insourced: Phase 6, Termination of relationship • if currently external activity is kept external: Phase 5, Managing relationship

The initial sourcing decision concerns the principal decision whether or not to outsource. The term sourcing means choosing a source to provide IS products or services: either internal or external IS suppliers. A few alternatives are considered for each group of IS activities, such as performing the activities internally, outsourcing to one strategic partner or outsourcing separate units of work to multiple IS suppliers.

5.1.1 Decide whether to initiate sourcing evaluation

A sourcing evaluation should only be initiated if the dissatisfaction with the current situation and the potential improvements from changing the sourcing are expected, intuitively, to outweigh the costs and the risks of the evaluation process.

Starting to evaluate the possibilities of IS outsourcing or insourcing is a decision in itself, which engenders costs and has certain advantages and disadvantages. Evaluating sourcing can be a very educative process that may provide a stimulus for improvement of the IS function, regardless of the outcome of the evaluation, but it engenders high costs and may provoke unrest among IS staff.

The most apparent advantage of evaluating IS outsourcing or insourcing is the possibility that outsourcing or insourcing may indeed appear to be a better option. Another advantage is that the organization learns from a sourcing evaluation, regardless of the outcome. After a critical and systematic sourcing evaluation, general managers may be more aware of the role of the IS function, IS managers will have compared the performance of the IS function to external IS suppliers and may have obtained a stimulus and new ideas for improvement, and users may be more aware of the necessity, or the lack of it, of their needs and wishes. Top management may initiate a sourcing evaluation to test the IS function's performance and keep IS management alert. The information that needs to be collected for a systematic evaluation may be very useful for improving the IS function.

A sourcing evaluation usually takes considerable time, engenders high costs and puts high demands on internal staff and management. The actual demand depends on the availability of the information needed and on the depth of the evaluation, for example, whether the evaluation goes as far as issuing a (tentative) tender.

Another disadvantage of initiating a sourcing evaluation is the uncertainty and unrest it may cause among the IS staff, especially when transferring staff to an IS supplier is considered. This may result in a significant reduction in productivity and in the motivation of the staff. IS functionaries may look for employment elsewhere, and the most qualified ones will usually succeed. Users may lose trust in the internal IS department, run ahead of the outcome of the evaluation and start performing IS activities themselves or outsourcing to other suppliers.

If large changes in business conditions are expected, such as moving into a new market or a merger or take-over, the outsourcing decision should be postponed until the consequences of these changes become clear.

5.1.2 Set up initial sourcing decision process

Determine decision makers for initial sourcing decision

The decision team must include enough authority, expertise and representatives to ensure good decisions and the power and commitment for implementation. This often requires the inclusion of top management, IS management and (representatives of) IS staff and users.

The decision makers in the initial sourcing decision process must have enough expertise to take a sound decision, have enough authority to have the decision be implemented, and represent all stakeholders to obtain commitment. The following areas of expertise are necessary to take sound sourcing decisions:

* *business process* expertise, to know the information needs of the business processes,
* IT expertise, to know the possibilities and limitations of IT,
* *IS planning and design* expertise, to translate business needs to IT requirements,
* IS market expertise, such as knowledge of IS suppliers, their specialisms and qualities, prices and lead times of activities, and availability of software packages.
* outsourcing expertise, to determine the consequences of outsourcing, and to perform tendering procedures, contract negotiation, and manage relationships with external suppliers,
* legal expertise, to write or evaluate IS outsourcing contracts,
* financial expertise, to evaluate the costs of different sourcing options.

These types of expertise are seldom united in one functionary or department. A decision making team will include several functionaries from different organizational units.

Top management must be included in the decision team, to ensure the authority necessary to take far reaching decisions that may involve large amounts of money and many jobs. Other stakeholders should however also be included, because top management seldom has all the types of expertise mentioned above and the commitment of other stakeholders is often necessary to ensure that the decision is accepted.

IS management should be included in the decision team, to bring in expertise on IT, IS planning and the IS market. Financial and legal specialists should be consulted for the activities that require specific financial or legal expertise. If the organization has no experience with IS outsourcing, an outsourcing specialist may be hired.

Representatives of the IS staff must be involved, or at least be informed, if the sourcing decision involves the transfer of staff. In the Netherlands, works councils, ondernemingsraden or dienstcommissies, have a legal right to be consulted or even to give binding advice in strategic decisions that influence the position of employees. The commitment of the IS staff is also necessary to ensure cooperation in a possible transfer.

Management of user departments should be included to bring in business expertise and to assess the state and the necessity of the IS products and services that are under consideration. If the users are not involved in the sourcing evaluation, they may run ahead of the decision process and internalize or outsource activities by themselves.

Determine relationship sourcing decision and information planning

Sourcing decisions are part of IS management and should be integrated with the information planning process.

Outsourcing decisions are related strongly to information planning. Much of the information needed for the initial sourcing decision may already be available in the information plan. Outsourcing is but one of the organizational decisions that can be taken to improve the IS function. Previous sourcing decisions determine to a large extent the number and nature of IS activities that can be planned. Outsourcing should not be a one-off, isolated decision, but an integral and recurrent consideration within the information planning cycle.

This does not imply that, in exceptional cases, a large outsourcing decision can not be taken outside the information planning cycle, or that a first time sourcing evaluation can not be a separate project; however, the relationship with other organizational decisions and with the information planning process should always be maintained.

Determine part of IS function considered in initial sourcing decision

Demarcate and if necessary divide the part of the IS function under consideration.

IS outsourcing decision making does not always involve the entire IS function. The part of the IS function that is the subject of the decision process should be demarcated unambiguously, by stating which information systems, IS activities and IS components are involved.

If the part of the IS function that is under consideration is large or heterogeneous, it should be divided into a number of logical groups, each of which can then be the subject of a separate outsourcing decision process. The relationships between these groups must be taken into account, because different sourcing decisions for related parts of the IS function will complicate coordination between these parts.

Determine time scope of initial sourcing decision

Include long term consequences in the decision process and look beyond the time scope of the (potential) contract and beyond the life cycle of the technology in use.

Outsourcing decisions have long term consequences and changes in sourcing can not always be performed at short notice. Decision makers must determine the time scope of the implementation of their decisions and the time scope of the consequences they include in their considerations.

Certain sourcing alternatives may be very attractive in the first year but less attractive in consecutive years. The outcome of financial analyses, such as calculating the return on investment, is influenced by the time scope considered. The distinction between fixed and variable costs is another notion that is relative to the time scope considered. Some costs may be fixed for a year, but can be changed over a few years. Personnel costs, for example, can be lowered by not replacing employees that leave the organization, but this process will only lower costs significantly over a number of years.

Loss of knowledge, one of the possible consequences of outsourcing, usually yields problems only after a few years, when technology has changed so radically that the existing knowledge is outdated. Changing staffing levels takes considerable time, as does changing the location of resources and the legal relationship with an IS supplier.

The improvements gained from outsourcing usually appear shortly after implementation, while the negative consequences often emerge only after a few years, for example at the time the contract must be renewed or terminated or when the organization wants to implement major changes in the business processes or in the information technology they use. The time scope of the decision process should exceed the duration of the (projected) contract. The decision makers should also look beyond the life cycle of the technology that is in use, and determine what they want to do when the technology becomes outdated and must be replaced by newer technology.

Determine role of variables in initial sourcing decision

Be aware of restrictions in decision options. Determine which variables can be changed, which must be taken as they are, and which are to be optimized.

Decision makers must determine which variables they can and want to influence directly. These variables are the decision variables. The variables that the decision makers cannot change, or do not want to change, are the situational factors. The variables that are to be optimized by the decisions are the goal variables. These categories of variables have been described more extensively in Chapter 2.

Some of the variables that can be decision variables, will sometimes be restricted or fixed by decisions taken earlier or by higher management, and become situational factors. Decision variables can, in other situations, also be goal variables, if higher management demands certain results to be achieved

The number of internal IS staff, for example, is a variable that can take different roles. If decision makers can and want to consider changing the staffing levels of the IS function, by hiring additional staff or by firing or outsourcing staff, staffing levels is a decision variable. If higher management has decided previously that the organization does not need an internal IS department, hiring staff is not an option and the current staffing levels are a situational factor. If higher management demands that IS staffing levels are reduced, the decision team must take decisions that lead to this reduction, and staffing levels is a goal variable.

The decision makers should determine whether the restrictions of the decision variables are acceptable, sensible and not contradictory. Some previous decisions or decisions made by higher management may exclude options that would be beneficial to the organization, or may be so restrictive that the decision makers can not take responsibility for the remaining options.

5.1.3 Determine goal variables

Goal variables must be specified to evaluate the performance of internal or external IS suppliers and to compare alternative sourcing options. The relative importance of these variables depends on the value of the IS function to the client organization.

Goal variables are the variables that the decision makers want to optimize in their decision situation. Goal variables are necessary to evaluate the current situation and the performance of the current internal or external IS suppliers. They are also needed to compare alternative future sourcing options. A number of goal variables that are

costs	the total costs of preparing and performing an activity
lead time	the time between the moment the requirements for an activity have been specified and the moment the result of the activity has been accepted
quality	the degree to which the specified requirements are met
flexibility	the degree to which IS activities that are needed can be started, changed and stopped at any time
controllability	the degree to which costs, lead time and quality can be predicted, measured and if necessary be enforced.
continuity	the probability that a certain product or service will be delivered as long as the client organization has a need for it.

Table 5.2 Goal variables

relevant in most sourcing decisions are listed in Table 5.2. Additional goal variables can be included if necessary.

Reducing staffing levels can be a goal variable, but is usually a decision variable that is assumed to decrease costs and increase flexibility. Going back to the core business is not a goal variable in itself, but a strategy to reduce costs and increase flexibility and controllability.

Goal variables can have a different nature in different circumstances. There may be a specific value a goal variable must meet, for example, if the budget for an activity is limited or the maximum lead time is pre-determined. Other variables may be maximized or minimized.

Sourcing options will often score well on certain goal variables and less well on others. The relative importance of the goal variables must be determined, to be able to trade off variables against each other. The relative importance of goal variables can often be derived from the organization's strategy and from the role of the information systems under consideration. If the organization has a low cost strategy or if the systems are not very important to the organization, costs will be the most important variable. If the organization has a high quality strategy, or the systems are very important or critical, then quality, controllability and continuity must be given the highest priority. If the organization has a turbulent environment, or the information systems are changed frequently, lead time and flexibility are paramount.

Attaching different weights to goal variables should not lead to a one-sided emphasis on one or a few goal variables. All goal variables must at least be taken into account. It is especially dangerous to fixate on reductions of costs and staffing levels, without including the consequences to the other goal variables

Decision makers attach different importance to goal variables.

The stakeholders in an outsourcing evaluation will often have different opinions as to the relative importance of goal variables. These differences should be made explicit and be discussed, to avoid unclear and conflicting demands. Common viewpoints of stakeholders are:

• General and financial top managers have a tendency to emphasize reductions in costs and staffing levels, and to value controllability of services and costs.
• Users put more weight on lead time, functional quality, flexibility and continuity of service.
• IS staff are concerned mostly with the technical quality and with continuity of employment.
• IS management may be 'stuck in the middle' if users demand superior quality and top management demands low costs.

5.1.4 Assess current situation and changes planned

Sourcing decisions should be based on a thorough analysis of the current situation, the future requirements for staff and resources, and the triggers that gave rise to considering changing the sourcing.

Describe current systems
The information systems that are in use currently and the IS components they contain should be depicted in a "systems versus components" table such as Table 5.3 (duplicated from chapter 2). Each information system is represented by a column. Each IS component is represented by a row. The cells can be marked to indicate that a specific IS component is part of a specific information system. A letter c can be placed in the cells of the data categories to indicate that the data category is created by the information system; a letter u indicates that the data category is used by the information system.

Table 5.3 is filled in as an example, representing the relationships between three information systems for licenses and inspections, and their components. Looking at the rows for hardware, one can see that the registry system and the planning system use one mini computer and the reporting system uses another mini computer, while all three systems use the personal computers. If the organization depicted in Table 5.3 decides to outsource the operation of the mini computers but not of the personal computers, then part of the hardware of the three systems resides with an external IS supplier and part of it is operated internally. Provision must be made to ensure that the connections between the mini computers and the personal computers function well.

If the organization decides to outsource the reporting system, then mini computer 2 can be outsourced without any problem, but the personal computers will have to be shared by two systems operated

Types of components	Examples of components	Examples of information systems		
		license registry system	license inspection planning system	license inspection reporting system
Hardware	AS/400 mini computer 1	x	x	
	AS/400 mini computer			x
	personal computers	x	x	x
Software	database tool X	x	x	x
	reporting tool Y			x
	license application	x		
	planning application	x		
	reporting application		x	
People	users at head office	x	x	
	users at bus. units	x	x	
	IS staff	x	x	x
Procedures	proc.s for commissioning	x		
	proc.s for inspection	x	x	
	proc.s for reporting	x		
Data	licenses	c	u	u
	inspections		c	u

x = component is part of information system
c = data category is created by information system
u = data category is used by information system

Table 5.3 Example of "systems versus components" table

internally and one system operated by an external IS supplier. Again, provision must be made to ensure proper functioning.

A "systems versus components" table such as Table 5.3 can also be used to distinguish between infrastructural and non-infrastructural parts of the IS function. If a certain row has a relatively large number of marked cells, then that component is considered to be part of the IS infrastructure. In the example, the personal computers are considered to be part of the IS infrastructure, because they are part of all three information systems. Mini computer 2 is used only by the reporting system, and is therefore not considered to be part of the IS infrastructure

Describe current activities

The relationships between information systems and IS activities can be depicted in a table such as Table 5.4 (duplicated from chapter 2). Each information system is represented by a column. Each IS activity is represented by a row. Each cell represents a specific IS activity that is performed on a specific information system. The cells are then filled in with the name of the organizational unit that performs the activity.

IS Activities	Examples of information systems		
	license registry system	license inspection planning system	license inspection reporting system
planning	central IS department	central IS department	central IS department
development	business unit's IS department	supplier A	supplier A
implementation	business unit's IS department	business unit's IS department	business unit's IS department
maintenance	business unit's IS department	supplier A	supplier A
operation	supplier B	supplier B	supplier B

Table 5.4 Example of "activities versus systems" table

An example of the relationships between three information systems and IS activities is given in Table 5.4. In this example, the registry system is developed by the business unit's IS department and the other two systems by supplier A. If the information systems must exchange information, the development activities of the business unit's IS department must be coordinated with the development activities of supplier A. The implementation of the planning and the reporting system performed by the business unit's IS department has to be coordinated with the development of these systems by supplier A.

Future systems and activities

Long term contracts should be based not only on the current situation, but also on plans to extend or terminate systems. The necessity of all systems must be evaluated.

Describing future systems and activities is necessary to determine changes that are expected and that influence sourcing options, and to determine the capacity and resources needed, through time, to establish and sustain these systems.

The future information systems and activities are described in a manner similar to that for the current systems and activities. This description should include all plans to develop new information systems, and sustain, extend or terminate existing systems within the time scope of the decision process. These plans can be described by the changes that are expected, or by the final state after the changes. In the latter case, it may be useful to describe the planned state at the end of the time scope and at a number of intermediate stages.

Special attention should be paid to termination of systems. Information systems are sometimes sustained even if the need for their use has decreased or disappeared, and sourcing decisions are then taken based on the capacity requirements of systems that are no longer needed. This occurs mostly if users do not have to pay for services that are provided by internal personnel using internal resources that are already present and paid for, or if no regular information planning cycle is present. All information systems should be discussed on a regular basis, evaluating all external and internal costs against the benefits of sustaining the system.

Derive total requirements for IS staff and resources

The total amount of internal or external IS staff and resources that is required, over time, can be derived from the current systems and activities and the changes planned for these systems.

The requirements for IS staff can be described by the total number of person years for each type of job, specialism and expertise. The quantitative requirements for processing capacity can be expressed by the number of CPU's (central processing units) of a specific type or the number of MIPS (million instructions per second) on a specific type of computer. Storage capacity can be described by the number of megabytes of data that needs to be stored and communication capacity by the number of megabytes of data per second that need to be communicated between processing units. These quantitative measures are only rough indicators of the need for IS staff and resources. A complete description of all types of activities and components required will be needed when a tendering procedure is started.

Evaluate current situation

Be critical towards the perceptions and triggers that initiated the sourcing evaluation. Compare the current situation to similar situations and to plans and objectives.

The aim of this phase is to evaluate the current IS function with regard to the goal variables. This is necessary to identify areas that need improvement and to have a point of reference for comparing sourcing options. A point of reference is always necessary, even if it has already been decided that the activities will be outsourced, because suppliers will often offer improvements relative to the current situation, such as reducing costs or lead times by a certain percentage.

Cost evaluation should be based on a complete overview of all costs and correct allocation of these costs to the pertinent activities. When evaluating the costs of internal IS activities, all indirect costs, fixed costs, transaction costs and costs incurred by non-IS employees should be included, and these costs should be allocated to pertinent parts of the IS function. Existing financial administrations are often not detailed enough and may use different cost allocation principles. Evaluation of the costs of external IS activities should include the internal costs of market research, tendering, negotiation, and management of the outsourcing relationship.

Evaluation of *lead times* should include the time to prepare the activity. With internal IS activities, this includes the time needed to hire or retrain IS staff, if necessary, and the time until the internal IS department has capacity available to start the activity. Lead times of external IS activities should include the time for tendering, contracting and familiarizing the IS supplier.

The *quality* of IS activities should be evaluated by comparing the performance to the requirements as specified. If requirements are not specified or are constantly changing, quality can not be measured objectively, and only a subjective judgment can be made.

Flexibility of IS activities can be evaluated at the level of the IS portfolio, i.e., how easy new activities and systems can be initiated, and at the level of the individual activities, i.e., how easy the requirements or the planning of the activities can be adapted. Evaluating flexibility of internal activities should include the possibility of retraining and using flexible employment arrangements. Evaluating the flexibility of external activities must include the possibilities and limitations of changing requirements during the activities.

Evaluation of the *continuity* of IS activities should be focused on the probability that the product or service will be delivered as long as the client organization has a need for it. Continuity should not be interpreted as the availability of operational systems, because that is part of the quality requirements for operational services. Continuity should not be restricted to the chance that a supplier goes bankrupt. The continuity of internal IS activities can be endangered by a high turnover of critical IS staff, by essential knowledge and skills being concentrated in one or a few employees, by the risk of not being able to attract and maintain enough qualified personnel, and by the risk that the internal demand for specific products or services decreases to a level that the product or service can no longer be delivered at reasonable costs. The continuity of external IS activities depends on the risk that the IS supplier goes bankrupt or gets involved in a merger or take-over, on the risk that the supplier stops releasing new versions of packages or tools, on the risk that the supplier withdraws from the pertinent market or product, and on the risk of high turnover of the supplier's staff.

The evaluation of the current situation must be compared to certain norms to judge the current performance. The current situation can be compared to the situation in previous years, to similar IS activities within the organization, to similar IS activities in similar organizations, or to current plans and objectives for the IS function.

Comparing internal and external services is useful only if the products or services considered are really similar. This is often very difficult, because information systems are not a homogeneous product and information technology changes very fast. When comparing the current situation with the situation in previous years, the portfolio of IS activities has often changed, for example because systems were terminated or performance requirements were increased. Comparing costs, lead times or quality of the total portfolio is then useless. The same holds for comparing with similar activities or similar organizations.

Decision makers should be careful when comparing the current situation with IS activities in similar organizations. This type of comparison is often called "*benchmarking.*" Comparative metric service companies, such as Real Decisions Inc., Compass and Nolan, Norton & Co., measure the efficiency of an organization's IS function against a database of companies in similar industries. These metrics can tell a company how it compares to its peers or to external IS suppliers. These benchmarks have only limited value, because the comparisons usually neglect differences in the IS products and services delivered and in other characteristics of the organization. Having higher IS costs than competitors is not necessarily a sign of inefficiency.

The triggers and perceptions that initiated the sourcing evaluation should be examined critically. Sourcing evaluations are often started because managers perceive the IS function to be expensive, uncontrollable or inflexible. These perceptions are not always founded on a thorough knowledge of the actual circumstances and comparable situations. Managers do not always know about the complexity of and efforts needed for IS activities and therefore, the costs and lead times that are reasonable for IS activities.

Analyze problems current situation

Watch out for choosing outsourcing if problems have been encountered. Many problems are not caused by insourcing and are not solved automatically by outsourcing.

If the evaluation of the current situation is unsatisfactory with regard to one or several goal variables, the conclusion should not always be to change the sourcing. Many problems are not caused by the source of provision and are not solved automatically by changing the sourcing. Analyze why the current situation is not satisfactory, what the causes may be, and what solutions may be considered, other than changing the sourcing. A number of common problems, causes and solutions are listed in Table 5.5.

5.1.5 Assess situational factors

The optimal sourcing decision depends on the specific situation. Situational factors determine whether outsourcing or insourcing is the best choice.

The aim of this phase is to analyze the situation at hand with regard to a number of factors that have proven to be relevant to outsourcing decision making. These factors are grouped into characteristics of the IS function and the information systems, the client

Problem	Possible causes	Solutions
high costs	wrong perception	• improve administration and allocation of IS costs • improve cost/benefit analyses • improve awareness of possibilities and costs of IS
	uncontrollable or unnecessary user requests	• improve cost awareness • introduce chargeback system • introduce method for evaluating IS investments • improve and regulate information planning cycle
	IS supplier performs unnecessary activities	• introduce or improve chargeback system
high lead times	IS supplier does not operate efficiently capacity is insufficient or is not used optimal	• consolidate IS units or IS resources • automate IS activities • increase capacity • evaluate necessity of all IS products and services • improve capacity planning and usage • require users to commit to capacity planning
	instable user requirements or unclear priorities	• have users commit to requirements • improve analysis of urgency of activities
	IS supplier does not operate efficiently	• improve project planning methods and techniques
low quality	wrong perception operate efficiently	• improve awareness of complexity of IS • describe requirements and report compliance
	requirements not met	• training of IS staff • increasing quality control • other quality improvement measures
low flexibility	high fixed costs	• lease or rent hardware and software • share IS resources among business units
	restrictions by current staff's, skills & capacity	• use flexible employment arrangements • have users plan changes in technology • encourage job rotation and retraining of IS staff
low controllability	insufficient planning, measuring or enforcing	• tight budgeting and reporting procedures. • improve incentives for high quality
low continuity	high turnover of IS staff	• increase career opportunities • adjust rewards to market values • improve image of IS department

Table 5.5 Causes and solutions of common problems with IS function

organization and the environment, and the IS market. Some of the factors are explained below. The other factors were described in Chapter 4.

Assess characteristics of the IS function and information systems

The situational factors of the IS function and current and future information systems are summarized in Table 5.6.

The *scale* of the IS activities refers to the scale at which the (average) IS supplier performs the pertinent IS activity, as compared to the scale at which the client organization needs the activity. *Scale advantages* is the degree to which the efficiency of the IS activity generally increases if the scale of the activity increases. *Barriers for re-use* are present if the client organization's requirements impede the IS supplier reusing knowledge, skills or resources deployed or acquired for the client organization.

Volume uncertainty is the lack of information about future changes in volume of use or required volume of resources. *Technical uncertainty* is the amount of uncertainty about future technological developments and the consequences for the organization. *Functional uncertainty* is the uncertainty about the functional requirements for the information systems.

---

scale of the IS activity
scale advantages of the IS activity
barriers for re-use
standardization of IS components
interconnectedness of information systems
measurability of the requirements
volume uncertainty
technical uncertainty
functional uncertainty
distribution of the IS components
heterogeneity of the IS components
specifiability of the requirements
human asset specificity
physical asset specificity
site specificity
frequency of the IS activity
switching costs of client
complexity of the information systems
innovativeness of the information systems
variability of the requirements
infrastructure
programmability of the IS activity
length of relationship with IS supplier
competitive use of IS
exactingness of technical requirements
confidentiality of software and data
criticality of information systems

Table 5.6 Situational factors of IS function and information systems

Distribution is the geographical dispersion of IS components. Distribution is high if hardware, data, or users are dispersed over many locations. Heterogeneity is the variety of the types of IS components that are in use or are needed.

Specifiability is whether the functional and technical requirements for systems or activities can be specified in enough detail and in advance. *Measurability* is whether the client organization can determine objectively and relatively easily whether the products or services delivered by the supplier meet the functional and technical requirements.

Interconnectedness is the number and complexity of relationships between the systems or activities under consideration and with other systems or other activities in the client organization. Relationships between information systems can be determined by filling in a "systems versus components" table. Infrastructure is the degree to which the components under consideration are used by many information systems.

Specificity is the degree to which a system is specific for the client organization, and needs investments by the supplier that can not be reused for other clients or activities. A system can be unique, common within the client organization's industry or common among all organizations. A supplier may need specific investments in location, knowledge and tools. Site specificity can be present for example if hardware needs extensive provisions, such as air conditioning and physical security measures, or if very regular contact is necessary between the client organization and the IS suppliers, such as help desk, system design, and consultancy. *Physical asset specificity* refers to how specific the IS resources must be, such as tools, hardware configurations. *Human asset specificity* is the amount of learning, specialization, learning on the job and knowledge of the client organization's processes that is required. *Switching costs* are the costs of outsourcing the pertinent activities to another supplier or re-internalizing the activities.

Innovativeness is the degree to which the activities required are new, either to the client organization, to the IS supplier or to both. Systems can for example be innovative in their functional or technical requirements, in the new combination of existing functions or technologies, or in their scale. *Variability* is the expected amount of change in volume and functional and technical requirements of the systems that are in use.

Exactingness is the severity of the technical requirements. Technical requirements, such as performance, security, reliability, maintainability, portability and usability, can be very high for example, for financial transaction systems, real time systems, or military intelligence systems. *Confidentiality* is a characteristic of data and software. These components are confidential if they concern confidential personal or company information.

Criticality is the degree to which the continuity and availability of systems are essential to the client organization. This can be determined by analyzing how much of the business processes and the revenues depend on the system and how long the systems can be down before the organization would face serious consequences.

Competitiveness is whether the systems or activities distinguish the company from its competitors. Competitiveness should be distinguished from criticality. A system can be critical but be non-competitive, and vice versa. To a supermarket, for example, the cash desk system is critical, because the supermarket can not function if the system is not available. The system is however usually not competitive, unless the supermarket has found a way to use the system for example, to obtain information on buyer behavior in a way that competitors have not thought of. Competitive is often opposed to commodity, but commodity refers to being widely available, which does not always coincide with being non-competitive. Systems can be non-competitive but still be non-available. Systems that are widely available however, are usually not competitive, because competitors can also obtain the systems.

Assess characteristics of the client organization and the environment

The situational factors of the client organization are summarized in Table 5.7 and explained below.

IS maturity is the users' and managers' experience with IT, their attitude towards IT, their ability to determine their information needs and identify useful applications of IT in their business processes, and their awareness of the importance and role of IT.

Structuredness of business processes can be determined by analyzing the degree of formalism or programmability. Processes can be very formalized, for example if the processes are governed by legal

---

IS maturity of user community
uncertainty of business processes
complexity of business processes
structuredness of business processes
variability of business processes
uniqueness of business processes
information intensity of business processes
heterogeneity of user community
buyer concentration
importance of volume for client
resource acquisition
IS use by competitors
IS outsourcing by competitors
competition in the client organization's industry

Table 5.7 Situational factors of client organization

or company regulations. Many operational processes in government organizations and structured information processes, such as accounting and financial and legal transactions, are very formalized, as opposed to for example, managerial decision making or research.

The variability, uncertainty, complexity and uniqueness of the business processes are operationalized analogous to the variability and so on of information systems.

Information intensity refers to the information content of the business process, as opposed to the physical content. Business processes can include physical transformation processes, such as transporting, welding, assembling. These physical transformation processes always have an informational component, for tracking the products and the resources and controlling the activities. Many of the critical business processes in manufacturing organizations can be characterized as service activities and consist of information processing. Other business processes do not have a physical component and deliver abstract products or services that are materialized in information, such as financial transactions, insurance policies, and court decisions. Other business processes are aimed at producing information in itself, such as market research, historical research, a statistics office and consultancy.

IS use by competitors refers to the way the client organization's competitors use IS and IT and whether competitors use IS to distinguish themselves from their competitors. IS outsourcing by competitors is whether competitors have outsourced their IS function.

Competition in the client organization's industry is the intensity and turbulence of competition in the client organization's market segments. The fierceness of competition determines the rate of change of business processes and the speed of change required.

Assess characteristics of the IS market

Conditions in the IS market influence the attractiveness of IS outsourcing. The situational factors of the IS market are summarized in Table 5.8. It is important to analyze these factors not for the total IS market but for the specific market segment to which the client organization is outsourcing or is considering to outsource to.

The number of adequate suppliers is the number of appropriate suppliers that can deliver the pertinent product or service. It is not a characteristic of the total IS market, but of the pertinent market segment. The total number of IS suppliers is generally large, but the number of suppliers that are able to deliver specific products or services and have the necessary skills and resources for the pertinent activities may be very small. Client organizations should determine how many suppliers are specialized in their business process, the technology they use and the activities they need. If an agricultural trade organization, for example, needs an order entry and manage-

---

number of adequate suppliers
supplier's barriers to entry and exit
availability of market information
risk aversion of suppliers
switching costs of suppliers
degree of subcontracting
supplier concentration
importance of volume for IS supplier
degree of uncertainty absorption
selective use of information

Table 5.8 Situational factors of IS market segment

ment system that needs to run on a specific mini computer with a specific database management system, they must determine how many IS suppliers have knowledge of agriculture, trade, order management systems, and the specific hardware and system software. Client organizations must also be aware of alliances between suppliers. If the number of suppliers seems fairly large, but many or these suppliers are interrelated, then the actual choice for the client organization is less than they may expect. The number of suppliers can be determined by conducting market research or by issuing a preliminary request for proposal. The number of adequate proposals received on an earlier request for proposal for a similar activity can also indicate the number of adequate suppliers.

The availability of market information is whether client organizations can obtain sufficient market information to select and assess suppliers. Market information that client organizations need includes information on suppliers, their specialisms and qualities, products and services available, and average prices and lead times for specific products and services. Client organizations must know the suppliers business records, that is, whether the suppliers have shown a steady and continuous growth and are healthy and coherent organizations.

Supplier concentration refers to the number and size distribution of the suppliers in the pertinent market segment and the scale at which these suppliers perform the pertinent activities.

Subcontracting is whether IS suppliers need to rely heavily on subcontractors to perform IS activities for a client organization. Subcontracting is not necessarily disadvantageous, as long as it is a deliberate strategy of the IS suppliers and they have a long term steady relationship with their subcontractors.

5.1.6 Determine attractiveness of outsourcing

The basic attractiveness of outsourcing can be derived from the situational factors described in the previous section. These factors influence intermediate variables and these intermediate variables can be used to determine the attractiveness of outsourcing.

Determine intermediate variables

The number of situational factors, decision variables and goal variables is too large to specify all the interrelationships between these variables. Therefore, a number of intermediate variables are distinguished. Each intermediate variable is influenced by a number of situational factors. In the following steps, the intermediate variables are used to determine the attractiveness of outsourcing and to design the most appropriate outsourcing relationship.

The relationships between the situational factors and the intermediate variables are summarized in Table 5.9. A cell marked with a + (plus sign) denotes a positive relationship, which means that a high value of the pertinent situational factor will result in a high value of the pertinent intermediate variable. A - (minus sign) indicates a negative relationship, where a high value of the situational factor means a lower value of the intermediate variable.

The positive relationship between number of suppliers and market pressure on supplier, for example, means that a higher number of IS suppliers will lead to higher market pressure on the supplier.

The negative relationship between uniqueness and supplier's economies of scale means that the higher the uniqueness of the systems or activities, the lower the supplier's economies of scale will be, because the supplier will not be able to use knowledge or resources from previous assignments for other client organizations and can not re-use the knowledge and systems for future assignments.

The values of the intermediate variables follow from filling in Table 5.9. Determine the value of each situational factor in the specific situation and fill in this value in the left-most column. Analyze each intermediate variable by considering each situational factor that has a relationship with that intermediate variable. A high value for the situational factor and a positive relationship means a high value of the intermediate variable. A low value and a positive relationship, or a high value and a negative relationship, yields a low value of the intermediate variable. An intermediate variable is influenced by several situational factors. The net result of the situational factors determines the value of the intermediate variable, which can be filled in the bottom row. Each of the intermediate variables is discussed below.

Strategicness
Strategicness concerns the role of the information systems in the organizational processes. Systems and the corresponding activities are called strategic if they are essential for the continuity of the organization. This is the case if the systems are critical to the organization or if they give the organization a competitive advantage.

	Situational factor	Value	econ.s of scale	market pressure	control	opportunism	inf. asymmetry	power	strategicness
Information systems and IS function	scale	...	+						
	scale advantages	...	+						
	barriers for re-use	...	-						
	standardization	...		+					
	interconnectedness	...	-						
	measurability	...			+	-			
	volume uncertainty	...			-	+	+		
	technical uncertainty	...			-	+	++		
	functional uncertainty	...			-	+	++		
	distribution	...	-						
	heterogeneity	...	-		-				
	specifiability	...			-				
	human asset specificity	...	-		+				
	physical asset specificity	...	-		+				
	site specificity	...	-		+				
	frequency	...			-				
	switching costs of client	...			+				
	complexity	...			+				
	innovativeness	...		-					
	variability	...		-					
	infrastructure	...		-					
	programmability	...				-			
	length of relationship	...				-			
	competitive use of IS	...	-					+	
	exactingness	...	+						
	criticality	...					-	+	
	confidentiality	...	-				-	+	
client organization and environment	IS maturity	...			+	-			
	uncertainty of business processes	...			-	+	+		
	complexity of business processes	...	-		-				
	structuredness of business processes	...			+				
	variability of business processes	...			-				
	information intensity	...				-		-	+
	heterogeneity of user community	...	-		-				
	buyer concentration	...						+	
	importance of volume for client	...						-	
	resource acquisition	...						+	
	IS use by competitors	...							+
	IS outsourcing by competitors	...	+						-
IS market and suppliers	number of adequate suppliers	...		+		-			
	suppliers' barriers to entry and exit	...		-					
	availability of market information	...		+					
	risk aversion of suppliers	...					+		
	switching costs of suppliers	...						+	
	degree of subcontracting	...			-				
	supplier concentration	...						-	
	importance of volume for IS supplier	...						+	
	absorbing uncertainty	...						-	
	selective use of information	...						-	
	Resulting value of intermediate variables	...	...	...	...	...	...	...	

+ = positive relationship	- = negative relationship

Table 5.9 Relationships between situational factors and intermediate variables

Situational factor	Value	econ.s of scale	market pressure	control	inform. asymmetry
scale	H	+			
standardization	L		+		
interconnectedness	H			-	
measurability	L				-
Resulting value of intermediate variables		H	L	L	H
+ = positive relationship		- = negative relationship			

Table 5.10 Example of deriving intermediate variables

Market pressure

External IS suppliers are often assumed to be more efficient because they face market pressure and will go bankrupt if they under perform. In practice, the IS market is not transparent enough. For most parts of the IS function, there is a limited number of suppliers, no homogeneous and specified products, no uniform terminology and not enough information on prices and lead time, and specialism of supplier. Many client organizations can not assess the quality and efficiency of their supplier. Significant switching costs often impair the client organization's options of choosing another supplier.

Market pressure is high if the number of suppliers, availability of market information and standardization and normalization is high and if uniqueness and the size of suppliers is low. Outsourcing is possible and sensible only if a sufficient number of IS suppliers deliver the services the company needs and have experience with the pertinent technology and activities as well as with the pertinent business processes and markets.

Information asymmetry

Information asymmetry refers to whether the client organization can obtain enough information to measure and evaluate the performance of the IS supplier. Information asymmetry is high if the measurability, programmability and the length of the relationship are low and if the uncertainty of the requirements or the business processes is high.

Opportunism

The risk of opportunism on the side of the IS supplier can be determined by analyzing the switching costs, site specificity, physical asset specificity and human asset specificity. These factors together determine to what degree the client organization will become dependent on the IS supplier.

Power
The power of the client organization relative to the supplier is high if the criticality and confidentiality of the systems, the information intensity and the importance of the volume to the client are low, and if the buyer concentration, the client's control over resource acquisition, the switching costs of the supplier and the importance of the volume for the supplier are high.

Control
Whether the client organization will remain in control over the supplier depends on how easy it is to specify the requirements, to measure compliance to these requirements, and on the degree of uncertainty, complexity, innovativeness, and the level of subcontracting.

Economies of scale
IS suppliers can only achieve economies of scale if they perform similar activities on a considerably larger scale than their clients, if the activities have inherent scale advantages and if there are no barriers for re-use. Economies of scale decrease if systems are distributed, heterogeneous, highly interconnected, or specific, and if confidentiality or competitiveness impede the IS supplier for reusing knowledge and resources.

Derive fitness for outsourcing
A decision scheme for the initial sourcing decision using the intermediate variables is depicted in Figure 5.2. This decision scheme is a very generalized and simplified scheme that should be used with care, and only gives a general indication of the attractiveness of outsourcing. The questions in the decision scheme correspond to the intermediate variables discussed above.

The decision scheme should be followed separately for each part of the IS function. Parts of the IS function can be classified using the three dimensions given in chapter 2: the information systems, the IS activities and the IS components. Typical differences between specific parts of the IS function, and the consequent fitness for outsourcing, are given in the following sections

Differences between information systems
In general, categories of information systems have different values for the situational factors. These factors, and the consequent fitness for outsourcing, are listed in Table 5.11. Primary systems and primary support systems, as defined in chapter 2, are usually more specific and critical and less stable than secondary systems. Primary systems will therefore be less attractive for outsourcing than primary support

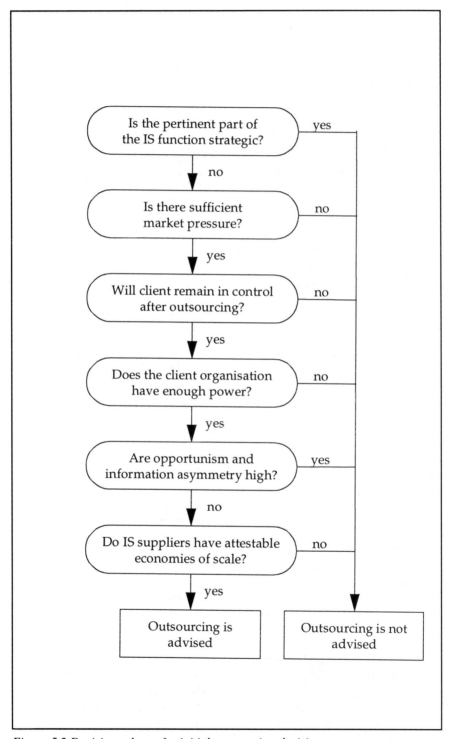

Figure 5.2 Decision scheme for initial outsourcing decision

	Primary systems	Primary support systems	Secondary systems
uncertainty	high	high	low
innovativeness	high	medium	low
specifiability	medium/low	medium/low	high
specificity	high	medium	low
exactingness	high	high	medium
criticality	high	high	medium
competitiveness	high	high	low
structuredness	medium	medium	high
number of suppliers	medium	medium	high
Fitness for outsourcing	Low	Medium	High

Table 5.11 Information systems' fitness for outsourcing

	Planning	Developm.	Implement.	Mainten.	Operation
uncertainty	high	high	high	medium	low
innovativeness	high	high	medium	medium	medium
specifiability	low	medium	low	medium	high
interconnectedness	high	high	medium	high	high
specificity	high	medium	high	medium	low
switching costs	medium	medium	high	high	high
exactingness	low	medium	high	high	high
confidentiality	high	medium	medium	medium	high
criticality	high	high	high	high	high
competitiveness	high	high	medium	medium	low
number of suppliers	medium	medium	medium	medium	high
Fitness for outsourcing	low	medium	low	medium	high

Table 5.12 IS activities' fitness for outsourcing

systems, which are in turn, less fit for outsourcing than secondary systems, which are widely available and non-specific.

Differences between IS activities

Activities also show a general pattern with regard to the situational factors (see Table 5.12). Planning is the most idiosyncratic and strategic activity, followed by development and to a lesser extent implementation and maintenance, while operation is the least specific and strategic activity.

Differences between IS components

The situational factors have different values for different IS components (see Table 5.13). Hardware is the least specific component. Software and procedures are widely available and non-specific for certain functions but require tailor-made solutions for other functions. Data and people are almost always organization-specific.

	Hardware	Software	Data	Procedures	Users
uncertainty	low	medium	high	high	high
innovativeness	low	high	high	high	medium
specifiability	high	high	medium	medium	medium
interconnectedness	high	medium	low	medium	ow
infrastructure	high	medium	low	low	high
specificity	low	med/high	high	high	high
switching costs	low	medium	high	high	high
exactingness	high	medium	medium	medium	medium
confidentiality	low	med/high	med/high	medium	medium
criticality	high	high	high	medium	medium
competitiveness	low	high	high	high	medium
number of IS suppliers	high	med/high	low	medium	low
Fitness for outsourcing	high	medium	low	medium	low

Table 5.13 IS component's fitness for outsourcing

5.1.7 Chose sourcing option

Include the alternatives of maintaining or improving the current situation. Evaluate each option with regard to the goal variables. Chose an alternative, based on the evaluation and the relative importance of the variables.

Develop alternative sourcing options

In this phase, a number of alternative internal and external sourcing options should be developed. It is important to include in this step the alternatives of maintaining the current situation and of improving the current situation without changing the sourcing. Maintaining the current situation has the advantage that no change costs and time is needed, no learning and familiarizing has to take place and there is no risk of failure or personnel leaving the organization. The disadvantage is that if the current situation is not satisfactory, these problems remain. Some managers might see deciding not to change to be a sign of a lack of decision power and want to change something, sometimes regardless of the consequences, to show their influence or advance their careers. Other managers might have the opinion that change or reorganization is necessary each couple of years to keep the organization alert and to provide an opportunity to change practices that could not be changed in a stable situation.

Options for improvement without changing sourcing have been given in section 5.1.4, especially for improvements in internal provision. Options for improving an already outsourced situation can be found in section 5.2, which covers designing the outsourcing relationship.

Changing the sourcing means outsourcing if the current situation is internal provision and insourcing if activities are currently outsourced. Several ways of sourcing can be included as decision alternatives, such

as transferring IS staff and other resources to a supplier or reemploy-
ing current staff and resources and outsourcing activities to several
suppliers.

External IS suppliers have to be evaluated as to their actual
performance and abilities instead of assuming superiority based on
theoretical considerations. The internal IS department and external IS
suppliers have to be compared on an equal basis. The comparison
should include the same products and services, at the same quality
level and within the same time constraints.

The internal IS department has to have a chance to include
improvements in their bid. Internal departments are sometimes
forced, by organizational politics, historical reasons or interference
from higher management, to satisfy individual users' idiosyncratic
needs and maintain certain inefficient practices. These requirements
are often not made to suppliers. If the department has the authority to
institute best practices, it might be able to operate better and more
cheaply. If the decision makers know how well the IS department could
operate, they can negotiate a better contract with an outside provider.

Evaluate alternative sourcing options

*Evaluate the internal and external alternatives on an equal basis.
Include the initial and the recurrent costs and efforts.*

The alternatives must be compared on an equal basis, which
means that the same activities are considered and that the same
requirements for the activities are made for all alternatives.

The alternatives that imply a change from the current situation
must be evaluated with regard to the initial costs and benefits of the
change and to the recurrent costs and benefits after implementation.
If yearly costs and recurrent savings are expected, a return on
investment or payback period can be calculated. Allocations over time
must be incorporated, by calculating net present value of cash flows
and by incorporating risks and uncertainties with regard to future
cash flows. If short term savings are expected but higher costs over the
long term, time preferences must be included.

The alternative sourcing options, including maintaining the initial
situation, can now be evaluated with regard to the goal variables. The
results can be summarized in a table such as Table 5.14. Each row
represents an alternative and each column is one of the goal variables.
The importance that is assigned to each of the goal variables is filled
in the first cell of each column. The scores of each alternative on each
goal variable can be filled in the pertinent cell.

Costs may also be represented by the actual amount of money
involved and the lead time by the actual time, if such information is
available or can be obtained easily. Detailed evaluation of external

Alternatives	Goal variable						Result
	Costs	Lead time	Quality	Control	Flexibility	Continuity	
Importance	*medium*	*medium*	*high*	*very high*	*high*	*medium*	
Keep internal	-	-	-	+	o	++	-
Consolidate internally	+	+	-	+	+	+	+
Outsource staff and resources	++	+	+	—	+	—	o
Selective outsourcing	+	o	+	+	++	+	+

Table 5.14 Example of evaluating alternatives

alternatives may require some market research or even issuing a (tentative) call for tender.

Choose sourcing option

Determine the alternative that scores best on the most important goal variables. A more quantitative evaluation is possible by attaching a numerical value to the importance of each of the goal variables, and to each cell of Table 5.14. The importance of a goal variable can for example be represented by a value between 1 and 5, with 1 signifying very low importance and 5 signifying very high importance. Each cell can be filled in with a score between 1 and 5 for the pertinent alternative with regard to the pertinent goal variable, with 1 signifying that the alternative scores very badly and 5 signifying the alternative scores very well with regard to that goal variable. An overall score can then be obtained by multiplying the scores by the weight factor of each goal variable and adding up the results. The result of each alternative can be filled in in the last column. The alternative with the highest overall result will be the most beneficial.

One must be careful, however, with this quantification, as it may suggest that the best alternative can be determined by simple calculation and may lead to overconfidence in the overall score

5.2 Designing the outsourcing arrangement

Phase 2	**Designing the outsourcing arrangement**
Purpose	The aim of this phase is to design the future outsourcing arrangement, maximizing the client organization's flexibility and control and ensuring that the improvements and goals of the outsourcing decision are achieved
Trigger	• a new IS activity is outsourced • an internal IS activity is outsourced • an outsourced IS activity might be outsourced more effectively • the IS supplier selected does not agree with the previous design

Activities	5.2.1 Design the outsourcing relationship
	5.2.2 Divide work among suppliers and contracts
	5.2.3 Design management structure
	5.2.4 Design operational structure
	5.2.5 Internal organization of outsourcing coordination
Results	A design for the future outsourcing arrangement, describing the future relationship, division among suppliers and contracts, management and operational structure and internal organization of the coordination.
Proceed with	• if a supplier has not yet been selected: phase 3, selecting the IS supplier
	• if a supplier has been selected and the supplier agrees with the design: phase 4, Implementation of the outsourcing decision

The previous steps may have resulted in a decision to pursue outsourcing or to improve an existing outsourcing situation. The new outsourcing situation must then be designed. The resulting design can be included in the tendering process and be implemented after choosing the IS supplier.

Two major objectives should be kept in mind when designing the outsourcing relationship. Decision makers should realize that the advantages and improvements that were the reason for choosing outsourcing can only be realized if the outsourcing relationship is designed in a way that enables these improvements to be achieved. A well-designed outsourcing arrangement increases the likelihood that expected improvements will be realized and potential dangers are avoided or dealt with.

The second objective is that the outsourcing relationship should be designed to maximize the client organization's flexibility and control and to ensure that the client organization remains able to deploy information systems to its advantage and adapt to changing circumstances and needs. Flexibility and control is maintained by maximizing competition; to this end, managers should take a selective approach towards outsourcing and outsource well-defined separate IS activities to multiple suppliers under separate contracts. The internal IS department and external IS suppliers then compete constantly to obtain assignments.

5.2.1 Design the outsourcing relationship

The outsourcing relationship determines the amount and type of control the client organization has over the IS supplier.

Determine legal relationship

The legal relationship between a client organization and an IS supplier can vary from the parties being part of the same legal entity to being totally separated legal entities. In between they can be separate but owned by the same parent company or the client organization can totally or partially own the IS supplier. The possible legal relationships and the advantages and disadvantages are listed in Table 5.15

All types of legal relationships except that with an independent supplier imply certain restrictions for the client and the supplier. A supplier within the same holding or otherwise owned by the client organization has very limited options for control but the client organization still bears the financial risk of the supplier. With a joint venture, the risk can be shared, but the benefits are also shared.

Economic relationship

The economic relationship refers to the percentage of the IS supplier's business volume generated by the client organization and to the percentage of the client organization's IS costs that are spent on the IS supplier. It is advisable to avoid large differences in these percentages to avoid an unequal power balance.

Outsourcing almost all activities to one supplier should be avoided, because that makes the client organization overly dependent on the supplier. This gives the supplier too much power and yields a large risk if the supplier goes bankrupt or decides to withdraw from the relationship.

A supplier that is dependent on one client organization for most of the revenues has other dangers. The client organization can not withdraw a significant part of the outsourced activities from the relationship without causing the bankruptcy of the supplier. The client may have social or ethical concerns about this and may suffer because of disruptions in the other activities performed by the supplier.

Legal relationship	Advantages	Disadvantages
same legal entity	maximum hierarchical control	client bears full risk of capacity
same holding	more business-like conflict resolution by holding	no real competition
client owns supplier	client can appoint top management and direct general strategy	client bears full risk but only has shareholder authorities
joint venture	risks and rewards are shared between client and supplier high commitment and motivation of client and supplier	limited flexibility and few economies of scale
independent supplier	full flexibility and possibilities for economies of scale	less commitment

Table 5.15 Considerations for legal relationships

Determine transactional relationship

A client organization may have an agreement with an IS supplier that spans multiple transactions. The transactional relationship refers to the type of agreement between the client and supplier. The possible transactional relationships and the advantages and disadvantages are listed in Table 5.16.

An informal working relationship is a result of previous collaborations between the client and the supplier. This is a very useful relationship, because the supplier is already familiar with the client organization and the client knows the qualities of the supplier.

Guaranteed spending, in which a client organization agrees to spend a certain amount of money over a certain number of years with the IS supplier, should be avoided as much as possible, as it is a major obstacle for real competition and does not motivate the staff to deliver high quality at low costs. IS suppliers that take over staff from a client organization often demand guaranteed spending in exchange for an employment guarantee for the IS staff taken over. High guaranteed spending should not be necessary if a supplier really achieves economies of scale, for example by having the staff work for other client organizations. If a guaranteed spending agreement can not be avoided, the following guidelines should be followed:

- the amount should be below the previous internal costs, preferably between 80 and 90%, and decrease quickly over a few years,

Transactional relationship	Advantages	Disadvantages
none	maximum flexibility	high costs of finding and acquainting supplier
informal working relationship	maximum flexibility reduced costs and time for familiarizing supplier	no savings on costs of contracting
cooperation agreement	reduced contract costs, only project-specific clauses necessary	
trust-based partnership	high flexibility no detailed contracts required	danger of loss of trust if trust is lost, client has no means to enforce performance of supplier
business partnership	high motivation for supplier	part of revenues go to supplier
guaranteed spending	necessary to guarantee employment of staff transferred to supplier	no competition, no motivation for supplier to deliver high quality and efficiency, no flexibility, no options to switch

Table 5.16 Considerations for transactional relationships

preferably to between 40 and 60% within three years,
- the amount should not be divided further into amounts for periods shorter than one year or into separate amounts for different IS activities,
- the client organization must retain the freedom to call for tender, to work with other suppliers and to re-internalize activities if wanted,
- tariffs have to be agreed for work above the guaranteed amount,
- the budget for the guaranteed spending must be allocated to or coordinated by a central unit, to avoid spending too much or too little.

Suppliers often offer to be strategic partners. They interpret partnership as a relationship based upon trust instead of the letters of the contract, and they offer to be a partner who assists the client organization in thinking about their IS strategy and suggesting new applications of IT in the client's business processes. These trust-based partnerships should be avoided, for the following reasons:

- Forming an IS strategy requires knowledge of new products, markets and strategies of the client organization, via both formal and informal channels. One may doubt whether the supplier can obtain and use this information and whether it is wise of the organization to share this information with its supplier, who may work for competitors.
- IS strategy formulation requires very different skills and knowledge from system development or operation. Suppliers that are good at operating large data centers are not necessarily good at facilitating IS strategy formulation.
- The supplier that performs many operational IS activities has an interest in certain outcomes of the IS strategy process and will not be objective. IS strategy should therefore be outsourced to an independent supplier who is specialized in this.
- Trust is a necessary but insufficient basis for an outsourcing relationship. Trust has to be earned, can be lost, and can not be enforced. As soon as the relationship gets under pressure, trust may be lost.

Though client and supplier do not usually have shared profit goals, complementary goals can be created, by establishing a measurable partnership where part of the benefits of a contract are shared between the client and supplier. If a supplier is being hired to develop a new application, for example, the contract might stipulate that the company and the supplier will share any profits that come from selling the application.

Choice of business partners
Business units can be obliged to take services from an internal IS department or be free to chose their IS supplier. Internal IS depart-

	Advantages	Disadvantages
Free to chose supplier	best supplier for each activity less switching costs easy to compare suppliers	Risk that internal IS department loses too many internal clients
Restricted to one supplier	no coordination between multiple suppliers	No competition No use of specialisms of suppliers difficult to compare to external suppliers
Free to offer	excess capacity can be sold market tests performance broadens experience	conflicts of priority between internal and external clients commercial overhead requires different management strategy
Restricted to one client	no marketing costs no conflicts of interest	difficult to compensate for fluctuations no market test

Table 5.17 Considerations for choice of business partners

ments can be restricted to work only for the internal business units or be allowed to offer products and services to external client organizations. The advantages and disadvantages of these options are listed in Table 5.17.

Business units should be free in their choice of IS supplier for activities that do not need to be kept internally. If however an outsourcing evaluation has led to the decision to keep certain activities within the organization, top management should support that decision and oblige users to take these services from the internal IS department. If the business units were first obliged and are then given the option to chose, the danger exists that they will all chose to outsource, and leave the internal IS department without work. By the time they find out that the internal department had certain advantages over external suppliers, the department will have been dismantled.

Having the IS department work for outside clients may utilize excess capacity of the internal IS department and is a test for the competitiveness of the department. It may however also lead to priority problems if external clients are perceived to be more important or to have more urgent needs than internal clients. It also takes a fundamentally different way of managing the IS department. It is advisable to put restrictions on the amount and type of products or services to be offered to outsiders and to make tight rules for priorities.

5.2.2 Divide work among suppliers and contracts

Clients obtain maximum flexibility and control by outsourcing pieces of IS work to multiple suppliers using separate contracts. The extra costs of contracting and coordinating are almost always outweighed by the advantages of flexibility.

Flexibility and controllability can be achieved by using short contracts for well-defined pieces of IS work, and by outsourcing those pieces to multiple IS suppliers, in a way that permits comparison between the IS suppliers and easy switching if one of the suppliers underperforms. Withholding a piece of the business as a carrot or splitting IS activities between two suppliers can provoke suppliers to deploy their best efforts and resources.

Number of IS suppliers

Client organizations can chose to outsource a portion of work to one IS supplier or divide the work into sections, solicit separate bids for each service and award them to multiple suppliers.

An advantage of putting several related activities in the hands of one supplier is that coordination between these activities is performed by the supplier. Coordination activities still have to be performed, but it is often easier to coordinate activities within one organization than between organizations.

The major disadvantage of outsourcing to one supplier is the lack of competition and comparison. If a client organization decides to outsource to one supplier, this supplier does not have to compete with other IS suppliers and the client organization has little basis for comparing the supplier to other suppliers. If the client organization is able to make a comparison, for example by conducting market research or issuing a call for tender, and other suppliers appear to be better at certain activities, the client organization can often not outsource to another suppliers because of contractual obligations.

The advantages of multiple suppliers almost always outweigh the advantages of outsourcing to one supplier. The advantages of outsourcing activities to multiple IS suppliers are:

- less dependent on one or a small number of IS suppliers
- strategic business knowledge is not in the hands of one IS supplier
- less switching costs
- better comparison between suppliers
- supplier may be motivated by threat of switching
- consecutive activities can be used as a carrot for the supplier
- activities can be outsourced to the supplier that is best suited to that activity

Client organizations divide activities among suppliers in numerous ways. Work is divided across different IS activities, information systems or IS components. Independence and comparison can be maximized by rewarding similar activities for groups of information systems to different suppliers. Client organizations should take advantage of the specialisms of suppliers. Suppliers are often specialized in certain activities, components or information systems. Data centers for example, specialize in operation, while software houses specialize in software development and maintenance.

If work is divided among multiple suppliers, the client organization must take extra care when defining each portion of work and the interfaces between them. If problems arise with the performance of information systems, it is often difficult to determine which activity or which component is causing the problems. Poor response time may for example, be caused by bad software development, but can also be caused by inappropriate network configuration or improper operation of central hardware.

Coordination between multiple suppliers can also be outsourced to a main supplier, which subcontracts the activities to each of the other suppliers. This does not eliminate the coordination costs, but moves them from the client organization to the main supplier.

Number of contracts

The IS activities that are outsourced to one IS supplier can be encompassed by one overall long term contract or can be governed by separate contracts for separate activities.

Separate contracts involve higher contracting costs and extra costs for coordinating between the contracts, but has many advantages that almost always outweigh these extra costs. The advantages of separate contracts are:

- Having separate contracts for separate systems or components makes it easier to change or terminate individual systems or components.
- Having separate contracts for separate activities or phases within these activities makes it easier to switch to another supplier or to bring an activity or phase back in-house if a supplier proves to be disappointing.
- Specifically for development, outsourcing of consecutive phases of system development with separate contracts forces the supplier to document the result of each phase in a way that can be transferred to another supplier, and allows for different sourcing designs for different phases, e.g., hiring a consultant to assist in the definition phase and outsource the actual development for a fixed fee.
- Even if eventually all activities or phases are outsourced to the same supplier, the threat that activities or phases could have been given to other suppliers stimulates the supplier to deploy its best efforts and resources.

The costs of writing multiple contracts can be reduced by making framework agreements with regular IS suppliers and by providing business units with standard contracts.

Contract duration

A company should also try, whenever possible, to sign short-term contracts. Most client organizations can not predict their business conditions more than three years ahead, and technologies will be outdated after that period. The contract duration should not be longer than the period the client organization can foresee its business conditions and the necessary technologies.

5.2.3 Design management structure

Controllability is determined mainly by the choice of the requirement specification, pricing, lead time and quality control mechanism and coordination mechanism.

Requirements definition

The first element that needs to be determined in designing the management structure of an outsourcing arrangement are the requirements that the outsourced activities must meet. These requirements describe the products or services the supplier must deliver to the client organization. The content of the activities is described by stating which activities must be performed on what components of which information systems. The requirements are described by product or service specifications. Development activities are specified by a (preliminary) design that includes the system specifications. Maintenance and operation activities are specified by a service description.

Requirements for outsourced activities can be defined in abstract or detailed terms and in functional or technical terms. Abstract functional terms are usually unfit to be the basis of a solid contract and can not be enforced. Defining activities in functional terms, such as "develop software that provides detailed information on sales in each quarter", will not be adequate, because compliance to these requirements can not be measured or enforced.

Pricing mechanism

The price the client organization has to pay to the IS supplier for certain activities can be determined in several ways. The advantages and disadvantages of pricing mechanisms are listed in Table 5.18.

No pricing usually occurs with internal IS departments that do not charge for their services to internal clients. This is not advisable, because then users are not confronted with the cost of their requirements and are not stimulated to make good cost/benefit analyses. Another disadvantage is that the internal IS department will then be judged with regard to its total costs instead of to its attractiveness to users and its contribution to the business processes. Systems or

	Advantages	**Disadvantages**
no pricing	no cost allocation overhead no barriers for innovation	users do not face costs of requests investment analysis not possible
time and materials	fee is never higher than actual costs	total costs not known in advance less motivation for efficiency
fixed fee	total costs are known in advance total costs are known approximately supplier is motivated to be efficient client organization benefits from efficiency	fee may be higher than actual costs incentive scheme part of benefits are shared
work load	flexible costs decrease when usage decreases	total costs not known in advance units of work load may not be clear to users
benefits to client	supplier is motivated to maximize benefits of information systems	difficult to determine contribution of supplier to benefits of client

Table 5.18 Considerations for pricing mechanism

components that top management sees as necessary for all business units, such as a uniform communication infrastructure or corporate data bases, and wants to be used by all units, can be provided for free or be paid for from central budgets.

A fixed price mechanism may suggest maximum control of costs, but this is only the case if the requirements for the activities can be specified in detail and need not be changed:

- If the requirements can not be specified in detail, it is difficult to determine whether the supplier has performed all of the work the fixed price was based on.
- If requirements are not stable and users change their demands during the project, the supplier will charge excess fees above the fixed fee.
- The client organization must be able to assess whether the price is reasonable. A supplier will have no trouble meeting cost and time limits if they are 50% above average.
- One may wonder what must be done if the work is not finished when the budget is used. If the client organization demands compliance, the supplier may scramble through the work or in the worst case go bankrupt.
- Suppliers will usually only agree with a fixed price mechanism if the activity is relatively predictable and straight-forward, while client organizations want this mechanism, especially for innovative and

uncertain activities.

The alternative of time and materials has other drawbacks. The client organization does not pay more than the time and materials actually used, but the supplier is less motivated to work efficiently and the total costs are not known in advance. It is therefore advisable to minimize the work that must be outsourced for time and materials and outsource the other activities in well-defined pieces for a fixed price and date. This may involve performing a pilot study or a definition study to define the actual activity in clear and measurable terms.

The fee plus incentive scheme is a good alternative, because it stimulates the supplier to work efficiently and returns part of the benefits of this efficiency to the client organization.

Lead time mechanism

The lead time of an activity can be fixed or be unlimited. The considerations for choosing between a fixed or unlimited lead time are the same as for choosing between a fixed fee or a time and material pricing mechanism. A fixed lead time should be chosen if the requirements for the activities can be specified in detail in advance.

If a fixed lead time is chosen, the client organization should determine what is to be done if the deadline is not met. The client organization may demand a penalty for each day the supplier is late.

For more or less continuous activities, such as operation and maintenance, two types of lead time must be specified: the time it takes the supplier to start the activity, including for example transferring information systems to the supplier's hardware, and the lead time of individual activities, such as the reaction time after the supplier has been notified of a disruption or the lead time for repairing a system.

Quality control mechanism

Quality is the degree to which the products or services a supplier delivers meet the requirements specified in advance. The client organization can chose different strategies for measuring and enforcing the quality of the products or services delivered (see Table 5.19). Quality control must also include measures to be taken if the quality delivered is not satisfactory. This may include giving the supplier a limited time to correct the deliverables and a penalty clause for not meeting the agreed quality.

Conflict resolution mechanism

Conflicts may arise between the client organization and the IS supplier and mechanisms must be determined to resolve these conflicts. Conflict resolution mechanisms and the advantages and disadvantages are listed in Table 5.20.

Conflict resolution by higher management is the most efficient and flexible way to resolve conflicts. This mechanism may, however,

	Advantages	Disadvantages
measure final deliverable	less effort required	may be too late to correct on time
measure intermediate deliverables	earlier detection of inadequacies	more effort
quality reports by supplier	less effort for client	supplier may not measure objectively
quality testing by client	increases involvement of client	requires efforts and skills of client supplier may not accept test results
quality audit by third party	objective and professional	costs are high

Table 5.19 Considerations for quality control strategies

	Advantages	Disadvantages
joint hierarchical authority	low costs, fast	not formalized influenced by internal politics time demands on top management
escalation procedures	no third parties needed low costs, fast	time demands on top management
third party arbitration	neutral, objective	fairly expensive
legal action	formalized enforceable	very high costs and long time before finished eventual deliverable will seldom be satisfactory and on time

Table 5.20 Considerations for conflict resolution mechanisms

demand considerable time from top management and is usually not available in outsourcing situations.

Escalation procedures and third party arbitration are preferred in outsourcing situations, and a combination is best. Legal action should only be used as a last resort, because of the high costs and time taken for legal action and the fact that it is unlikely that the client will get satisfactory products or services that are on time. Escalation procedures and third party arbitration are faster and cheaper and do less damage to the relationship. Legal action should however always be possible, to pose a final threat and thereby make it in the best interest of both parties to resolve conflicts outside court. Legal action is possible only if measurable and detailed requirements are specified that can be enforced by law.

Coordination mechanisms	Advantages	Disadvantages
Mutual adjustment	very flexible and fast	time-consuming less business-like
Direct supervision	high controllability	time-consuming
Standardization of work processes	high controllability	requires thorough knowledge of work processes does not guarantee result
Standardization of output	requires little effort	output can not always be specified or measured
Standardization of skills	requires little effort	difficult to assess
Standardization of values	does not require detailed coordination	not enforceable

Table 5.21 Considerations for coordination mechanisms

Coordination mechanisms

The client organization can monitor and control the IS supplier basically by specifying the desired outcomes or by coordinating the processes to achieve the desired results. These and other coordination mechanisms are listed in Table 5.21.

In outsourcing situations, standardization of output is the most applicable coordination mechanism. Standardization of skills may be added by selecting the supplier and staff with the best skills for the pertinent activities; and standardization of work processes, by demanding that certain project management strategies, development methodologies, or quality systems be used by the supplier.

Not all activities are however, suited to be controlled solely by skills and output. Many IS activities are not standardized enough and can not be specified to enough detail in advance. In these cases, mutual adjustment and more detailed control of work processes is required, for example by having very regular meetings between client and supplier, and having the supplier conduct many interviews with (future) users. This requires the client organization to be capable of managing IS activities.

5.2.4 Design operational structure

The location, ownership and exclusiveness of the IS components and who employs the IS staff determine to a large extent whether economies of scale and cost reductions can be achieved.

Location

Hardware can be placed and personnel can work at the supplier's or the customer's site. Placing hardware and personnel at the supplier's site can lead to lower costs if office space at the customer's site is scarce or expensive, and to savings being made due to the possibility of using hardware and personnel for multiple clients. Client organizations may chose to keep hardware and personnel at their site, to have (a feeling of) more control over the resources.

Ownership

Hardware and software can be owned by the customer or the supplier. Supplier ownership of hardware and software allows for shared use of resources and can generate cash infusions if client resources are sold to the supplier. Client's ownership of resources may increase control but will increase fixed costs and decrease the flexibility of the IS activities portfolio.

Employment

IS personnel can have an employment relationship with the client organization or with the IS supplier. In the latter case, the supplier's personnel works for the client organization in a contractor relationship instead of an employment relationship.

Staff employed by an external IS supplier is available to multiple client organizations, which allows the supplier to achieve economies of scale and specialization. A supplier can have full time specialists for functions that each individual client organization only needs occasionally.

Internal IS staff are often more committed to the client organization that employs them and are more acquainted with the organization's business processes. Internal staff have more and easier access to formal and informal channels and are generally more loyal to the organization's goals.

Exclusiveness

If hardware or software is owned and the personnel are employed by the IS supplier, the client organization can chose to have dedicated, exclusive use of these resources, or let the supplier share these resources between multiple clients. Dedicated use may be chosen for security reasons, to protect intellectual rights or to maintain competitive use of software. Shared use will lower costs by increasing the possibility of economies of scale and increase flexibility.

Shared use of hardware means that a client rents hardware capacity measured by some unit of usage instead of having a number of dedicated pieces of hardware operated. Renting capacity has the advantage that the client has only to pay for the capacity that is actually used and that fluctuations in the processing volume do not yield problems with a shortage or abundance of processing capacity. This should be chosen if the client has high fluctuations in capacity demand or wants to be very flexible.

Shared use of software means that the supplier sells the same software to multiple clients. This may involve ready made packages the supplier has developed at their own risk or software that was originally developed for one client organization and appeared to be useful to other clients. In the latter case, the original client should demand a reduction in the costs of development or a share of the revenues. Selling tailor-made software means that the client for which the software was developed initially can no longer keep a unique advantage. This option should not be chosen for software that distinguishes the organization or contains confidential business information.

If ready-made packages that meet requirements are available, then the initial costs will usually be much less than the costs of developing tailor-made software. Other advantages of ready-made packages include the fact that the software has been tested extensively by previous clients and that no development time is needed. Disadvantages include a lack of flexibility, as the software will only be updated if and when a considerable number of clients want a certain change, and the time and effort required to select the package that suits the organization best. Another risk of packages is the fact that many packages have far more options than most client organizations need and that users will start to experiment or even to use functions they are not supposed to be using.

If a package does not meet the client's requirements completely, the supplier can be asked to make a dedicated version for the client and to make the necessary adaptations. This is however an option that has all the disadvantages of packages but none of the advantages, because the adaptations will take time and need to be tested and corrected, and the organization still has no control over the standard functions of the package.

5.2.5 Internal organization of outsourcing coordination

IS activities that are outsourced require as much coordination effort as internal activities. Outsourcing coordination is not trivial and requires significant staff and resources. Managing an outsourcing relationship requires fundamentally different skills than managing an internal IS department.

An outsourcing relationship must be managed and controlled by the client organization, to ensure that the relationship is designed and operated in the interests of the client. Outsourcing coordination activities include the activities described in each of the phases of this model. These activities must all be organized by the client organization.

Decentralization

Outsourcing coordination can be centralized in one unit that coordinates all outsourcing relationships that the client organization has, or can be decentralized so that the business units manage their own outsourcing relationships.

It is advisable to have a central unit within the organization that can assist business units in performing these specialized activities. Today the responsibility for support processes, such as the IS function, is often decentralized to business units. Business units that outsource their IS activities however often make the same elementary mistakes with specifying requirements, evaluating reactions on tenders, negotiating contracts and managing external suppliers. Business units will usually only outsource one or a few activities a year and do not get the chance to become familiar with managing outsourcing. A central unit that assists all business units with outsourcing obtains experience and is better able to perform specialized activities such as market research, tendering, negotiating and writing a contract and assessing the quality of the product or service delivered. The business units must however determine the functionality of the systems and activities they outsource. Managers must stay committed to the outsourcing and act as principals. They should be supported by a central unit, but the central unit must not become the client, because that may result in a loss of commitment of users and a result that does not comply to their wishes or is otherwise not acceptable.

Line versus staff

Outsourcing coordination can be allocated to line managers and users or to staff units. The considerations for centralizing certain specialized activities also apply to the division between line and staff. Line management should act as principals and determine functionality; staff functionaries may assist in specialized activities.

Outsourcing of outsourcing coordination

The capacity and skills required for outsourcing coordination may not be available within the client organization, however, some of the outsourcing coordination activities can also be outsourced. This would mean that an external organization or expert assists the client organization and designs and manages the outsourcing relationship on behalf of the client organization. This expert should of course be independent from the IS supplier.

Outsourcing experts can be hired to assist in developing a sourcing strategy. Legal experts with experience in IS outsourcing can be hired for drawing a good contract. Managing external suppliers can be outsourced to a main supplier. This is especially beneficial if the client organization has many external suppliers, that deliver products and services that are required to interact.

5.3 Selecting the IS supplier

Phase 3	Selecting the IS supplier
Purpose	The aim of this phase is to select an IS supplier that is able to perform the activities the client organization wants to outsource
Trigger	• existing or new activities are outsourced
Activities	5.3.1 Set up the selection process 5.3.2 Write call for tender 5.3.3 Choose potential suppliers to invite to tender 5.3.4 Evaluate tender responses 5.3.5 Write the contract
Results	The selection of a supplier that is most likely to perform the activities according to the requirements
Proceed with decision	• if no adequate supplier is found: phase 1, Initial sourcing • if an adequate supplier is selected, but the design of the outsourcing arrangement is not agreed: phase 2, Design outsourcing arrangement • if an supplier has been selected and the design is agreed: phase 4, implementation of outsourcing

Tendering is the phase where the client organization issues a call for tender, also called a request for proposal (RFP), in which the desired products or services are described and suppliers are invited to make an offer containing the conditions under which they are willing to provide these products or services to the client organization. The client organization chooses between the tender responses received and negotiates a contract with one or more IS suppliers. Tendering is necessary when a client organization decides to outsource existing or new activities.

Tendering is not necessary if the supplier has already been chosen, for example because the users are obliged to take services from the internal IS department, or because the client organization has a relationship with one IS supplier that obliges them to outsource to that supplier.

The selection process proposed in this section is a highly formalized and structured process. A supplier can also be selected informally, based on impressions and personal contacts, but this is strongly discouraged, because of the risk that important criteria or very good suppliers will be overlooked.

5.3.1 Set up the selection process

The selection team should include the specialized knowledge and skills that are required for the selection process.

Determine whether public tendering is required.

Public sector organizations that reside within the European Union are subject to European rules regarding public procurement of services, and must issue a public tender if the value of the procurement, or aggregation of procurements, is above the EC/GATT threshold. The threshold for services is 200.000 ECU excluding V.A.T. Public tenders must be published in the European Journal and are subject to the regulations of the European Community (rule 92/50/EC June 18, 1992), that prescribe procedures for tendering and evaluation of tender responses.

Splitting work that exceeds the threshold into parts that are below the threshold usually does not avoid the obligation for public tendering. The extra effort and time needed for public tendering is relatively small and the structuredness of the prescribed procedures can be helpful to the client organization.

Set up the selection team

The selection process requires up to date knowledge of the IS market, IS suppliers and their qualities, knowledge of and experience with tendering procedures, and the skill to select an appropriate supplier and negotiate a good contract. The tendering team should include this expertise and have enough organizational authority to take the decisions involved.

Identify risks

Some situational factors may imply risks for the tendering process or the outsourcing relationship. One of the possible risks for IS development is that the initial state, for example a problem description, and the final state, for example a complete implemented information system, are too far apart to be covered in one project with one contract. It may be necessary to split the project into separate phases or to conduct a pilot study.

Other risks include high innovativeness or uncertainty and the possibility of large changes in the business processes or mergers. If the current situation is unclear or not well documented, the supplier does not have enough information on which to base the tender response. This might mean that the client organization has to improve the documentation of the current situation before starting the tendering process.

Determine steps

If public tendering is required, the steps to be taken are largely prescribed. Otherwise, the tendering team must decide which of the steps suggested in this section will be performed and in what order.

The client organization has the option to split the tendering process into a pre-selection and a selection phase. A pre-selection phase means that the client organization asks a large number of IS suppliers to answer certain questions, and then selects a short-list of suppliers that conform to a pre-defined set of criteria. This can be useful if the client organization is not familiar with suppliers for a specific IS activity or does not want responses from inappropriate suppliers.

5.3.2 Write call for tender

A detailed and comprehensive call for tender is essential for the supplier to write a realistic tender response and for the client organization to select the best supplier. It also facilitates contracting considerably.

Substantial time and care should always be invested in formulating a call for tender. The process of writing the call for tender helps clients clarify their thoughts and agree on exactly what they wish to outsource, and what some of their terms and conditions are. Responses to a well-written call for tender allow clients to get sufficient information from each vendor to allow them to determine which supplier will be the best fit for the future partnership. It also levels the playing field among suppliers, by ensuring that all vendors receive the same information. A good call for tender can make writing the final contract easier, since most issues will already have been spelled out, or at least outlined, in the call for tender or the responses. The elements essential in a call for tender are listed in Table 5.22. Each of these elements is described below.

Include a description of the current situation in the call for tender

It is necessary to describe the current situation, because suppliers need to know where they start and which systems and documents will be provided as input to their activities. A call for tender for development must include whether there is an approved definition study or basic design and what the state of the existing system is that needs to be replaced and whether it is properly documented. A call for

---

description of current situation
functional and technical requirements
organization of the outsourcing relationship
planning of meetings and intermediate and final products and reports
format and content of tender responses
procedures for the tendering process

Table 5.22 Elements of a call for tender

tender for operation requires a description of the current systems and the current operation organization.

Include functional and technical requirements in the call for tender

The requirements should be specified as comprehensively as possible, to allow the supplier to provide a well-considered response. A cost/benefit analysis must be made for each requirement. Clients often see outsourcing as an opportunity to fulfill all their wishes for a particular product or service, without realizing what the costs of their requirements are.

Suppliers may have effective ways to provide a solution that the client has not thought of. Creative supplier responses should however be limited, and each supplier should offer a proposal for implementing the client's requirements, to avoid it being impossible to compare the proposals of different suppliers. Alternative solutions should be proposed separately from the requested solution.

Include the organization of the outsourcing relationship in the call for tender

The client organization should specify how the outsourcing relationship must be organized, for example whether the client wants the supplier's staff to work at the client's premises. Requirements for each of the decision variables from the previous section are included in the call for tender, if the client organization has specific wishes with regard to the variables. It can also be left to the supplier to make a proposal, but this may again, result in responses that are difficult to compare.

Include the contents and format for tender responses in the call for tender

Determine what information IS suppliers have to provide in the tender response and prescribe the format of the tender response. Demanding a uniform format for the tender responses will facilitate comparing the responses. The information asked from the suppliers must be sufficient to evaluate the tender responses with regard to criteria that are given in the next section. The tender response should contain information to assess whether the supplier will be able to perform the activities required, and whether the goal variables, i.e., the costs, lead time, quality, flexibility, controllability, and continuity, will be met satisfactory.

One of the items the supplier must provide is the price the supplier will ask for providing the services. The client organization must define exactly which services are included in the price offered by the supplier and which services will be charged as extras. Many client organizations have faced hidden or unexpected costs for services they assumed were included in the base line.

The client organization can demand a certain lead time or it can be left to the suppliers to offer a lead time. The client organization must also ask how long it will take the supplier to start the activity and define what is included in the lead time, e.g., whether testing and correcting is included or will be performed after the deadline. For operations, the client must ask the lead time for implementation or transfer of systems to the supplier.

The quality of the services can be determined directly, by asking whether all requirements will be met or indirectly by asking for the supplier's experience in the market segment and references from other clients.

Continuity, the probability that a supplier will deliver the services for as long as needed and not go bankrupt or withdraw from business, is usually measured by determining the financial position of the supplier and the number of years the supplier has been in the pertinent business.

Include the selection procedure in the call for tender

The call for tender should also include the procedure that the client organization will follow to select a supplier. These procedures include the planning of the tendering process and the communication between the client and the suppliers.

The potential suppliers must be given enough time to make a well-considered tender response. Some client organizations spend over a year planning an activity and then give suppliers two weeks to produce a tender response. This will lead to responses that are not well thought through, which is not in the interest of either of the parties.

The client organization must decide how to handle requests for additional information. A procedure that is often used is that of holding a meeting with the suppliers that have shown interest in the tender, giving them the information and giving them the opportunity to ask questions. An alternative is to allow written inquiries only and to send all questions and answers to all the potential suppliers.

The procedures should also cover the legal status of the call for tender, the costs and obligations of tender responses and an agreement on the confidentiality of information provided.

5.3.3 Choose potential suppliers to invite to tender

The client organization should issue a formal call for tender to three or more potential suppliers. The client organization should not invite too many suppliers, because it will take the tendering team considerable time to evaluate a large number of responses and it wastes the time of suppliers that have little or no chance of being chosen.

If the client organization does not know the IS market well enough to select a small number of potential suppliers, pre-selection can be used, by inviting a large number of suppliers to answer a few general questions that make it possible for the client organization to select a short-list of potential suppliers. The questions asked in a pre-selection should be of a general nature, such as some key facts about the suppliers and their relevant experience, and it must be possible to answer the questions and process the answers in a short time. Detailed information about the activities that are to be outsourced should not be included in a pre-selection.

If the client organization has an internal IS department, the department should also be invited to offer a tender response. Many client organizations compare external bids to the current performance of the internal IS department, but the internal IS department is often limited by internal politics and may be able to improve significantly if they get the freedom to apply the same measures that external suppliers use. Public sector organizations in the European Communities however are not allowed to invite their internal departments to tender.

5.3.4 Evaluate tender responses

Determine selection criteria

Determine the criteria that will be used to evaluate the tender responses. Keep the goals of the outsourcing decision in mind. Continuity and potential quality are characteristics of the supplier. Cost, lead time and actual quality are characteristics of the product or service offered. Flexibility and controllability are influenced mostly by the design of the outsourcing relationship.

Determine relative importance

The importance of each of the selection criteria depends on the specific situation. The importance of the selection criteria can often be derived from the importance of the goal variables as determined in section 5.1.3. All criteria must receive adequate attention, and a one-sided emphasis on, for example, costs or lead time is not advisable.

Client organizations buying ready-made software packages, software tools, or hardware should not attach low importance to the continuity of the supplier. This may be dangerous, because the client organization will need to be serviced and need new versions after the initial purchase.

Determine required values

It is good negotiating practice to start with determining the desired and minimum result, instead of being satisfied with the best offer received. Otherwise, the client organization may end up choosing the cheapest of five bids, while that bid is not as efficient as possible, or the amount is still 20% higher than the budget available for the activities.

The required or desired values can be derived from internal restrictions on the budget and time limits, and data on previous, similar projects. External sources include comparison with similar projects in similar organizations, assessment by a benchmarking firm, and expert opinions.

Evaluate each proposal to criteria

The tender responses should be evaluated on each of the criteria. The evaluation can be summarized in a table such as Table 5.23. Each member of the tendering team should evaluate the proposals independently before comparing the members' preferences.

A supplier not keeping to the required format for the tender response or the procedures of the call for tender can be a signal that the supplier is not willing or able to accommodate to the client's needs and situation.

The tender responses should be evaluated on their actual conditions, and not by general abstract reasoning about why external suppliers or this supplier will be better or cheaper, nor by personal impressions of persuasive oral or written presentations. It is necessary to assess the probability that the supplier is willing and able to actually deliver what they are offering.

Perform a critical analysis of the best bids

If the best bids are considerably better than the current situation or than the bid of the internal IS department, analyze how the suppliers achieve these improvements, and assert that it is not by reducing quality, leaving out requirements, or using creative accounting methods. Suppliers sometimes make offers that save costs in the short term but are more expensive in the long term, so the deal looks attractive when comparing the internal situation with the first year of the contract. Suppliers offer these deals to win the tendering process and often recoup their profit in later years or when the client organization wants to change or extend use or services. Suppliers make much of their profit on additional time and materials work and additional

Responses	Criteria						Result
	costs	lead time	quality	control	flexibility	continuity	
importance	*medium*	*medium*	*high*	*very high*	*high*	*medium*	
supplier A	-	-	-	+	o	++	-
supplier B	+	+	-	+	+	+	+
supplier C	++	+	+	—	+	—	o
internal IS department	+	o	+	+	++	+	+

Table 5.23 Example of evaluating tender responses

processing charges beyond the scope of the original contract.

If the selection has come to one or a few remaining responses, references should be checked intensively, because these are often the most valuable sources of information on the supplier's performance. When selecting a ready-made software package, a client can ask for demonstrations or even implementation of business cases, which means that part of the client organization's real data and processes is implemented in the package. When outsourcing operations, a visit to the data center may reveal additional information and give an impression of the supplier's way of working.

Negotiations can be started with the two or three most adequate suppliers. Suppliers often push for exclusive negotiations in an early stage, but it is better to negotiate with two or more suppliers for as long as possible before making a final choice, because this gives the client organization more bargaining power.

The negotiation team must include someone with the experience and skills to negotiate. This expertise is often present in the procurement department. Most suppliers object to having to deal with a functionary from the client organization's procurement department, for obvious reasons. Suppliers hold that IS outsourcing is about partnership and trust instead of tight price negotiations. This should not stop the client organization from negotiating for the best result. The IS and line managers in the team should guard against an overemphasis on cost reduction, as most procurers focus mainly on low costs.

If none of the tender responses is adequate, then the decision makers should ask themselves whether it is sensible to outsource at all. The decision process should proceed with a reevaluation the initial sourcing decision.

If the selected IS supplier does not agree with the client's design of the outsourcing relationship, then the decision makers should return to phase 2 and negotiate a new design that is acceptable to both parties.

5.3.5 Write the contract

A solid and detailed contract is necessary to guarantee adequate performance of the supplier. Using standard contracts and framework contracts increases the efficiency and effectiveness of contracting.

The contract between the client organization and the IS supplier documents the decisions and negotiation results from the previous phases. Both sides should try to draft a contract that it is clear and complete. Potential areas of contention should not be left to chance, or worse, resolved during a crisis, when tempers are high and attention must be focused on solving the crisis. Nor should the parties leave certain clauses incomplete, assuming they will be inserted after the contract is signed. The contract should be future-oriented. A common tendency is to focus on today's environment, rather than tomorrow's; however, the major challenges to the relationship will come about as requirements, volume or technology change.

The contract negotiation team should consist of at least one representative from each of the following groups: senior business management, financial, legal, technical, user community and human resources. It may be useful to hire an outside lawyer experienced in writing outsourcing contracts, to assist in writing the contract, or even with writing the request for proposal. No matter how experienced the client's IS or legal staff are, IS suppliers typically have more experience with this type of agreement. The external lawyer should work with in-house counsels, because they understand the client's business environment better.

The client organization should not accept the suppliers standard contract, not even as a starting point for drafting a new contract. Suppliers' contracts are usually biased towards the suppliers' interests. Writing a contract is also an educational exercise that may lead to useful insights about the outsourcing relationship..

The contract should specify all elements of the design of the outsourcing relationship that were specified in phase 2. The contract must cover all consecutive phases of outsourcing:

- Arrangements for the implementation or transition phase
- Arrangements for the continuous management of the outsourced activities
- Arrangements for intermediate changes in requirements
- Arrangements for early termination before the end of the contract
- Arrangements for regular termination at the end of the contract

The functional and technical requirements should be specified in detail and in measurable terms. Arrangements must be made for measuring and reporting compliance to these requirements and the contract must specify measures in case of non-compliance, such as penalty clauses. Many managers want to describe their requirements in broad business terms and expect their supplier to find the best technical solution and implement that solution under reasonable conditions. This approach is not advised, for the following reasons:

- information technology is not standardized enough to define requirements only in high-level functional terms,
- systems must connect to other systems, functionally and technically,
- technology sets limitations to the possible functional requirements

and the possibilities of technology may inspire additional functional requirements,
- functional requirements are not always stable and often only become clear as technical details are worked out or prototypes are built,
- client managers can not judge the fairness of prices and lead times offered if they do not have knowledge of the technology and the operational activities.

Issues that may change during the outsourcing relationship should be agreed in as flexible a manner as possible, by arranging procedures and clauses for change management. These clauses should also define what actions the supplier should take after a change request and under what conditions these changes will be performed. If the client organization for example has outsourced the development of certain software and wants extra functionality above the requirements agreed in the initial contract, parties can agree that the supplier will perform these changes at the same tariff or for a price that is proportional to the percentage of the system that is changed or extended.

Contracts should not be restricted to Service Level Agreements (SLAs), which are agreements specifying service levels for operating hardware and networks. SLAs usually only address operation and maintenance activities. Most SLAs in practice focus only on specifying service availability, response time, mean time between failure (MTBF) and mean time to repair (MTTR), while SLAs and other contracts should also include other technical requirements, such as security and change procedures, and functional requirements.

5.4 Implementation of the outsourcing decision

Phase 4	Implementation of the outsourcing decision
Purpose	The aim of this phase is to implement the outsourcing relationship
Trigger	• the client organization has signed a contract with an IS supplier
Activities	5.4.1 Transfer staff and other resources 5.4.2 Transfer systems and specifications
Results	All requirements for starting the execution of the outsourced activities are met
Proceed with	• phase 5, Management of the outsourcing relationship

The descriptions of the remaining phases are considerably shorter than the first three phases, because the emphasis of the research was on the first phases and because good preparation in the previous phases will facilitate the remaining phases to a great extent. If a systematic initial sourcing decision is followed by a thorough design of the outsourcing relationship and critical supplier selection, then most of the important decisions with regard to the consecutive phases have been taken. Implementing, managing and terminating the outsourcing relationship will then require much less effort and most potential problems can be avoided.

5.4.1 Transfer staff and other resources

The implementation of the outsourcing decision may imply, depending on the decisions taken, changing the location, ownership or employment of IS staff and other resources.

Transferring IS staff implies that employees resign from the client organization and are reemployed by the supplier. The IS staff usually demands that they get comparable employment conditions. Some of the employees may chose to look for employment elsewhere.

5.4.2 Transfer systems and specifications

The implementation of outsourcing of development requires that the design of the system to be developed is transferred to the supplier. If the system replaces an existing system, then the existing system and the documentation should also be handed over to the supplier.

Implementation of outsourcing of maintenance includes transferring the documentation of the system to be operated. Implementation of outsourcing the operation of a new system involves transferring the system and documentation from the development organization to the operation organization.

Operating existing systems involves transferring the systems to the new operation environment, converting the systems if necessary, and meanwhile minimizing the disruptions caused by the transfer. Enough time should be planned for this step, as it usually takes more time than managers think and suppliers suggest. The average time needed to transfer hardware and operational systems is over three months.

5.5 Management of the outsourcing relationship

Phase 5	Management of the outsourcing relationship
Purpose	The aim of this phase is to measure and control the performance of the IS supplier and to manage changes in the requirements and in the outsourcing relationship.
Trigger	• an outsourcing relationship has been designed and implemented

Activities	5.5.1 Maintain internal capacity 5.5.2 Measure compliance to requirements 5.5.3 Enforce compliance
Results	The activity that was outsourced has been finished or is no longer needed, or the contract has ended or has been terminated.
Proceed with	• if the relationship is not to be prolonged: phase 6, Termination of the outsourcing relationship

The outsourcing relationship must be managed by the client organization, to ensure that the supplier performs the activities according to the specified requirements and that the expected improvements are achieved. Prolonging a contract on the same conditions is considered part of management of the outsourcing relationship. If the contract ends and the client organization wants to reconsider the outsourcing relationship, then the decision makers should continue with phase 6, Termination of the outsourcing relationship.

5.5.1 Maintain internal capacity

Enough IS staff should be kept to monitor and control the IS supplier, and to keep up to date with the IS market. The knowledge and skills of the staff should be kept current. It is advisable to maintain a certain amount of operational staff and resources internally, regardless of the degree and type of outsourcing that is chosen. This staff and resources are necessary:

• to know the opportunities and limitations of current and future information technologies,
• to conceptualize new applications of IT in the business processes,
• to issue tenders and evaluate supplier responses,
• to specify technical and functional requirements,
• to assess what are reasonable costs and lead times,
• to be up to date on IS suppliers and their qualities,
• to negotiate conditions and contracts,
• to evaluate IS suppliers' progress, intermediate results and final deliveries,
• to be able to perform some IS activities within the organization, permanently or temporarily, if necessary,
• to do small or urgent jobs that can not wait for a tendering process.

The knowledge and skills of the internal IS staff can be kept up to date by performing part of the IS activities internally. Internal IS staff should meet with supplier's staff regularly, or even take part in a job rotation scheme with the supplier; internal IS staff may work for the supplier occasionally and vice versa.

The users should provide the input and information on the business processes that the supplier needs to perform the activities. Client organizations sometimes think that user involvement is not necessary, especially with development. Users sometimes can not free time from their daily work to provide input. This may result in a system being delivered that does not meet users' requirements. Therefore, users should be committed to deliver the required input.

5.5.2 Measure compliance to requirements

The intermediate and final products or services delivered should be checked to determine whether the results comply with the requirements. Progress and resource usage should be according to the planning. Some clients make considerable efforts to define functional and technical requirements but do not measure whether the supplier complies to these requirements, or they do not measure sufficiently often and accurately.

If requirements are stated in terms of percentages and averages, measurement should comply to statistical rules. If availability is for example, guaranteed for a certain percentage of service time, then the client organization must measure the availability during the service periods often enough to ensure that the reliability of the measurements is within acceptable confidence intervals.

If provisions for (early) termination have been agreed, then compliance to these provisions should be measured. If the supplier has for example, agreed to transfer all system documentation in case of termination of the relationship, the client organization should check regularly whether documentation is kept up to date, because insufficient documentation can not be brought up to date in the case of bankruptcy of the supplier.

5.5.3 Enforce compliance

If the supplier does not comply to the requirements, the measures that have been agreed to enforce compliance should be used. Some client organizations negotiate penalty clauses or other compliance measures, but do not want to use these measures, because they are afraid to harm the good working relationship. Compliance measures are however regular business agreements that put the burden of non-compliance on the party that caused it.

5.6 Termination of the outsourcing relationship

Phase 6	Termination of the outsourcing relationship
Purpose	The aim of this phase is to terminate the outsourcing relation ship, in a way that causes the least possible disruption and ensures a smooth transition to the new situation

Trigger	• initial sourcing decision resulted in decision to insource external activities • outsourcing contract ended • client organization wants to terminate outsourcing contract
Activities	5.6.2 Evaluate final deliverables 5.6.3 Transfer staff, resources and systems
Results	The outsourcing relationship is terminated
Proceed with	if the activity is still needed: phase 1, Initial sourcing decision

The outsourcing relationship will end at some time, either as planned in the contract or earlier if both parties agree or if the client organization is strongly dissatisfied and demands the termination of the contract. In case of early termination by mutual agreement, the supplier will demand compensation for lost profit. Termination may also include reconsidering the outsourcing relationship, possibly resulting in prolonging the relationship with the same supplier but under different conditions, or in choosing another supplier or another design for the outsourcing relationship.

5.6.1 Prepare for early termination

Client organizations should be prepared to terminate the outsourcing relationship. Provisions should be made to renegotiate and change the contract if requirements or circumstances change. These provisions should include periodic reviews and evaluations that may result in changes in the contract or the tariffs. There must also be emergency procedures in case the supplier goes bankrupt, is taken over or delivers gross nonfulfillment. The supplier should be obliged to cooperate when transferring the systems and data to another supplier or to the client organization.

5.6.2 Evaluate final deliverables

If the activity was aimed at delivering a product, this product must be tested, either by the users, by the client organization's IS staff or by an external party. If testing is outsourced to an external party, this party should not have any relationship with the supplier. Compliance to the functional requirements should always also be tested by the users.

5.6.3 Transfer staff, resources and systems

Terminating an outsourcing relationship may include transferring staff and resources back from the IS supplier to the client organization.

If outsourcing of planning, development or implementation is terminated, the final result must be transferred to the client. The result may be an information plan, a system design, a developed system or an implemented system.

If outsourcing of maintenance or operation is terminated, and the systems operated are still needed by the client organization, the systems must be transferred to the new operation environment, with the client organization or with another supplier. If the systems are no longer necessary, the data often needs to be transferred or converted to a new environment.

CHAPTER 6

Strategies for
IS suppliers

The market for IS products and services has become very dynamic and turbulent. IS suppliers change their marketing strategy frequently and enter mergers, alliances and takeovers. New products, services and types of outsourcing arrangements arise. Market pressure is increasing, as client organizations become more aware and knowledgeable of the possibilities and limitations of information technology, become more critical toward IS investments, and put higher demands on their IS suppliers. In this chapter, recommendations for IS suppliers are given, that can be used when developing marketing strategies and strategies for the acquisition and tendering process.

6.1 Introduction

It is important that demand and supply of IS products and services match for the IS market to function properly. Client organizations and IS suppliers benefit if IS suppliers offer what client organizations have a need for, if good matches come about between individual clients and suppliers, and if the resultant cooperation succeeds.

Some IS suppliers are very successful in their marketing strategy and in approaching client organizations, while other suppliers sometimes seem to be offering IS products or services that are not needed or offering them in a way that annoys the decision makers of client organizations instead of attracting them.

This research project was aimed mainly at supporting management of client organizations when making IS outsourcing decisions and managing IS outsourcing relationships. The knowledge gained in this research can however, also benefit IS suppliers, who can use insights into the considerations of client organizations. Suppliers and client organizations have similar information needs on IS outsourcing, and suppliers benefit from knowledge about their competitors.

The guidelines in this chapter are based on indications from the case studies described in chapter 4. The guidelines are based on the remarks of the interviewees and on examples of strategies that suppliers used in the cases investigated. The recommendations of Van der Vlis (1992) are also included. He has investigated IS outsourcing from the perspective of both the client organization and the IS supplier, and has made recommendations for IS suppliers. The recommendations for marketing strategies are based mainly on marketing literature, such as Verhage and Cunningham (1984), because the suppliers entered the case studies after they had determined their marketing strategies.

This chapter contains only guidelines that are beneficial to both parties in an outsourcing relationship. It is assumed that the IS supplier strives for a long term relationship based on customer satisfaction, instead of short term profits by creating and exploiting dependencies. Some of the strategies used by suppliers in the cases investigated delivered a short term advantage to the supplier, but harmed the client organization. These strategies are not included in this chapter.

The guidelines presented in this chapter are aimed primarily at external IS suppliers, but may also be useful to internal IS departments that are offering products and services to internal or external clients. IS departments may also benefit from this chapter when they are confronted with an outsourcing decision and want to offer a competitive proposal.

This chapter is structured along the strategy development process of IS suppliers. This process starts with deciding in which product-market combinations (PMCs) the IS supplier wants to do business, and establishing a strategy for each PMC. The next step is acquiring client organizations and assignments. Then the IS supplier has to manage the interaction with individual client organizations in the tendering process and in designing, implementing, managing and terminating the outsourcing relationship. In practice, these steps will not be performed in this order. The steps are interdependent and will be performed recurrently and simultaneously.

6.2 Marketing strategies

Existing IS suppliers are active in one or more PMCs, which means that they offer specific products or services to specific types of client organizations. IS suppliers can continue to do business in their current PMCs, they can decide to increase, decrease or terminate their market share in PMCs, and they can enter new PMCs.

If suppliers decide to enter a new PMC or want to extend in their current PMCs, they must choose a strategy for entry and determine their marketing mix.

6.2.1 Specialist or total solutions provider

The first basic choice an IS supplier has to make is between being a specialist in a few PMCs or being a total solutions provider that can offer all IS products and services client organizations may need.

Client organizations that chose total solutions providers do this mainly to avoid having to deal with many different suppliers. IS products and services that are bought from different IS suppliers often have to interconnect. The activities of the suppliers must therefore be coordinated, and this usually takes a lot of effort and has the risk that suppliers blame each other for malfunctioning systems.

If suppliers decide to be a total solutions provider, they should be aware that client organizations probably selected them because they want to have a single point of entry for all IS activities. The supplier should make sure that the client really has to deal with only one person or department and that internal specialization should be transparent to the client organization.

Client organizations may be skeptical of a supplier that claims to be good at everything. Client organizations may chose to outsource separate activities to different suppliers for a number of reasons, each of which requires a different approach from the supplier. They may want to make use of the different specialties of different suppliers and chose the best supplier for each IS activity they want to outsource. Other clients chose multiple suppliers to be able to compare suppliers that work for them and motivate suppliers to remain competitive. Another reason can be that outsourcing to multiple suppliers reduces switching costs and dependency on one supplier, because other suppliers can take over part of the activities relatively easily if they already perform other activities for the client organization.

To IS suppliers, the advantage of being a total solutions provider is that it spreads the risk of fluctuations in individual PMCs. Only very large IS suppliers can afford to be total solutions providers. Smaller IS suppliers may offer total solutions by being a main supplier and subcontracting the activities they can not provide to other suppliers. IS suppliers that chose not to be total solutions provider can for example specialize in:

- specific IS activities: planning, development, implementation, operation, or maintenance,
- specific IS components: hardware, software, procedures, users, data,
- specific types of information systems, such as decision support

systems, financial systems or geographical information systems,
* specific brands of hardware or system software,
* specific client industries, such as agriculture, retail or hospitals,
* specific client sizes, such as large multinationals, medium or small firms,
* specific regions and serve clients in a specific area.

6.2.2 Market segmentation

When analyzing the attractiveness of PMCs, suppliers should divide the IS market into market segments. A large diversity of market segments can be found in the literature, and new products and services are constantly shifting the boundaries between segments (Borgers, 1995). A division into segments that is used often in IS market research reports is given in Table 6.1.

Existing IS suppliers are often active in more than one market segment and are moving out of and into other segments. Most large IS suppliers also offer consultancy services, especially software development suppliers. Hardware suppliers are moving into computer services and sometimes software development. Computer services companies become total solutions providers. If IS suppliers extend their services, they often enter market segments held by other IS suppliers in the supply chain. These are often their former partners with whom they had joint agreements to supply a product and the accompanying services to a client organization. Organizations that are not IS suppliers by origin, such as providers of telecommunication services and user organizations from other industries, are entering the IS market.

Market segments	Description	Examples
consultancy	advising management of client organizations with a wide orientation from strategic advise to guiding implementation of systems	Andersen Consulting, Coopers & Lybrand, KPMG, Moret Ernst & Young
software development	developing tailor-made software and body shopping	Cap Volmac, CMG, Logica, Origin
software packages	developing and selling ready-made software packages, often in conjunction with hardware and systems software	Baan Info Systems, Exact, Multihouse, Westmount
computer services	delivering hardware, operation, maintenance of hardware and software, back up services, help desk, and other operational activities	EDS, Getronics, Pink Elephant, Roccade Group
hardware	producing and selling hardware	Compaq, DEC, IBM, Tandem

Table 6.1 Traditional segmentation of IS market (Borgers, 1995)

They offer the services of their IS departments to external clients, or even set up new IS business units.

6.2.3 Analysis of market segments

Each market segment, or product market combination, that the supplier is in or might be attractive to enter can be analyzed by performing the following steps.

Analysis of supply
The amount and nature of the supply in a specific market segment can be analyzed by determining the number and size of suppliers offering products or services in the market segment, the total volume of supply, and the expected growth of supply. Qualitative analysis might include determining the qualities, specialties and tariffs of the current suppliers in the market segment, and analyzing trends in the type of product or service offered.

IS market analysis is difficult, because not much market research is available. The research reports that are available are not always useful, for a number of reasons. Research institutes often use different definitions and segmentations of the market. The terminology in the reports is not clear, and the sample size, response rate and research design are often not provided (Borgers, 1994). International clients and suppliers do not have data separated per country. Specific IS activities are often included in large-scope contracts and not separated. Suppliers do not publish their revenues per market segment and clients do not always want to make public the fact that they are outsourcing.

Analysis of demand
Determining the potential demand in a specific market segment is even more difficult than determining supply. A supplier's current clients can be a valuable source of information on the needs of client organizations for existing or new products or services. The research reports on the demand side are often based on client organization's estimations of future IS spendings in specific areas.

Analysis of profitability
Whether it is profitable for a supplier to stay within or enter a PMC is determined by:

• Current prices for the pertinent products or services and the effect of (changes in) prices on total sales volume. The relationship between price and sales volume is the price elasticity.
• The supplier's production costs and the effect of (changes in) the supplier's production volume on the production costs per unit. The relationship between the volume of production and the costs of

production, or the use of resources, is the production function. If costs per unit decrease with increasing volume, economies of scale are present.

The profitability of a PMC for a specific IS supplier is the difference between the price per unit of production and the supplier's production costs per unit, at a certain volume of production. In practice, it is often very difficult to determine price elasticity. If a supplier is considering entering a new PMC, then production costs are also hard to predict.

Analysis of stage in product life cycle

The product life cycle is a concept from marketing literature (Levitt, 1965; Verhage and Cunningham, 1984) and describes the stages a successful product or service goes through. The product life cycle has a number of phases, often called development, growth, maturity and decline. The total revenues, profit margins and the most effective marketing strategy differ per phase. Future developments in the market for a specific product can be predicted to some extent if the product life cycle stage of the product can be determined.

Each IS product or service is in a specific phase of the product life cycle. A number of traditional IS services are in their maturity phase, which is characterized by a stagnating total demand, many suppliers try to keep or increase their market share by competing on price, and low profit margins. These traditional IS services include pay roll processing, programming and service bureau, that is, operating ready-made packages for multiple clients.

Many suppliers try to extend their services portfolio with services that are in the development or growth phase. Taking over IS staff, providing consultancy, and taking responsibility for a major part of a client's IS function, are considered to be more profitable (Borgers, 1994).

Analysis of feasibility

The feasibility of being able to enter or extend a PMC depends on whether the supplier will be able to deliver the product or service and whether the supplier can get new or existing clients to buy the product or service.

Whether an IS supplier will be able to produce a new product or service depends partly on the innovativeness of the product or service. Generally, suppliers can be innovative in three dimensions: delivering a new product, changing the production process or selling the product to a new market. Innovations have the highest success rate, though not necessarily the highest returns, if the innovation is new in only one of these three dimensions, e.g., introducing a new product using existing production processes and selling these products to existing clients. Trying to sell a new product which requires a new production process to new clients is very risky (Verhage and Cunningham, 1984).

Providing new services using resources that are already available is very beneficial, especially if these resources have excess capacity that can not be deployed by increasing the usage already made of it. Services that build a long term relationship with a client can lead to additional revenues. Operating hardware and applications may for example result in additional work for software development, application maintenance and consultancy.

6.2.4 Strategies for entering or extending market segments

IS suppliers may, after analysis of the attractiveness of market segments, decide to extend their activities and market share in certain market segments or even to enter new market segments. Entering market segments and extending activities in a market segment requires a strategy to enter.

Basic strategy: make or buy

The first decision an IS supplier has to make is the choice between setting up or extending an internal unit to provide or extend the new product or service, versus acquiring or cooperating with an existing firm with an existing market share. In marketing literature, this is called the make or buy decision for new products (Verhage and Cunningham, 1984).

Buying a market share, through merger or take-over, is a fast way of entering a market segment, with less risk and less start-up time. It is also a way of obtaining the necessary knowledge, skills and resources for the new market segment. Making, or internal development, can lead to higher profits, because the supplier does not have to pay for the entrepreneurial risk and the goodwill already built. There are also no problems resulting from redundant management positions after acquisition.

Intermediate forms may have the advantages of both. An IS supplier can, for example, buy an existing firm that has a small but established share in a new market segment, and extend the firm's market share quickly through the marketing channels of the IS supplier.

Nowadays, a strong trend towards concentration can be observed, with many mergers and takeovers. Increasing scale is viewed as being essential for survival and to cope with the demand for projects of an ever increasing size and complexity. Mergers and takeovers are also pursued to extend expertise in specific market segments and eliminate competitors and increase market share. Suppliers assume that higher scales give them better chances for survival and lowers the risks that changing circumstances pose. For clients this means that suppliers are able to deliver a wider portfolio of services, but that the choice among suppliers is less. For certain areas, clients can chose from only a few suppliers. The market for software packages for municipalities is, for example, dominated by the *Roccade group*, that has taken over *CSC/Raet decentrale overheden* and *L+T*, and thereby has a very high market share in that market segment.

Types of entry

The basic strategies of make or buy give rise to a number of varieties and intermediate forms, each of which has certain advantages.

An IS supplier can extend or enter a market segment by autonomous growth either by offering more or new products or services using the existing staff and resources, or by hiring more staff and buying additional resources. The first option is usually faster and cheaper, but the existing staff and resources must have excess capacity to allow for the extra production.

An IS supplier can pursue a *take-over of another IS supplier* that already has a market share in, or at least staff and resources for, the pertinent market segment. This gives the IS supplier a (increased) market share instantaneously.

A *take-over of IS staff and resources of a client organization* usually does not give the IS supplier a market share, unless the client organization's IS department already offers products and services to other client organizations. It does, however, generate a certain and continuous revenue for a number of years that is usually large enough to deploy the majority of the staff and resources taken over. Service contracts, especially with the long term guarantees that are customary after taking over a client organization's staff, can be a way to ensure a continuous revenue for years ahead, compared to the uncertainty of small projects. Taking over staff can also be pursued by suppliers that have difficulty recruiting enough qualified staff.

An IS supplier may offer itself to be taken over by another IS supplier, or even by a client organization, if the management of the supplier thinks this is necessary for survival or to extend the business.

A *merger* with another IS supplier does not necessarily increase the profit of the individual IS supplier but it does increase the scale and may thereby increase viability or even be essential for survival.

Another option is a *joint venture* with another IS supplier or with a client organization. This usually involves setting up a separate organization owned and managed by both parties.

A *strategic alliance* is a long term cooperation agreement between IS suppliers. Strategic alliances are usually agreed between IS suppliers with complementary product and service portfolio's, to be able to offer total solutions to their clients.

Alliances on a project basis usually involve an IS supplier that acts as a main supplier for a client organization and subcontracts part of the activities the supplier has no capacity for to other suppliers.

Integrate or keep separate

If IS suppliers extend or enter a market segment by merger or take-over, they have the option of integrating the unit taken over with their existing units or keeping the unit as a separate business unit.

If a unit is taken over to enter a new market segment or because of the specialized skills and resources, integration is not necessary. Staff and resources taken over from a client organization are often not specialized and served all needs of the client organization. Integration will then be necessary to achieve economies of scale and other improvements. Client organizations and the IS staff will however often demand that the staff remains together as a recognizable unit. This impedes many potential improvements.

It is often very difficult to integrate units that are former competitors. Employees are uneasy in cooperating with people and organizations that were competitors, and competitors often have a very different way of working and different and explicit cultures.

6.2.5 Internal organization

Client organizations today expect their suppliers to know their business processes and industry. This requires that suppliers specialize in a certain group of clients, or if the supplier chooses to serve a broad group of clients, that the supplier organizes along client groups instead of functional and technical disciplines. This holds at least for 'front end' services, such as consultancy, system design, user support, and to a lesser extent to 'back end' services, such as data center operation and programming.

6.2.6 Marketing mix

When suppliers have decided which PMCs they want to maintain, extend or enter, and the strategy for entering or extending, they must determine a marketing mix for each market segment. A marketing mix has four basic components, often called the "four P's": product, price, promotion and place (Verhage and Cunningham, 1984).

Product

A product or service offered by a supplier has certain characteristics that distinguish it from the products or services of other suppliers. IS suppliers decide on the exact characteristics, specifications and qualities of the products and services they offer.

Price

The price or tariff of products and services is another important element in the marketing mix. According to Porter (1985), firms can chose between two basic strategies when offering services. They can either try to obtain *cost leadership*, by providing services at the lowest price, or chose for *differentiation*, which means providing products or services that distinguish themselves from competitors' products and services in a way that customers are prepared to pay a higher price. Differentiation can be achieved by differentiating the product, the associated service, the distribution, the image, the brand name, and so on.

Porter states that firms should strive for cost leadership or differentiation and that an intermediate position, which he calls 'stuck in the middle', will fail. In practice, the required level of quality and service differentiation will differ between market segments and parties within client organizations. Clients may require certain services at a specific quality level and seek to obtain those services at the lowest price, or have a limited budget and try to get the best service, or they want the best price/performance ratio. Suppliers do however have to make a decision about what level of quality and differentiation they want to offer, and they have to make sure that their price is competitive with other suppliers offering similar quality.

Price may also be a mechanism for entering or deterring entry to a market segment. A supplier can enter a new market by setting a low price, e.g., just above the variable costs of providing the service. Existing suppliers may deter new entrants by setting prices so low that new entrants can not regain their initial investments.

Promotion

Promotion and public relations can be realized by personal sales techniques, advertising, publicity, sales promotion and person-to-person communication (Verhage and Cunningham, 1984). Advertisement and slogans are often less important for selling directly than for creating an image and brand familiarity. Client organizations know IS suppliers mostly from the experience of colleagues, articles in trade magazines, and presentations at conferences and trade fairs.

Suppliers can chose between promoting their products or their organization. Simon (1989) distinguishes organizations with a product function and a capacity function. Organizations with a product function produce a standardized product for an anonymous market and should promote the characteristics of their products. Organizations with a capacity function produce tailor-made products for individual clients and should promote the characteristics of their organization, because the characteristics of the product are more difficult to promote and the products have not been produced at the time the client organization chooses the supplier.

IS suppliers with a product function include suppliers selling hardware, systems software, ready-made software packages and standardized services such as pay roll processing and direct mailing. Suppliers delivering labor-intensive, unique or tailor-made products, and almost all services, have a capacity function. They should promote their capacities, the qualities of their staff and resources, the work methods they use, and prior successes with other clients.

Place

The marketing instrument of place, or distribution of the product or service, consists of the physical distribution of products and services and the network of organizations that ensure the product or service finds its way from the producer to the consumer.

Geographical coverage of IS suppliers is an important issue today. Client organizations that operate in several countries or even world-wide often demand that their IS supplier has at least the same geographical scope. Globalization is a trend among all types of organizations, and this demand will therefore be made increasingly to IS suppliers.

Physical proximity is necessary especially for labor-intensive activities that can not be performed remotely, such as consulting, cooperative system design and certain types of user support. Certain business areas require specific knowledge of the national or regional regulations, circumstances or culture. This is especially required for serving client organizations in the public sector.

Distribution channels with dealers and retailer networks are relevant mainly for hardware, system software, networks and ready-made software packages.

6.3 Strategies for acquisition

IS suppliers can react to requests for proposals, but they can also be proactive and can take the initiative to approach clients. Well-known suppliers are often approached by client organizations, but less well-known suppliers or suppliers with a shortage of work or excess capacity must approach potential clients themselves. Many IS suppliers today have changed their strategy to identifying and approaching clients more proactively.

6.3.1 Identifying potential clients

IS suppliers can use several ways to identify potential client organizations that are planning to outsource IS activities. There is a large difference between selling new products and services to existing clients and obtaining new clients. Maintaining existing clients takes considerably less effort and a very different approach from that required to obtain new clients.

Sources to identify new potential clients include informal networks, established during conferences and lectures, news and articles in IT magazines, annual reports, and personnel advertisements. If client organizations appear to have problems with their IS function, or if they want to cut costs or can not attract enough qualified staff, a supplier may propose outsourcing as a solution to these problems. This should be done carefully, as many client organizations do not appreciate being approached based on negative publicity.

Direct mailing is usually not successful for obtaining long term service contracts. One of the suppliers involved in the case study research had held a large direct mailing campaign, aimed at top managers and with very intensive follow up; this resulted in only two reactions and no new clients.

Direct personal contact appears to be the most successful way of extending business opportunities. With existing client organizations, this contact is maintained mainly by staff that work at or often visit the client's site, such as account managers, consultants and body shoppers. Services that will most likely lead to more business are long term activities, such as infrastructural services and system operation, problem management, user support and user training. Selling ready-made packages can lead to a demand for operating these packages for client organizations. Identifying potential clients is easier for suppliers that focus on a particular group of clients than for generalized suppliers. Some suppliers do not identify clients themselves, but get clients handed over by the parent company.

6.3.2 Approaching potential clients

Approaching a potential client organization may take place in different stages of the client organization's decision process and at different organizational levels.

Suppliers may approach client organizations even before the client organization has decided to outsource. Top managers of large client organizations are often approached by IS suppliers that offer to take over the entire IS department and solve the client organization's problems with the IS function.

It is important to know how the client organization will react to the outsourcing decision, in which phase, and how far the client already is in this process. This determines how the supplier should approach the client and how much investigation the client and the supplier have to do. If the client organization has little IS expertise, then the supplier has to make a greater effort in the process and the process will take longer.

Suppliers should also find out whether the client is considering multiple alternatives and in what phase the client will chose a supplier: before or after designing the outsourcing relationship and before or after negotiations. Suppliers often approach the client at top management level, certainly with smaller clients. Large clients often form a project team with functionaries from the client and supplier.

Clients sometimes ask suppliers to write a proposal only to

determine whether the internal department is competitive and to get ideas for improvement. In these cases, it is often the IS manager who approaches the supplier, to prove to top management that the department is functioning well.

Suppliers should be aware that stakeholders within the client organization may be in different stages of the decision process. It might be that top management has made a decision, but that the staff is still in doubt. This requires a different approach for dealing with these different stakeholders. There is often one stakeholder who has initiated the outsourcing decision process. This may be top management, IS management or user management. One or more stakeholders, often the initiators, are strong proponents of outsourcing. A good relationship with this stakeholder is essential for the success of the acquisition. The supplier may assist this proponent in selling outsourcing within the organization.

Client organizations form their impression of a supplier based on the supplier's first approaches. A number of strategies appeared to increase the probability of successful acquisition. Avoid the 'fast' image of the supplier who solves all problems instantaneously. Outsourcing involves trust and reliability and a low-key profile is generally more appreciated. Emphasize how reversibility is guaranteed. Present a clear financial situation. Point the client to the many advantages and extra services the organization can deliver. Assist the client in solving personnel problems. Assist the decision makers to 'sell' outsourcing to the rest of the organization. Do not push a certain solution but investigate the client's situation and problems.

6.3.3 Analyzing the client organization's situation

There are several reasons for analyzing the client organization's situation: to determine whether tendering is beneficial for the supplier, to adjust the supplier's approach to the specific situation of the client, and to make a tender bid that will be beneficial for the supplier and has a high chance of being accepted by the client.

Determine the trigger for outsourcing

One of the most important points to analyze is the reason why the client organization has decided to outsource. What was the trigger for the client to consider outsourcing? What is the client's problem? What were the client's reasons behind the decision? What improvements and dangers does the client expect? Knowing the client's considerations allows the supplier to tailor the tender bid and the approach to the client's situation. It is not effective to offer for example, a low cost scenario if the client is interested in improving quality and flexibility.

If a client organization has chosen outsourcing to *implement a major technical change* for which the client lacks the necessary skills or capacity, then the supplier should offer short term assistance for implementing the new technology. The supplier may offer that the client's internal staff will be trained on the job to take over the new technology as soon as the old technology can be terminated. Emphasize that the client gains much time by outsourcing the implementation of the new technology, because no training time is needed. The supplier can also offer to operate the old technology during the training and transition time, and to assist in the conversion of the systems and data to the new infrastructure.

If managers in a client organization decide to outsource to *reduce the demands on management time,* the supplier should offer to take over a large part of the responsibility, to appoint one or a few competent account managers, and to provide high-level solutions in business terms and guarantee to develop the best technological implementation without hassling the client with technical details. If managers are afraid that the supplier will not act in their best interest and that they can not monitor their supplier in detail, the supplier may offer to have an independent firm perform external audits to verify the efficiency and the quality of the services.

If *increasing the quality* of IS products and services is the reason for outsourcing, suppliers should emphasize the skills of their employees, propose tangible quality improvement measures, and explain the quality assurance mechanisms the supplier uses.

Obtaining a cash infusion from selling assets is another possible motive for outsourcing. A supplier can adapt to this motive by offering to buy the client's hardware, software and goodwill. The cash infusion can be increased by offering a high initial payment, compensated for by a higher annual tariff. Payments for hardware often can not be increased, but payments for software and for goodwill can be negotiated.

Client organizations may chose outsourcing to *reduce* the costs of their IS function. A supplier may then offer outsourcing arrangements that take maximum advantage of the supplier's economies of scale, for example by offering to integrate the client's hardware operation with that of other clients, or to consolidate the hardware of multiple clients and place them at the supplier's location and its ownership. If the client organization's software is useful to other organizations, the supplier may offer to sell the software and share the revenues.

If *increasing the flexibility* of the IS function is the client's motive, then offering limited short term contracts with flexible change options has the best chance of producing an acceptable tender bid. A contract for software maintenance may for example, offer unlimited capacity usage and a guarantee that maintenance will be started within 24 hours after a maintenance request.

Determine expected disadvantages

Clients will also expect certain disadvantages and risks when outsourcing. Clients try to avoid these disadvantages by making demands on themselves, on the supplier, on the service, and on the design of the outsourcing relationship. If the supplier foresees these expectations and is able to make a tender bid that ensures the client that his interests are guarded, then the supplier's chances of being awarded the contract increase.

The client organization's largest fear is the risk of becoming overly *dependent* on a supplier. They often fear that they will not or do not have the option to switch to another supplier or to change or terminate activities. This is especially the case if the client outsources critical or strategic information systems. They fear that the supplier may go bankrupt or go out of the pertinent market segment, or that the supplier may take advantage of the powerful position they are in as a result of the client's dependency. The fear of discontinuity can be reduced by having the client organization sign the contract with the parent company of the supplier instead of the local subsidiary.

Another danger some clients expect is a *loss of flexibility*, because they will be tied to the contractual arrangements. This anticipated danger can be minimized by offering flexible contracts in which the client has enough options to change activities and requirements.

Client organizations realize that if they transfer IS staff, they *lose critical knowledge* that may be essential for managing their IS function. The supplier should advise the client organization to maintain an internal department that has the skills and capacity to determine the organization's IS strategy and to identify and specify new applications of IT in the business processes. It is in the interest of both parties that the client organization has a strong IS function and remains able to develop an IS strategy. The supplier might offer to have regular meetings with the client's internal staff, or to devise a job rotation scheme between the client and the supplier to keep the client's IS knowledge and skills up to date.

Increasing costs in the future is another common concern. The costs of specific hardware and system software usually decreases over the years, but the tariffs of suppliers are often fixed and are increased annually according to 'cost of living' measures. A supplier may offer to agree annually decreasing tariffs for hardware, or annual renegotiations based on external audits. Most cost increases are caused by increases in user requirements and by additional opportunities for applying IT in the client's business processes.

A disadvantage related to dependency and inflexibility is the danger of *irreversibility*. Client organizations are often afraid that they can not re-internalize their IS function if they are not satisfied with their IS supplier. If a client organization has this fear, the supplier may suggest the client does not sell the software and perhaps also hardware to the supplier and that they will maintain the hardware at the client's site. Suppliers should offer to include extensive termination provisions in the contract. It is not enough to ensure that the client can get rid of a supplier, because this does not guarantee that the services can be continued.

Some client organizations fear that they will lose the *competitive advantage* they have obtained from their information systems and IS function. Some clients consider it to be an advantage that their IS supplier has experience in their industry and has worked for competitors. Other clients fear that their supplier will use the knowledge gained while working for them, and make their competitive advantage available to competitors. It is often not sufficient for an IS supplier to guarantee the client organization that the systems developed or operated by them will not be sold to other clients, because the supplier's staff will have gained knowledge that can be deployed easily for competitors. If a client organization is really afraid of losing their competitive advantage, then the only option is that the supplier guarantees not to take assignments from the client organization's competitors.

Clients that do not take the IS function seriously or do not have a strong IS department are a risk, because these clients are not good at specifying what they want, which poses the risk that the client is not satisfied at the end. If this is the case, then advise the client to develop a thorough IS strategy and to improve its IS knowledge. Abusing the lack of knowledge and skills of the client organization usually leads to dissatisfaction and major problems in the long term.

Anticipate client organizations' demands

Client organizations have become more mature, more aware of the possibilities and limitations of information technology and consequently more critical towards IS suppliers. and as a consequence, they make increasing demands on their IS suppliers.

Client organizations want to be independent of their IS suppliers. They demand technical independence by requiring that suppliers use relatively open systems, conform to international standards and develop portable applications. Organizational independence is enforced by demanding explicit arrangements for re-internalizing or changing to another supplier and for changing activities and requirements.

The risks of IS projects are transferred increasingly to IS suppliers. Suppliers have reacted by covering these risks with tight contractual agreements, insuring against risks, tight planning, standardization, quality assurance and quality system certification.

Large client organizations strive to have a limited number of preferred suppliers. They build long term relationships, to reduce learning time and to enable the supplier to develop and use knowledge of the client's industry.

Client organizations demand that their IS supplier is familiar with their business processes and with their market. Many small IS suppliers therefore specialize in a certain industry, and large IS suppliers are reorganizing into business units that are focused on specific market segments.

Clients do not want account management to delay having small jobs performed and be an extra layer in the communication with the supplier's IS staff, especially if account managers do not have enough operational knowledge of IS and if they are difficult to reach. Client organizations do not like account managers that are only interested in maximizing profit rather than in delivering a good service.

6.3.4 Determining the attractiveness of prospect

Before IS suppliers offer a tender bid to a client organization, they should determine whether the potential assignment, often called a prospect, is attractive to them. The attractiveness of a prospect is determined by the expected costs for the supplier, the expected revenues, the risk of the project and the timing and suitability of the work for the supplier's capacity planning.

If clients have unrealistic expectations or outsource for reasons that the supplier can not comply to, the supplier may chose not to submit a bid. The demands and expectations of client organizations can be very high and conflicting. Suppliers are often tempted to go outside their specialties if an attractive prospect comes by, but this appears to be very risky.

If taking over staff and resources is part of the deal, then suppliers have to decide whether they can deploy the staff and resources. Client organizations usually do not accept the supplier selecting staff and taking over only the best employees. Some of the employees the client wants to transfer will not accept the supplier's offer and seek employment elsewhere. The supplier may be able to deploy a possible surplus of staff and resources for new clients. External suppliers may be better able to discharge personnel if they have less favorable employment conditions or if they use job counseling and outplacement services. Many client organizations have ethical objections to using these options. If an IS supplier is asked to take over employees from a client organization and guarantee the staff's employment for a certain period, then the supplier should demand a certain amount of guaranteed spending from the client organization. If the supplier expects to achieve efficiency gains and to obtain additional assignments to deploy the staff taken over, then the supplier should demand guaranteed spendings below the initial costs of the staff, because client organizations usually object to high and long term guaranteed spending agreements.

6.4 Strategies for tendering

Most client organizations will organize a formal tendering procedure to select a supplier. It is again essential that the supplier knows the motives and expectations of the client organization and adjusts the tender bid to the client organization's specific situation. It is remarkable how many suppliers claim that each client is unique to them, but submit almost identical tender bids to all potential clients.

6.4.1 Writing the proposal

Client organizations are becoming more skeptical towards general claims that outsourcing will lead always and automatically to lower costs, higher quality and flexibility and more focus on their core business. Suppliers should demonstrate improvements with explicit measures and guarantees.

Suppliers should comply to the procedural requirements of the tendering process as specified by the client organizations. Client organizations often view this as a signal of the willingness and ability of the supplier to study and accommodate to the client's situation. Client organizations often demand a specific format for the tender bid, to facilitate comparing the bids of different IS suppliers.

Client organizations often do not realize what information a supplier needs to develop a thorough tender bid. It is better to ask the client organization for clarification than to guess what the situation will be. Some client organizations may demand that questions are asked in writing and distribute the questions and answers to all participants in the tendering process.

6.4.2 Presenting the proposal

Before or after the formal written proposal, client organizations often invite suppliers to a meeting where the suppliers can present their bids and intentions.

Special attention should be paid to presenting the cost calculations. The costs of external services are often higher than clients expect, because they compare the bids to their internal costs and do not include all fixed costs and overhead in their calculation. Clients are often afraid that they have not included all services and will have to pay extra for unexpected activities. Give a clear presentation of which services are and which are not included in the tender bid. Present the financial consequences of alternative future scenarios, for example if the volume of usage of specific services increases or decreases.

6.4.3 Awarding the contract

The criteria that client organizations use for selecting the supplier, and the relative importance of these criteria, depends again on their motives for outsourcing. Client organizations that chose outsourcing to reduce costs will for example, put a high emphasis on the price of the tender bids. Many client organizations have the policy to select the bids that meet the functional and technical requirements and then chose the cheapest of these bids. Some client organizations however reconsider this strategy if there is a bid that nearly meets all requirements but is considerably cheaper.

A qualitative criterion that many client organizations use is the willingness of the IS supplier to study the client organization's specific situation and to offer a dedicated solution, concentrating on the wishes of the client instead of their own abilities. Client organizations also appreciate a supplier's willingness to take a share of the risk, as demonstrated for example by investing in the pre-bid phases, by offering a tender bid with a fixed price, or by proposing a pricing scheme based on some outcome or performance measure.

6.4.4 Contract negotiation

A supplier's contract is often not accepted by the client organization. Clients want to use published standard contracts that have been developed with the client's interests in mind, or they want to develop or use their own IS contracts. Lawyers specialized in IS outsourcing are sometimes hired to negotiate and write outsourcing contracts. Client organizations include increasingly a procurer in the negotiation team, despite some suppliers objections that outsourcing is a matter of strategic partnership instead of price negotiation.

6.5 Conclusions

The basic strategic choice of an IS supplier is between being a specialist or a total solutions provider. There is a trend towards providing total solutions, either by mergers and takeovers between suppliers, or by strategic alliances between independent suppliers. Suppliers increase their scale to reduce risks, to be competitive with international suppliers and to become international partners. Economies of scale can only be achieved if the units taken over are integrated with the other units of the supplier.

Client organizations nowadays are more critical towards IS suppliers. They demand that their IS suppliers have a thorough knowledge of their products, markets and business processes. Suppliers can meet that demand by specializing in a specific client group, or by reorganizing from being organized along functions and technical disciplines to independent units serving specific client groups.

Suppliers extend their business by moving into products or services that are in the earlier and more profitable stages of the product life cycle. IS suppliers should be very careful when entering new product market combinations that are outside their current areas and require fundamentally different skills and resources.

Long term service contracts are the best basis for obtaining additional revenues from existing clients. The employees that are physically present at the client's site very often, such as the account manager, consultants, help desk employees and system designers, very often are the best sources and initiators of additional assignments.

The paramount recommendation for approaching client organizations and for the tendering process is that the IS supplier must know the motives and expectations of the client organization and accommodate to the client's situation. A client organization that outsources for example, to increase the flexibility of the IS function should be approached in a fundamentally different manner from a client organization looking for improvements in quality or cost reductions. Determine which dangers and risks the client may expect and incorporate measures and arguments to alleviate these fears. It is also important to determine in which phase of the decision process the client organization is, and to realize that different stakeholders within client organizations may be at a different phase and have different preferences.

Tender bids should emphasize the aspects that the client values most and must demonstrate improvements instead of referring to abstract speculations about the advantages of outsourcing in general. Continuity, knowledge of the client's business, and a willingness to study and accommodate to the client situation are the most important qualitative criteria clients use to select a tender bid. Conforming to the client's procedural and format requirements is taken as a signal that the supplier is willing to accommodate to the client. Clients do not always accept the supplier's contract and often involve a professional procurer in the negotiation team.

CHAPTER 7

Conclusions

The issue of information systems (IS) outsourcing is addressed in this book. IS outsourcing, that is, commissioning part or all of the IS activities an organization needs to external IS suppliers, is a decision that has a major impact on the future performance of the organization's IS function. Some client organizations have very high expectations of IS outsourcing, fed by positive media attention and eloquent suppliers. Other clients doubt whether the improvements attributed to outsourcing will arise and fear that they will become overly dependent on external suppliers. The main conclusion of this research is that outsourcing only leads to the improvements decision makers expect if specific conditions are fulfilled, and that it may otherwise even appear to be detrimental to the organization. Improvements from outsourcing are never achieved automatically but must be supervised, and enforced if necessary, by the client organization.

The objectives of the research were to support management of client organizations when making the decision whether or not to outsource (parts of) the organization's IS function, and when designing and managing an IS outsourcing relationship. Another was to support IS suppliers when developing their marketing strategies. The research design and the research questions are reviewed, and directions for future research are given, in this final chapter.

7.1 Research design

A number of research strategies were used, to meet the objectives of the research project. The design and execution of the research strategies are recapitulated in this section.

7.1.1 Pilot study

The research project started in 1992 with a pilot study (see section 1.3.1) consisting of 30 interviews with functionaries of client organizations and IS suppliers involved in IS outsourcing decisions. The pilot study yielded very valuable information with regard to current practice in IS outsourcing decision making and to the need for decision support, and was also used as a guide for the consecutive research phases.

7.1.2 Developing a framework

The terminology used in IS outsourcing appeared to be far from clear; researchers and practitioners use many different terms and concepts in ambiguous ways. This leads to difficulties with comparing research results and to disagreements between client organizations and IS suppliers. Therefore, a descriptional framework was developed (see chapter 2), that can be used to describe systematically different types of outsourcing and other variables that are relevant in outsourcing decision making processes. The framework appeared to be very useful for structuring the findings from established organizational theories, for describing the case studies and for developing the prescriptive model for IS outsourcing decision making.

7.1.3 Analyzing organizational theories

IS outsourcing decision makers can benefit from established organizational theories. A number of these theories were analyzed (see chapter 3), and the useful elements were adapted to IS outsourcing decision making. Elements of theories on division of labor and coordination were used, transaction costs economics and agency theory appeared to be applicable and the literature on competitive strategy produced a number of guidelines.

7.1.4 Case studies

Most empirical research undertaken by other researchers has focused on the expectations and opinions of stakeholders before or shortly after outsourcing decisions. The pilot study revealed that most consequences of outsourcing only arise one or a few years after the implementation. In this research the actual consequences of 23 outsourcing decisions in the Netherlands were investigated, retrospectively up to ten years back, and longitudinally over a period of two years (see chapter 4).

7.1.5 Developing a decision model for client organizations

The decision models currently available do not comply to the criteria that a decision model should meet to give adequate support to client organizations in all phases of IS outsourcing decision making. The model developed in this research project does meet these criteria (see chapter 5). It is based on established theories and on systematic empirical research and covers all phases of IS outsourcing, from the initial sourcing decision to the management and termination of outsourcing. Differences between different types of outsourcing are incorporated in the model. The model recognizes that the attractiveness of and approach to outsourcing depends on the specific situation of the client organization and guidelines are given for analyzing situational factors. The model is intended to be applicable during the outsourcing decision processes.

7.1.6 Developing strategies for IS suppliers

Client organizations and IS suppliers both have an interest in a smoothly functioning IS market, in which suppliers offer products and services that client organizations have a need for, and where good matches and resultant cooperation between clients and suppliers evolve. The case studies yielded a lot of information that is also useful to suppliers. This information was used to give guidelines to IS suppliers to assist them in determining attractive product market combinations, entering new market segments, identifying and approaching client organizations, and responding to calls for tender (see chapter 6).

7.2 Research findings

The conclusions from the research project are recapitulated in this section. The section is structured along the line of the research questions given in chapter 1.

7.2.1 Framework

The first research question addresses the need for consistent and systematic terminology to be able to describe different types of outsourcing:

1. *How can the variables that are relevant for IS outsourcing be described systematically?*

Based on a systems theory perspective, the concepts relevant to IS outsourcing are divided into situational factors, decision variables and goal variables (see section 2.4). Situational factors are the characteristics of the IS function, the client organization and the environment that are relevant to IS outsourcing decision making. Decision variables are the variables that decision makers can, and want to, influence. Goal variables are the variables that indicate the actual or required performance of the IS function.

This classification of variables is not fixed, and specific variables can take different roles depending on the specific situation. In specific decision processes, decision makers should decide which variables they must, or want to, take as situational factors, which decision variables they can and want to change, and which goal variables they want to optimize. The roles of the variables can change during the decision processes, for example if previous demarcations appear to be too strict or if the authority of the decision makers has changed.

Conclusion 1
Variables in IS outsourcing can be classified into situational factors, decision variables and goal variables. Specific variables have different roles in different decision situations, and can change roles during the decision process.

7.2.2 Consequences of IS outsourcing

The research was aimed at determining the actual consequences, in practice, of IS outsourcing and of sourcing decisions, instead of asking stakeholders for their opinions and expectations shortly after taking outsourcing decisions.

2. What are the actual consequences of IS sourcing decisions in the short and long term?

IS outsourcing has significant consequences for the performance of the IS function. The consequences of the outsourcing decisions investigated ranged from evident successes, where results were achieved that could not have been realized without external suppliers, to clear failures, where client organizations faced many problems and did not achieve the objectives of their outsourcing decisions. In many cases, however, mixed results were achieved. Outsourcing decisions were beneficial in certain respects but not in other aspects, and stakeholders often had different opinions as to the success of the outsourcing operations (see section 4.6).

Generally, IS outsourcing appeared to lead to higher *flexibility* of the IS portfolio. Activities could be started at almost any time, given that there were suppliers that had the necessary skills and resources. Flexibility during activities however generally decreased. Once the requirements were specified and the contracts were signed, it was more difficult to change requirements or delay or speed up outsourced activities than internal activities. Changes had to be renegotiated and suppliers sometimes demanded more favorable conditions for the excess work because they were in a better position to negotiate.

Decision makers often expected higher *controllability* because the supplier's performance could be enforced by a contract, but they were often disappointed in this respect. Many contracts were not specific enough to describe all the necessary requirements. It is also usually not sufficient for a client organization if the suppliers confine themselves to the minimum effort needed to comply to the contractual agreement. The extra effort needed to deliver a satisfactory instead of a minimum result can not be enforced by a contract. The contract is but one of the power resources. Some client organizations depended so much on their IS suppliers that they could not afford to enforce their contractual agreements. None of the client organizations in the case studies took legal action against their suppliers, even though some suppliers did not comply to certain contractual agreements.

Controllability often did not increase or decrease with outsourcing, but changed, because control changed from managing internal staff and resources to managing contract relationships. This requires fundamentally different management skills that were not always present at the client organizations.

No conclusive results were obtained with respect to *costs* of internal versus outsourced activities. Existing financial administrations were often not adequate for comparing the costs of individual IS activities before and after implementation of outsourcing decisions. If decision makers quantified their expectations of cost reduction at all, they often quantified expected reductions at the level of the IS department's total costs, and not at the level of individual activities. Cost awareness of users was only increased if the costs of their requests were actually charged to their budgets and if budgets were tight. Even if suppliers managed to reduce costs, they did not always charge a lower price.

When analyzing *lead times*, decision makers often did not include preparation time. After outsourcing, they were disappointed in the time it took before the actual work began. Requirement specification, market research, tendering, contract negotiation and acquainting the supplier often took much more time than decision makers had expected. The lead times of the actual work sometimes improved by outsourcing, but this advantage was lost due to the extra time needed for setting up the transaction. Lead times of outsourced activities were significantly shorter only if the client organization did not have the necessary staff and resources and would otherwise have had to hire or retrain staff and acquire resources to perform the activity.

Whether the *quality* of outsourced IS activities increased or decreased was also difficult to assess, mainly because requirements were not always defined clearly in advance, especially not in the initial internal situation.

Continuity of the IS activities appeared to depend not only on the probability that the IS supplier would go bankrupt, but was also endangered by the fact that suppliers sometimes decided to stop releasing new versions of software packages or system software, or even withdrew from the client organization's market segment. Other clients experienced problems with continuity if the supplier changed regularly the staff deployed for the client.

Conclusion 2
Generally, IS outsourcing leads to higher *flexibility* of the IS portfolio, but to less flexibility during activities. *Controllability* changes from managing internal staff and resources to managing contract relationships. Costs, *lead time* and *quality* may increase or decrease in practice, depending on the choice of supplier and the type of outsourcing arrangement.

7.2.3 Situational factors

The research is based on the contingency approach, which states that no single solution is optimal in all circumstances, and that situational factors determine the most appropriate choices. This led to the following research question:

3. *What situational factors are relevant for IS outsourcing decision making and how should these factors be taken into account?*

Situational factors were found mainly in the organizational theories. The case studies led to a number of additional factors. The relevance of most situational factors was demonstrated by the case studies (see section 4.7).

Outsourcing is sensible only if the information systems are not strategic, if IS activities can be separated, if requirements can be specified in detail and in advance, and if compliance to these requirements can be measured and enforced. Sufficient suppliers must be available that offer the pertinent product or service, because otherwise there is no actual market for the product or service and consequently no market pressure.

Outsourcing is beneficial only if suppliers have characteristics that give them the opportunity to perform better than the client organization's internal department, and if the client organization will be able to enforce the improvements and obtain some of the benefits. These conditions are present if a supplier performs similar activities for multiple client organizations and on a considerably larger scale than the client organization, and integrates the activities performed for multiple clients in one organizational unit.

> *Conclusion 3*
> Outsourcing is *sensible* only if activities are measurable, if suffi-
> cient IS suppliers offer the pertinent product, and if the client can
> remain independent.
> Outsourcing is *beneficial* only if the supplier has attestable
> economies of scale or has experience and resources available that
> a client needs.

7.2.4 Decision variables

The fourth research question addresses the outsourcing arrangement that must be designed and managed if client organizations have
decided to outsource part of their IS function.

4. *What are the options for designing and managing an outsourcing
   arrangement, and what options should be chosen in a specific
   situation?*

There are many different types of outsourcing and new forms are
evolving constantly. The first element in describing an outsourcing
situation is to demarcate the part of the IS function that is to be
outsourced. An organization's IS function, that is, the aggregate of
activities and resources needed to establish and sustain the information systems required by the organization, can be classified using three
dimensions: the *information systems* the IS function provides, the *IS
components* that make up the information systems, and the *IS
activities* necessary to establish and sustain the information systems
(see section 2.4).

Specific outsourcing arrangements can be described using a
number of variables, grouped in five categories. The type of *relationship*
between a client organization and a supplier is described by the legal,
economic and transactional relationship and the freedom to chose
business partners. The *division among suppliers and contracts* is
whether and how IS activities are separated among multiple suppliers,
and whether and how IS activities outsourced to an IS supplier are
governed by separate contracts. The *management structure* is determined by the type of requirement specification, the mechanisms for
pricing, lead time, quality control, conflict resolution and coordination. The *operational structure* is the location, ownership, employment
and exclusiveness of the IS components. The *internal organization of
the outsourcing coordination* includes the degree of centralization and
the distribution among line management and staff of the activities and
skills needed for coordinating outsourcing, and whether (part of) the
outsourcing coordination is outsourced.

Conclusion 4.1
Types of outsourcing can be described systematically by denoting which IS activities are outsourced with regard to which IS components of which information systems, and by describing the outsourcing arrangement using the decision variables summarized above.

In the cases where outsourcing led to considerable and attestable improvements, these improvements did not arise automatically, but were enforced by the client organization. Decision makers had designed the outsourcing arrangements in a way that allowed and stimulated the supplier to achieve savings and other improvements and enforced that at least part of these benefits went to the client organization (see section 4.8).

Guaranteed spending should be avoided or minimized, because they impair competition and provide no incentive at all for suppliers to deliver good products and services under reasonable conditions. The cost awareness of the users also does not increase, because the money guaranteed must be spent, whether it is necessary or not. Guaranteed spending agreements are usually demanded by suppliers if a client organization wants to outsource IS staff and wants the supplier to guarantee the employment of the staff, but the amount guaranteed should start below the client's initial costs and decrease fast over a few years.

It is advisable to establish framework contracts and cooperation agreements with a few regular suppliers, because this decreases the costs of contracting, increases the quality of the contracts and thereby leads to outsourcing arrangements that are better manageable. If user departments want to outsource IS activities, they only need to specify the requirements and they can refer to the general conditions of the contract. Having regular suppliers also decreases the costs incurred when familiarizing new suppliers. The regular suppliers obtain and maintain knowledge of the client organization and its business processes.

Outsourcing of clearly demarcated and well defined activities to multiple suppliers under separate contracts increases flexibility and control and maximizes competition. Client organizations can then specify requirements and measure compliance, and can switch to other suppliers more easily if one supplier under performs. If suppliers know that they are really competing with other suppliers, that changing suppliers is feasible, and that they have to perform well to obtain consecutive assignments, they are more motivated to deploy their best efforts, staff and resources.

Conclusion 4.2
Guaranteed spending should be avoided or minimized. Establishing framework contracts and cooperation agreements is advised.

Outsourcing of clearly demarcated and well defined activities to multiple suppliers under separate contracts increases flexibility and control and maximizes competition.

Suppliers can achieve economies of scale best if the IS components are owned by the supplier and located at the supplier's site and if the client organization does not demand exclusiveness (see section 4.8). Client organizations may however, have reasons to keep the components in their ownership at their own sites, for example because they think this improves security and confidentiality. If client organizations do not demand exclusive use of resources, then the supplier can sell the products or services to other clients. This decreases the costs, but also decreases the client organization's ability to use the products or services to gain advantage over their competitors. The ready-made products and services may not meet the specific needs of a client organization.

Specialized outsourcing activities, such as market research, tendering, contracting and quality assessment should be performed by a central staff unit. These activities require specialized knowledge and skills, and individual user departments do not outsource often enough to establish and sustain these capacities. A central unit can coordinate all outsourced activities, build the necessary skills, and assist user departments if they want to outsource IS activities. The user departments however should maintain the role of the client, determine the functional requirements and make the actual assignments. If the central staff unit takes the role of the client, then the involvement of the client's user department decreases and the final result may not be accepted by the users.

Conclusion 4.3
Economies of scale can be achieved best if IS components are owned by the supplier, located at the supplier's site and if the client organization does not demand exclusive use of resources. A central staff unit should support user departments in performing specialized outsourcing activities.

The case studies included six cases of outsourcing of the client organization's central IS department. Most of the stakeholders in these client organization were more or less dissatisfied with the outsourcing, for various reasons. None of the suppliers integrated the IS departments taken over with their other units, so economies of scale, additional clients for the IS departments and new expertise for the client organization were not realized. In most cases, some top managers were replaced and account managers were appointed from other units of the supplier, but the supplier made no other effort to improve the IS department and exploited the guaranteed spendings that have been agreed. Client organizations often expected that the department would be transformed from a bureaucratic internal staff department to an innovative and customer-oriented organization, but since they were served by their former employees and the supplier had not tried to or succeeded in transforming the department, hardly any changes were noted (see section 4.8).

The main reason that the IS suppliers in these cases were not stimulated or forced to achieve improvements was the fact that in all these cases high levels of long term guaranteed spending had been agreed. The suppliers had guaranteed revenues for a number of years that were enough to cover all costs of the departments taken over, regardless of how well the departments performed. Since a significant percentage of the former employees sought employment elsewhere at the time of the outsourcing implementation or afterwards, the suppliers gained a large margin on the departments.

One significant exception was an outsourcing operation that was initially not very successful, because the supplier was not cooperative and focused on short time revenues instead of customer satisfaction. The supplier went bankrupt some time after the outsourcing operation. The former department was sold to a small holding that had a genuine interest in the department itself, reinstalled the cooperative culture and used its marketing channels and the expertise of other units to improve the department and to obtain new clients.

Conclusion 4.4
Outsourcing of an entire IS department only leads to improvements if the department is integrated with the other units and also serves other clients. This can be stimulated by not agreeing to a high level of guaranteed spending and by choosing a supplier with a genuine interest in improving the department instead of one that sees it merely as a financial investment.

7.2.5 Outsourcing decision making

The research was aimed at supporting decision makers in practice, not only by giving guidelines for the actual decisions to be taken, but also by providing a decision model to support the decision processes that are needed to take sound sourcing decisions.

5.   *How should the outsourcing decision process be organized?*

Many large outsourcing decisions in the case study organizations were taken mainly by top management in a relatively short time without a thorough analysis of the triggers and problems that gave rise to considering outsourcing and all external and internal alternatives for solving these problems.

The decision model described in chapter 5 contains guidelines for the outsourcing decision process, and is divided into six phases. The recommendations for each of these phases are recapitulated below.

Phase 1: Initial sourcing decision

A sourcing evaluation should only be initiated if the dissatisfaction with the current situation and the potential improvements to be gained from changing the sourcing are expected to outweigh the costs and the risks of the evaluation process (see section 5.1).

The decision team must include enough authority, expertise and representation to ensure good decisions and the power and commitment for implementation. The expertise needed for IS outsourcing decision making includes business process expertise, IT expertise, IS planning and design expertise, IS market expertise, outsourcing expertise, legal expertise, and financial expertise. This often requires the inclusion of top management, IS management and (representatives of) IS staff and users.

Outsourcing decisions are strongly related to information planning. Outsourcing is but one of the organizational decisions that can be taken to improve the IS function. Previous sourcing decisions determine to a large extent the number and nature of IS activities that can be planned. Outsourcing should not be a one-off isolated decision, but an integral and recurrent consideration within the information planning cycle.

IS outsourcing decision making does not always involve the entire IS function. The part of the IS function that is subject of the decision process should be demarcated unambiguously, by stating which information systems, IS activities and IS components are involved.

Decision makers should include long term consequences in the decision process and look beyond the time scope of the (potential) contract and beyond the life cycle of the technology in use. Goal variables must be specified to evaluate the performance of internal or external IS suppliers and to compare alternative sourcing options. The relative importance of these variables depends on the role and value of the IS function to the client organization. Attaching different weights to goal variables should not lead to a one-sided emphasis on one or a few goal variables. All goal variables must at least be taken into account. It is especially dangerous to fixate on reductions in costs and staffing levels, without including the consequences to the other goal variables.

The total requirements for IS staff and resources can be determined by analyzing the current information systems and IS activities and any plans for developing new systems and sustaining, changing or terminating existing systems. The need for and usage of all the systems in use must be evaluated.

Decision makers should be critical towards the perceptions and triggers that initiated the sourcing evaluation. If some problems were encountered when analyzing the initial situation, decision makers should not immediately chose outsourcing as the only solution. Many problems are not caused by insourcing and are not solved automatically by outsourcing.

Decision makers should develop and analyze a number of internal and external alternatives for improving the IS function. They should include the alternatives of maintaining or improving the current situation. Evaluate each option with regard to the goal variables. Chose an alternative, based on the evaluation and the relative importance of the variables.

External IS suppliers have to be evaluated on their actual performance and abilities instead of assuming superiority based on theoretical considerations. The internal IS department and external IS suppliers have to be compared on an equal basis. The comparison should include the same products and services, at the same quality level and within the same time constraints. Include all the initial and the recurrent costs and efforts.

Conclusion 5.1
IS sourcing decisions should be integral part of the IS planning and strategy development process. External and internal alternatives for improving the IS function should be analyzed on an equal basis and with regard to their actual short and long term consequences.

Phase 2: Designing the outsourcing arrangement
Two major objectives should be kept in mind when designing the outsourcing relationship. First, decision makers should realize that the advantages and improvements that were the reason for choosing outsourcing can only be realized if the outsourcing relationship is designed in a way that enables and enforces these improvements. A well designed outsourcing arrangement increases the likelihood that expected improvements will be realized and potential dangers are avoided or dealt with (see section 5.2).

Second, the outsourcing relationship should be designed to maximize the client organization's flexibility and control and to ensure that the client organization remains able to deploy information systems to its advantage and adapt to changing circumstances and needs. Flexibility and control is maintained by maximizing competition. To that end, decision makers should take a selective approach toward outsourcing and outsource well defined separate IS activities to multiple suppliers under separate contracts. The internal IS department and external IS suppliers are then competing constantly to obtain assignments.

Decision makers should have a clear view of the preferred outsourcing arrangement before starting tendering procedures After selecting an IS supplier, however, the arrangement must be negotiated with the supplier. It may be that the supplier does not accept the design as desired. The supplier's claims may be justified, for example because the design impedes the supplier achieving certain improvements the client wants, but it can also be a tactic to obtain an arrangement that is more to their benefit.

Conclusion 5.2
The design of the outsourcing arrangement is the most important factor that determines whether improvements by outsourcing will actually be achieved. Decision makers should have a clear view of the preferred outsourcing arrangement before starting tendering procedures.

Phase 3: Selecting the IS supplier
The selection process proposed in section 5.3 is a highly formalized and structured process. A supplier can also be selected informally, based on impressions and personal contacts, but this is strongly discouraged, because of the risk that important criteria or very good suppliers are overlooked (see section 5.3).

A detailed and comprehensive call for tender is essential for the supplier to write a realistic tender bid and for the client organization to select the best supplier. It also facilitates contracting considerably. A call for tender should include a description of the current situation, functional and technical requirements, the design of the outsourcing arrangement, schedule of meetings and intermediate and final products and reports, format and content of tender bids, and procedures for the tendering process.

If the client organization does not know the IS market well enough to select a small number of potential suppliers, pre-selection can be used, by inviting a large number of suppliers to answer a few general questions that make it possible for the client organization to select a short-list of potential suppliers.

If the client organization has an internal IS department, the department should also be invited to offer a tender response. Many client organizations compare external bids to the current performance of the internal IS department. The internal IS department has to have the chance to include improvements in their bid. Internal departments are sometimes forced, by organizational politics, historical reasons or interference from higher management, to satisfy individual users' idiosyncratic needs and maintain certain inefficient practices. These requirements are often not made to suppliers. If the department has the authority to institute best practices, it might be able to improve significantly if they get the freedom to apply the same measures that external suppliers will use.

It is good negotiating practice to start with determining the desired and minimum result, instead of being satisfied with the best offer received. Otherwise, the client organization might end up, for example, choosing the cheapest of five bids, while that bid is not as efficient as is possible or the amount is still 20% higher than the budget available for the activities.

Each member of the tendering team should evaluate the proposals independently before comparing the members' preferences. If the best bids are considerably better than the current situation or than the bid of the internal IS department, decision makers should analyze how the suppliers achieve these improvements, and make sure that it is not by lowering quality, leaving out requirements, or using creative accounting methods. If the selection has come down to one or a few remaining responses, references should be checked intensively, because these are often the most valuable sources of information on the supplier's performance. Suppliers often push for exclusive negotiations in an early stage, but it is better to negotiate with two or more suppliers for as long as possible before making a final choice, because that gives the client organization more bargaining power.

A solid and detailed contract is necessary to enforce adequate performance by the supplier. Using standard or framework contracts increases the efficiency and effectiveness of contracting. The client organization should not accept the suppliers standard contract, not even as a starting point for drafting a new contract. Suppliers' contracts are usually biased towards the suppliers' interests. Writing a contract is also an educational exercise that may lead to useful insights about the outsourcing relationship.

The contract must cover all consecutive phases of outsourcing and include arrangements for the implementation or transition phase, for the continuous management of the outsourced activities, for intermediate changes in requirements, for early termination before the end of the contract, and for regular termination at the end of the contract.

The functional and technical requirements should be specified in detail and in measurable terms. Arrangements must be made for measuring and reporting compliance to these requirements and the contract must specify measures in case of non-compliance, such as penalty clauses.

Conclusion 5.3
A structured tendering process and a detailed and comprehensive call for tender improve the selection and contracting process. The internal IS department should be invited to offer a tender bid which includes internal improvements.

Phase 4: Implementing outsourcing decision
Good preparation in the previous phases will facilitate the remain-

ing phases to a great extent. If a systematic initial sourcing decision is followed by a thorough design of the outsourcing relationship and critical supplier selection, then most of the important decisions with regard to the consecutive phases have been taken. Implementing, managing, renewing, extending and terminating the outsourcing relationship will then require much less effort and most potential problems will be avoided.

Implementation of a sourcing decision may involve transferring the location, ownership or employment of the IS staff and other IS resources. The systems and knowledge necessary for the supplier to perform the outsourced activities should also be transferred. Considerable time should be planned for transferring the information systems, as this usually takes more time than decision makers expect and suppliers imply (see section 5.4).

Conclusion 5.4
Considerable time and resources should be planned for transferring the information systems.

Phase 5: Managing the outsourcing relationship
An outsourcing relationship must be managed and controlled actively by the client organization, to ensure that the relationship is designed and operated in the interests of the client (see section 5.5).

IS activities that are outsourced require as much coordination effort as internal activities. Outsourcing coordination is not trivial and requires significant staff and resources. Managing an outsourcing relationship requires fundamentally different management skills from that of managing an internal IS department.

The client organization should keep enough IS staff to develop the IS strategy, to monitor and control the IS supplier and the IS market. The client organization should maintain knowledge and skills: to know the opportunities and limitations of current and future information technologies; to conceptualize new applications of IT in their business processes; to issue tenders and evaluate supplier responses; to specify technical and functional requirements; to assess what are reasonable costs and lead times; to be up to date with available IS suppliers and their qualities; to negotiate conditions and contracts; to evaluate IS suppliers' progress, intermediate results and final deliveries; to be able to perform some IS activities internal, permanently or temporarily, if necessary; and to do small or urgent jobs that can not wait for a tendering process.

The knowledge and skills of the internal IS staff can be kept up to date by performing part of the IS activities internally. Internal IS staff should meet with supplier's staff regularly, or even take part in a job rotation scheme with the supplier. Internal IS staff may work for the supplier occasionally and vice versa.

The users should provide the input and information on the business processes that the supplier needs to perform the activities. The intermediate and final products or services delivered should be checked to determine whether the results comply with the requirements. Progress and resource usage should be according to the planning. Some clients make considerable effort to define functional and technical requirements but do not measure whether the supplier complies to these requirements or measure insufficiently. If requirements are stated in terms of percentages and averages, measurement should comply to statistical rules.

If the supplier does not comply to the requirements, the measures that are agreed to enforce compliance should be used. Some client organizations have negotiated penalty clauses or other compliance measures, but do not want to use these measures, because they are afraid to harm the good working relationship. Compliance measures are however regular business agreements that are used to place the burden of non-compliance on the party that caused it.

Conclusion 5.5
Keep enough IS staff and resources internally to remain a critical and competent principal. Keep the knowledge and skills of the IS staff up to date by performing part of the operational IS activities in-house and by arranging regular meetings or even job rotation with the IS supplier.

Phase 6: Terminating the outsourcing relationship
At the end of the contract period, client organizations may decide to renew the contract, change to another supplier, change the design of the outsourcing relationship, or terminate the outsourcing relationship completely. Conditions for termination should be arranged before the outsourcing arrangement is implemented. Compliance to provisions for (early) termination should be measured during the entire activity. If the supplier has for example agreed to transfer all system documentation in case of termination of the relationship, the client organization should check regularly whether documentation is kept up to date, because insufficient documentation can not be brought up in the case of bankruptcy of the supplier (see section 5.6).

Conclusion 5.6
Provisions for termination should be arranged in advance and checked during the entire activity.

7.2.6 Strategies for IS suppliers

Client organizations and IS suppliers both have an interest in a smoothly functioning IS market, in which supply and demand for IS products and services are complementary. Both parties have similar information needs, and the information gathered in this research may also benefit IS suppliers (see chapter 6).

6. How can IS suppliers use the answers to the previous questions when developing their marketing strategies?

The basic strategic choice of an IS supplier is between being a specialist or a total solutions provider. There is a trend towards providing total solutions, either by mergers and takeovers between suppliers, or by strategic alliances between independent suppliers. Suppliers increase their scale to reduce risks, to be competitive with international suppliers and to become international partners themselves. Economies of scale can only be achieved if the units taken over are integrated with the other units of the supplier.

Suppliers extend their business into products or services that are in an earlier and more profitable stage of the product life cycle. IS suppliers should be very careful when entering new product market combinations (PMCs) that are outside their current areas and require fundamentally different skills and resources.

Long term service contracts are the best basis for obtaining additional revenues from existing clients. The employees that are physically present at the client's site, such as the account manager, consultants, help desk employees and system designers, are the best sources and initiators of additional assignments.

The paramount recommendation for approaching client organizations and for the tendering process is that the IS supplier must know the motives and expectations of the client organization and accommodate to the client's situation. A client organization that outsources for example to increase the flexibility of the IS function should be approached in a fundamentally different manner from a client organization looking for improvements in quality or cost reductions. Determine which dangers and risks the client may expect and incorporate measures and arguments to alleviate these fears. It is also important to determine in which phase of the decision process the client organization is, and to realize that different stakeholders within client organizations may be at a different phase and have different preferences.

Tender bids should emphasize the aspects that the client values most and must demonstrate improvements instead of referring to abstract speculations about the advantages of outsourcing in general. Continuity, knowledge of the client's business, and a willingness to study and accommodate to the client situation are the most important qualitative criteria clients use to select a tender bid. Conforming to the client's procedural and format requirements is taken as a signal that the supplier is willing to accommodate to the client.

Client organizations nowadays are more critical towards IS suppliers. They demand that their IS suppliers have a thorough knowledge of their products, markets and business processes. Suppliers can meet that demand by specializing in a specific client group, or by reorganizing from being organized along functions and technical disciplines to independent units serving specific client groups. Clients do not always accept the supplier's contract and often involve a procurer in the negotiation team.

Conclusion 6:
IS suppliers must determine the motives and expectations of a client organization and focus their approach and their proposal on these motives. Client organizations chose an IS supplier mainly based on continuity and the willingness of the supplier to study and accommodate to the client's situation.

7.3 Further research

7.3.1 Testing the utility of the model

Time constraints have impeded testing the utility of model in practice. The utility of the model can be investigated by applying the model in actual IS outsourcing decision making processes, to determine whether the format and structure of the model matches the needs of decision makers in practice.

7.3.2 Outsourcing the use of information systems

Outsourcing of the use of information systems, which implies outsourcing entire informational processes, was not investigated in this research. It is however a very relevant phenomenon with high potential impact on the organization of informational processes. It would be a very useful extension of this research to investigate the considerations and consequences of outsourcing informational processes.

Historically, pay roll processing and book keeping were about the only structured informational processes that were outsourced to service bureaus and accountants. Nowadays many other structured and unstructured informational processes can and are being outsourced, such as market research, consultancy, billing and factoring, processing of forms, direct mailing, order entry and even entire order processing.

Client organizations show an increasing tendency to outsource informational processes, especially large-scale, structured, routine processes. IS suppliers increasingly offer to take over informational processes. It is mainly the IS suppliers offering mainframe capacity and operation of hardware and system software that offer these services, maybe because previous large scale outsourcing operations and takeovers of data centers and IS departments have left them with data entry personnel.

7.3.3 A comprehensive method for IS management

IS outsourcing is only one of the organizational parameters in IS management. The logical steps that are taken in IS management are listed below. These steps do not occur in this chronological order, but form mutually dependent aspects of IS management. The steps are:

1. developing an IS strategy, in interaction with the organization's overall business strategy,
2. identifying and selecting information systems that are to be developed, adapted, sustained or terminated,
3. deciding which of the consequent IS activities are to be performed internally and which are to be outsourced,
4. organizing and managing the internal IS activities,
5. organizing and managing the outsourced IS activities.

This research was aimed at steps 3 and 5. Work has been undertaken in each of the other areas by other researchers, and guidelines and methods are available for each step. There are however many relationships between these steps, logically and chronologically. The IS strategy, for example, should support the organization's overall business strategy, which should in turn consider the limitations and the new opportunities provided by information technology and IS strategies. The information systems currently in use determine to some extent the possibilities for changing the IS strategy. The degree of outsourcing and the internal IS resources determine how many and which information systems can be developed and adapted. A comprehensive method for IS management should support all of these steps, and most importantly, the interaction between the steps.

A start has been made towards integrating steps 3, 4 and 5, by combining the findings of this research with the findings of Mantelaers (1995) on organizing the internal IS function, into a course on effective design of the IS function (Mantelaers and De Looff, 1996).

REFERENCES

Ang, S. (1994) Towards Conceptual Clarity of Outsourcing. *Proceedings of the IFIP TC8 Open Conference on Business Process Reengineering,* Gold Coast Queensland, Australia, May 8-11.

Ang, S. and C.M. Beath (1993) Hierarchical Elements in Software Contracts. *Journal of Organisational Computing,* 3, 3, pp. 329-361.

Arnett, K.P. and M.C. Jones (1994) Firms that choose outsourcing: A profile. *Information & Management,* 26.

Aubert, B.A., S. Rivard and M. Patry (1993) A Transaction Costs Approach to Outsourcing: Some Empirical Evidence. *Proceedings of the ASAC IS Division,* Lake Louise.

Aubert, B.A., S. Rivard and M. Patry (1994) Development of measures to assess dimensions of IS operation transactions. *Proceedings of the Fifteenth International Conference on Information Systems,* Vancouver, Canada, December 14-17.

Aubert, B.A. (1994) *Outsourcing of Information Services; A Transaction Cost analysis,* PhD thesis, Ecole des Hautes Etudes Commmerciales, Montreal, Canada.

Auwers, T. and D. DeSchoolmeester (1993) The Dynamics of an Outsourcing Relationship: a case in the Belgian Food Industry. *Outsourcing of Information Systems Services Workshop,* Twente, The Netherlands, May 20-22.

Beath, C.M. (1987) Managing the User Relationship in IS Development Projects: A Transaction Governance Approach. *Proceedings of the 8th International Conference on Information Systems,* Pittsburgh, PA.

Benbasat, I, D.K. Goldstein and M. Mead (1987) The Case Research Strategy in Studies of Information Systems. *MIS Quarterly,* 11, 3, 369-386.

Beulen, E.J.J., P. Ribbers and J. Roos (1994) *Outsourcing van IT-dienstverlening: een make or buy beslissing.* Kluwer, Deventer (in Dutch).

Berghout, E.W. and T.J.W. Renkema (1994) *Evaluating information system investment proposals: a comparative review of current methodologies.* Research report 94-27, Delft University of Technology.

Borgers, N.J.W. (1995) *Strategiebepaling op de markt voor Facilities Management-dienstverlening.* Master's Thesis, Eindhoven University of Technology (in Dutch).

Broek, J.G.A. van den (1990), Uitbesteding van informatievoorzieningstaken; een demagogische verhandeling, in: J.G.A. van den Broek, G. Jager, J. Steegh (red.), *Voor een informaticus zonder computer; Vriendenboek aangeboden aan de heer B.K. Brussaard bij zijn afscheid van de rijksdienst,* Ministerie van Binnenlandse Zaken, 's-Gravenhage (in Dutch).

Brussaard, B.K. (1992) Large Scale Information Systems: A Comparative Analysis. P.H.A. Frissen, V.J.J.M. Bekkers, B.K. Brussaard, I.T M. Snellen and M. Wolters (eds.), *European Public Administration and Informatization, a comparative research project into policies, systems, infrastructures and projects,* IOS Press, Amsterdam, The Netherlands.

Brussaard, B.K. (1995) *Information Systems in Theory.* Exaugural Lecture, Delft University Press (in Dutch).

Buck-Lew, M. (1992) To outsource or Not? *International Journal of Information Management,* 12, 3-20.

Buijs, P. and C. van der Kraa (1996) Uitgangspunten bij outsourcing. *Outsourcing in Nederland; een onderzoek naar de bedrijfsmatige structurering van IT en uitbesteding,* Giarte Publishing, Amsterdam (in Dutch).

CCOI (Centrale Commissie Overheidsinformatievoorziening) (1990), *Uitbesteding van informatievoorzieningstaken; aanbeveling in het kader van het besluit IVR,* 's Gravenhage.

Cash Jr., J. and B.R. Konsynski (1985) IS redraws competitive boundaries. *Harvard Business Review,* 63, 2.

Cheon, M.J., V. Grover and J.T.C. Teng (1995) Theoretical perspectives on the outsourcing of information systems. *Journal of Information Technology,* 10, 209-219.

Coase, R.H. (1973) The nature of the firm. *Economica,* 4, 386-405.

CCTA (Central Computer and Telecommunications Agency) (1994) *IT Infrastructure Library,* Norwich, England.

Deitz, R. (1996) IT investeringen tussen berekening en inspiratie. PhD Thesis, Eindhoven University of Technology (in Dutch).

Douma, S. and H. Schreuder (1992) *Economic Approaches to Organisations.* Prentice Hall, Englewood Cliffs, New Jersey.

Douglass, D.P. (ed.) (1993) New Wrinkles in IS Outsourcing. *I/S Analyzer,* 31, 9.

Earl, M.J. (1989) *Management Strategies for Information Technology.* Prentice Hall, Englewood Cliffs, New Jersey.

Eggleton, D. and G. Otter (1991) Outsourcing Information Systems

Services. Research Report, Butler Cox Foundation, London.

Eisenhardt, K.M. (1989) Building Theories from Case Study Research. *Academy of Management Review*, 14, 532-550.

Eisenhardt, K.M. (1989) Agency theory: An Assessment and Review. *Academy of Management Review*, 14, 57-74.

Euromethod consortium (1994) Euromethod.

Fama, E.F. (1980) Agency problems and the theory of the firm. *Journal of Political Economics*, 80, 21, 288-307.

Fitzgerald, G. (1994) *The Outsourcing of Information Technology: Revenge of the Business Manager or Legitimate Strategic Option?* Inaugural Lecture, Birkbeck College, 19th October.

Fitzgerald, G. and L. Willcocks (1994) *Information Technology Outsourcing Practice: A UK survey.* Business Intelligence, London.

Fitzgerald, G. and Willcocks, L. (1994) Contracts and Partnerships in the Outsourcing of IT. *Proceedings of the Fifteenth International Conference on Information Systems*, Vancouver, Canada.

Galbraith, J.R. (1973) *Designing Complex Organizations.* Addison-Wesley, Reading, Massachusetts.

Galbraith, J.R. (1977) *Organization Design.* Addison-Wesley, Reading, Massachusetts.

Galliers, R.D. and F.F. Land (1987) Choosing Appropriate Information Systems Research Methodologies. *Communications of the ACM*, 30, 11.

Gantz, J. (1990) Outsourcing: threat or salvation? *Networking Management*, 10.

Ginzberg, A. and N. Venkatraman (1985) Contingency perspectives of organizational strategy: a critical review of empirical research. *Academy of Management Review*, 10, 421-434.

Griese, J. (1993) Outsourcing of Information Systems in Switzerland; A Status Report. *Outsourcing of Information Systems Services Workshop*, Twente, The Netherlands, May 20-22.

Gurbaxani, V. and S. Whang (1991) The impact of information systems on organisations and markets. *Communications of the ACM*, 34, 1, 59-73.

Harrington, J. (1990) *Organizational structure and information technology.* Prentice Hall, London.

Heinzl, A. (1993) Outsourcing the Information Systems Function within the Company - an empirical study. *Outsourcing of Information Systems Services Workshop,* Twente, The Netherlands, May 20-22.

Hewett, W.G. (1994) If Outsourcing IT is the answer - What is the Question? *Proceedings of the IFIP TC8 Open Conference on business Process Re-engineering: Information System Opportunities and Challenges,* Gold Coast Queensland, Australia, May 8-11, 1994, North-Holland, Amsterdam.

Hoogeveen, D. (1994) *Outsourcing,* Kluwer, Deventer.

Huber, R. (1993) How Continental Bank Outsourced its 'Crown Jewels'. *Harvard Business Review*, 71, 1, 121-129.

IDC Nederland (1990) *Facilities Management in Nederland: de vraagkant.* Amsterdam (in Dutch).

IJpelaar, D.P.N.M. (1993) *Beslissingsondersteuning bij het bepalen van een informatiestrategie.* Moret Ernst & Young Management Consultants, Utrecht (in Dutch).

Jensen, M.C. and Meckling, W.H. (1976) Theory of the firm: managerial behaviour, agency costs and ownership structure. *Journal of Financial Economics*, 3, 305-360.

Kaplan, B. and D. Duchon (1988) Combining Qualitative and Quantitative Methods in Information Systems Research: A Case Study. *MIS Quarterly*, 12, 571-586.

Kennedy, M.M. (1979) Generalizing from single case studies. *Evaluation Quarterly*, 3, 4, 661-678.

Ketler, K. and J. Walstrom (1993) The Outsourcing Decision. *International Journal of Information Management*, 13.

Ketler, K. and J. Walstrom (1994) An Overview of the Outsourcing Decision. M. Khosrowpour (ed.), *Information Technology and Organizations; challenges of new technologies*, Idea Group Publishing, Harrisburg.

Klepper, R. (1995) The management of partnering development in I/S outsourcing. *Journal of Information Technology*, Theme Issue Information Technology Outsourcing: Theory and Practice, 10, 4, 249-258.

Kraljic, P. (1983) Purchasing Must Become Supply Management. *Harvard Business Review*, 61, 6, 109-117

Lacity, M.C. (1992) *The Information Systems Outsourcing Bandwagon: Look Before You Leap.* University of Missouri.

Lacity, M.C. and R. Hirschheim (1993) *Information Systems Outsourcing; Myths, Metaphors and Realities.* Wiley, Chichester, England.

Lacity, M.C. and R. Hirschheim (1994) IS outsourcing evaluations: lessons from the field. *Proceedings of the IFIP TC8 Open Conference on business Process Re-engineering*, Gold Coast Queensland, Australia, May 8-11.

Lacity, M.C. and R. Hirschheim (1995) *Beyond the Information Systems Outsourcing Bandwagon.* Wiley, Chichester, England.

Lacity, M.C., L. Willcocks and D.F. Feeny (1995) IT Outsourcing: Maximize Flexibility and Control. *Harvard Business Review*, 73, 3, 84-93.

Lee, A.S. (1989) A Scientific Methodology for MIS Case Studies. *MIS Quarterly*, 33-50.

Leeuw, A.C.J. de (1982) *Organisaties: management, analyse, ontwerp en verandering.* Van Gorcum, Assen.

Leeuw, A.C.J. de (1990) Een boekje over bedrijfskundige methodologie.

Van Gorcum, Assen.

Loh, L. and Venkatraman, N. (1992a) Stock market reaction to information technology outsourcing: an event study. Working Paper No 3499-92BPS, Massachusetts Institute of Technology.

Loh, L. and Venkatraman, N. (1992b) Determinants of Information Technology Outsourcing: A Cross-Sectional Analysis. *Journal of Management Information Systems*, 9, 1, 7-24.

Loh, L., N. Venkatraman (1992c) Diffusion of Information Technology Outsourcing: influence sources and the Kodak effect. *Information Systems Research*, 3, 4, 334-358.

Loh, L. (1994) An Organisational-Economic Blueprint for Information Technology Outsourcing: Concepts and Evidence. *Proceedings of the Fifteenth International Conference on Information Systems*, Vancouver, Canada.

Looff, L.A. de (1994) Decision Support for Outsourcing the IS function. *Proceedings of the Ernst and Young/ICIS Doctoral Consortium of the Fifteenth Annual International Conference on Information Systems*, Vancouver, Canada.

Looff, L.A. de (1995a) Information Systems Outsourcing Decision Making; A Framework, Organisational Theories and Case Studies. *Journal of Information Technology*, Theme Issue Information Technology Outsourcing: Theory and Practice, 10, 4, 281-297.

Looff, L.A. de (1995b) Uitbesteden: verbeteringen komen niet altijd en nooit vanzelf. H.R. Stol, P.E. Wisse, J.C. Op de Coul en L.A. de Looff (eds.) *Organisatie-verandering en informatie-architectuur*, Samsom, Alphen aan den Rijn (in Dutch).

Looff, L.A. de (1996a) Information Systems Outsourcing: Innovative Concept for Leaner Information Systems Management? *Proceedings of the 1996 Information Resources Management Association International Conference*, Washington, 22-25 May, Idea Group Publishing, Harrisburg.

Looff, L.A. de (1996b) IS Outsourcing by Public Sector Organisations. *International Federation for Information Processing World Conference on Advanced IT Tools*, Canberra, Australia, 2-6 September.

Looff, L.A. de (1996c) The Impact of Outsourcing on Information Systems Management, *Information Resources Management Journal* (forthcoming).

Looff, L.A. de (1996d) Information Systems Outsourcing Decision Making; A Framework, Organisational Theories and Case Studies. L. Willcocks and M.C. Lacity (eds.) *Information Technology Outsourcing: theory and practice*, Oxford University Press, 1996 (forthcoming).

Looff, L.A. de (1996e) *A Model for Information Systems Outsourcing Decision Making*. PhD Thesis, Delft University of Technology.

Looff, L.A. de, and Berghout, E.W. (1994) *Research Strategies in IS. Research Report* TWI 94-17, Delft University of Technology, Delft, (in Dutch).

Looijen, M. (1996) *Information Systems, Management, Control and Maintenance* (forthcoming).

Malone, T., J. Yates and R. Benjamin (1987) Electronic Markets and electronic Hierarchies. *Communications of the ACM*, 30, 6, 484-497.

Mantelaers, P.A.H.M. (1995) *Information Capacity Engineering.* PhD Thesis, Delft University of Technology, Delft (in Dutch).

Mantelaers, P.A.H.M. and L.A. de Looff (1996) *Effective design of the IT organisation, course material,* Delft University of Technology, 1996.

McFarlan, F. W. (1984) Information technology changes the way you compete, *Harvard Business Review*, 62, 3.

Merchant, K.A. (1989) *Rewarding Results. Motivating Profit Center Managers,* Harvard Business School Press, Boston.

Minoli, D. (1995) *Analyzing Outsourcing: Re-engineering Information and Communication Systems,* McGraw-Hill, New York.

Mintzberg, H. (1979) *The Structuring of Organisations.* Prentice-Hall, Englewood Cliffs, New Jersey.

Nissen, H.-E., Klein, H.K., and Hirschheim, R. (eds) (1991) Information Systems Research: Contemporary Approaches and Emergent Traditions. *Proceedings of the IFIP TC8/WG 8.2 Working Conference,* Copenhagen, Denmark.

Perrow, C. (1986) *Complex Organizations.* Random House, New York.

Pfeffer, J. (1981) *Power in Organisations.* Pitman, Marshfield, Massachusetts.

Porter, M.E. and V.E. Millar (1985) How information gives you competitive advantage. *Harvard Business Review*, 63, 4, 59-81.

Porter, M.E. (1980) *Competitive Strategy: Techniques for analyzing Industries and Competitors.* The Free Press, New York.

Porter, M.E. (1985) *Competitive Advantage; Creating and Sustaining Superior Performance.* The Free Press, New York.

Prahalad, C.K. and G. Hamel (1990) The Core Competence of the Corporation. *Harvard Business Review*, 68, 79-91.

Quinn, J.B., Th.L. Doorley and P.C. Paquette (1990a) Beyond Products: Services-Based Strategy. *Harvard Business Review*, 68, 58-67.

Quinn, J.B., Th.L. Doorley and P.C. Paquette (1990b) Technology in Services: Rethinking Strategic Focus. *Sloan Management Review,* Winter, 79-87.

Radding, A. (1990) The Outsourcing Experience. *Bank Management,* September.

Rands, T. (1992) The key role of applications software make-or-buy decisions. *Journal of Strategic Information Systems,* 1, 4, 215-223.

Rands, T. (1993) A framework for managing software make or buy. *European Journal of Information Systems,* 2, 4.

Renkema, Th.J.W. (1995) Managing the information infrastructure for business value. B Farbey and V. Serafeimidis (eds) *Proceedings of the Information Systems Evaluation Workshop,* 3rd European Conference on Information Systems, Athens 1-3 June.

Richmond, W.B., A. Seidmann and A.B. Whinston (1992) Incomplete contracting issues in information systems development outsourcing. *Decision Support Systems,* 8, 1992.

Rochester, J.B. and D.P. Douglass (eds.), Taking an objective look at Outsourcing. *I/S Analyzer,* 28, 9.

Ross, S. (1973) The economic theory of agency: The principal's problem. *American Economic Review,* 63, 134-139.

Ryan, B., R.W. Scapens and M. Theobald (1992) *Research method and methodology in finance and accounting.* Academic Press.

Saarinen, T. and M. Saaksjarvi (1993) Empirical Evaluation of Two Different IS outsourcing strategies in the Finnish Wood Working Industry. *Outsourcing of Information Systems Services Workshop,* Twente, The Netherlands, May 20-22.

Simon, H.A. (1961) *The New Science of Management Decision,* Harper & Row, New York.

Simon, M. (1989) *De strategische functie typologie; functioneel denkraam voor management.* Kluwer, Deventer, The Netherlands (in Dutch).

Stevens, D.J.L. (1994) Privatising data gathering activities; a study at the Central Bureau of Statistics. Master's thesis, Delft University of Technology (in Dutch).

Terdiman R. (1991) *Outsourcing: threat or salvation?* Gartner Group Industry Service report R-980-108.

Tushman, M. (1977) *A Political Approach to Organizations: A Review and Rationale.* Academy of Management Review, 2, 2, 206-216.

Verhage and Cunningham (1984) Foundations of Marketing Management, Stenfert Kroese, Leiden (in Dutch).

Verhoef, D. and V. van Swede (1995) *Euromethod; voor heldere afspraken tussen klant en leverancier in IT-projecten.* Kluwer, Deventer (in Dutch).

Vlis, P.K. van der (1993) *Outsourcing the IS function.* Master's Thesis, Delft University of Technology (in Dutch).

Vlis, P.K. van der, L.A. de Looff, and E.W. Berghout (1993) Mutual Trust is Essential; Research on Outsourcing Decisions. *Computable* November 5th, 17-21 (in Dutch).

Vries, M.S. de (1993) *Calculeren met beleid; theorie en praktijk van multi-criteria-evaluaties.* Van Gorcum, Assen, 1993 (in Dutch).

Vollmer, R. (1993) Outsourcing als Symptom der Legitimationskrise. *Online,* April (in German).

Waes, R.M.C. van (1991) *Architectures for information management,* Thesis Publishers Amsterdam.

Wagner, J.L. (1992) Issues in outsourcing. *1992 IRMA Conference Proceedings,* Idea Group Publishing, Harrisburg.

Walker, G. en D. Weber (1984) A Transaction Cost Approach to Make-or-Buy Decisions. *Administrative Science Quarterly,* 29.

Weele, A.J. van (1992) *Inkoop in strategisch perspectief; analyse, planning en praktijk* (2e druk). Samsom, Alphen aan den Rijn (in Dutch).

Wierda F.W. (1991) *Developing interorganizational information systems.* PhD Thesis, Delft University of Technology.

Wijs, C. de (1995) *Information systems management in complex organizations.* PhD Thesis, Delft University of Technology.

Winkels, A.M. (1995) *Outsourcing (parts of) the IS function; a case study at DSM.* Master's Thesis, Delft University of Technology (in Dutch).

Willcocks, L. (1992) Assessing the outsourcing option. *OXIIM Research Day at Templeton College,* 7th. December.

Willcocks, L. and G. Fitzgerald (1993) Market as opportunity? Case studies in outsourcing information technology and services. *Journal of Strategic Information Systems,* 2, 3, 223-242.

Willcocks, L. and G. Fitzgerald (1994) Towards the Residual IS Organisation? Research on IT outsourcing experiences in the United Kingdom. *IFIP WG8.2 Conference,* Ann Arbor, Michigan, 11-13 August.

Willcocks, L., M.C. Lacity and G. Fitzgerald (1995) *IT Outsourcing in Europe and the USA: Assessment Issues.* Research and discussion paper RDP95/2, Templeton College, Oxford.

Williamson, O.E. (1975) *Markets and Hierarchies.* MacMillan, New York.

Williamson, O.E. (1979) Transaction Cost Economics: The Governance of Contractual Relations. *Journal of Law and Economics,* 22, 2.

Williamson, O.E. (1985) *The Economic Institutions of Capitalism.* Free Press, New York.

Yin, R.K. (1984) *Case study research: design and methods.* Sage, Newbury Park.

Zoetmulder, E. (1995) *Information Planning and Outsourcing.* Research document, Delft University of Technology.

Zwaan, A.H. van der (1990) *Organisatie-onderzoek.* Van Gorcum, Assen (in Dutch).

INDEX

ABOUT THE AUTHOR

Leon de Looff was born in Kats, The Netherlands, on January 10, 1969. After graduating from the 'Buys Ballot College' in Goes in 1987, he studied Information Systems at Delft University of Technology. His final year project concerned the design of the internal information systems function of the Dutch Ministry of Housing, Physical Planning and Environment. During his study, he worked as an assistant for practical assignments at Delft University of Technology and taught information systems courses at an institute for computer education.

In 1992 he started the research for this thesis at the department of Information Systems at Delft University of Technology. He has taught sections of courses on information management and information economics, and he has guided several Master's students at the department in producing their final year thesis. He has contributed to post-academic courses and has given lectures at Dutch and international conferences.

His publications include articles in international journals and book chapters. In 1994 he was selected to take part in the Ernst & Young/ICIS Doctoral Consortium of the International Conference on Information Systems in Vancouver, Canada. He has presented papers at the International Federation of Information Processing (IFIP) 1996 World Conference on Advanced IT Tools in Canberra, Australia, and at the 1996 Information Resources Management Association (IRMA) International Conference in Washington D.C., where he received the Best Paper Award.